Also by Maggie Scarf

INTIMATE WORLDS

BODY, MIND, BEHAVIOR

INTIMATE PARTNERS

UNFINISHED BUSINESS

SECRETS, LIES, BETRAYALS

SECRETS, LIES,

RANDOM HOUSE

NEW YORK

BETRAYALS

HOW THE BODY HOLDS THE SECRETS OF A LIFE AND HOW TO UNLOCK THEM

 Published in the United States by Random House, an imprint of The Random House Publishing Group, a division of Random House, Inc., New York, and simultaneously in Canada by Random House of Canada Limited, Toronto.

RANDOM HOUSE and colophon are registered trademarks of Random House, Inc.

Library of Congress Cataloging-in-Publication Data

Scarf, Maggie.
Secrets, lies, betrayals : how the body holds the secrets of a life, and how to unlock them / by Maggie Scarf.
p. cm.
Includes index.
ISBN 0-679-45703-8
1. Mind and body therapies. 2. Mind and body. 3. Symptoms. 4. Medicine, Psychosomatic. 5. Recollection (Psychology). 6. Recovered memory. 7. Reminiscing. 8. Memory. I. Title.
RC489.M53S3535 2004
616.89'14—dc22 2003069317

Printed in the United States of America on acid-free paper

Random House website address: www.atrandom.com

9 8 7 6 5 4 3 2 1

FIRST EDITION

For my beloved husband, Herb,

and for the dear family we created together

Acknowledgments

THE LONGEST JOURNEY BEGINS WITH A SINGLE STEP," according to the ancient Chinese proverb. But although taking that first step into the unknown is clearly a pivotal act, it's also vitally important that one move off in the correct direction. I feel fortunate to have had the road map pointed out to me, early on in this project, by Dr. Bessel van der Kolk, M.D., who is Medical Director of the Trauma Center in Boston and a Professor of Psychiatry at Boston University School of Medicine. Bessel van der Kolk is an internationally renowned trauma expert—many people consider him to be the father of present-day research in the field—and he has pioneered the use of the body-oriented forms of therapy described in this book. My series of important conversations with him has served to guide and orient me throughout the course of this work; indeed, Bessel van der Kolk's knowledgeable, supportive presence is to be found everywhere in these pages, and for this I wish to express my heartfelt thanks and deep gratitude.

During my years of research and writing, I have also been assisted greatly by a number of other researchers and therapists. Those with whom I have had one, several, or a great many enlightening and helpful conversations include: Jim Hopper, Ph.D., Research Fellow in Psychology at McLean Hospital and Harvard Medical School; Dr. J. Douglas Bremner, M.D., Director of Emory University's Center for Positron Emission Tomography and Associate Professor of Psychiatry and Radiology at Emory's school of medicine; Steven M. Southwick, M.D., Professor of Psychiatry at Yale University School of Medicine; Julian Ford, Ph.D., Director, Center for Trauma Response, Recovery and Preparedness (CTRP) and Associate Professor, University of Connecticut Health Center; Peter A. Levine,

Ph.D., Distiguished Faculty, Santa Barbara Graduate Institute and President, Foundation for Human Enrichment; Babette Rothschild, M.S.W., psychotherapist and body-psychotherapist; Susan Gombos, M.S.W., Steven Lazrove, M.D., Leslie Weiss, Ph.D., Carol Nadelson, M.D., Professor of Psychiatry at Harvard and Director of the Partners Office for Women's Careers at Brigham and Women's Hospital in Boston; and Gary Tucker, M.D., Professor Emeritus in the Department of Psychiatry and Behavioral Sciences, University of Washington, and Editor of *Psychiatry Journal Watch.* I should add that Gary Tucker is a friend and mentor of long standing and that he served in a particularly valuable capacity as the expert commentator on and reviewer of my discussion of recent work in the area of brain research.

My very special thanks go to Francine Shapiro, Ph.D., the founder and guiding spirit of the reprocessing (Eye Movement Desensitization and Reprocessing or EMDR) movement, who offered me access to her Level I and Level II training sessions and generous amounts of her private time as well. I am also grateful to William Zangwill, Ph.D., therapist and EMDR instructor, and to Patti Levin, Ph.D., who has been my steadfast adviser, sometime therapist, and who became a dear friend of mine along the way. I am indebted, too, to Katherine Davis, M.S.W., C.S.W., for many intriguing, wide-ranging conversations filled with clinical wisdom and insight.

For those parts of the book that have to do with the recent scientific findings on human memory, my thanks go to the eminent memory researcher Larry Squire, Ph.D., whose own highly original work is discussed here, and who was an ever-obliging reader and reviewer. For those parts of the book that are concerned with infidelity, my debt to the late, incomparable psychologist Shirley Glass, Ph.D., is enormous. Shirley and I talked long, both in person and on the telephone, about the impact of sexual betrayal in general and in particular about the story of marital infidelity described in this book. I also benefited greatly from interviews with other experts in the field of extramarital sex—most particularly from conversations with psychologist Don Lusterman, Ph.D., and Janis Abrahms-Spring, Ph.D.

I am also deeply indebted to Al Pesso and Diane Boyden for welcoming me into their psychomotor (Pesso Boyden System Psychomotor or

PBSP) training programs with such enthusiasm. The Pessos generously facilitated my learning of a body-oriented theory and therapy that they had developed over years of work and experience but which I was trying to absorb at high speed. My grateful thanks go, too, to Lowijs N. M. Perquin, M.D., psychiatrist and co-director of the Institute for Psychiatric Training, Free University, Amsterdam, and Trainer in Pesso Boyden System Psychomotor (PBSP).

I would also like to express my gratitude to Dr. Janet Geller, who invited me to sit in on her course on partner abuse—a series of lectures designed primarily for therapists dealing with people in emotionally and/or physically violent relationships—which I found remarkably edifying. And thanks go to Charles V. Ford, M.D., Professor of Psychiatry and Neurobiology at the University of Alabama's School of Medicine, and to Evan Imber-Black, Ph.D., Professor of Psychiatry at the Albert Einstein College of Medicine, in New York. Both Ford and Imber-Black have made "secrets, lies, and betrayals" the subject of intensive, rigorous study, and my conversations with each of them proved extremely productive and illuminating.

So, too, did my periodic consultations with family therapist W. Leonard Hill, Jr., L.C.S.W., Assistant Professor of Clinical Psychiatry at Yale University and Director of the Adult Day Program at Yale–New Haven Hospital, with Hannah Fox, M.S.W., and with psychologist Jesse D. Geller, Ph.D., who is an Assistant Professor of Psychiatry at Yale and Columbia Universities. These clinicians were not only wonderful sounding boards for my own thoughts and ideas; they were also nothing short of *ingenious* at helping to tease out the underlying dynamics of the many secrets I was hearing.

As always, a fond word of appreciation is due to my assistant, Felicia Dickinson, who came to work with me when she was a graduate student—I have a vivid picture of a pretty dark-haired young woman flouncing up my front walk—and who has remained with me throughout my entire researching and writing career. Thanks are also due to my library assistant, the dauntless, determined Jean Emmons, who has never entertained the thought that there could be an out-of-print book or obscure scientific paper that she was unable to locate.

Lastly, I cannot fail to say a word of thanks to Susan Cheever, who invited me to sit in on her wonderfully enjoyable writing class at Yale—a class that, at the outset of my work on the manuscript, helped me to get my starter motor running. And I am grateful to my agent, Amanda Urban, for her enthusiastic readings of the book, in its several incarnations, and for the advice and encouragement she offered as the manuscript moved from its initial seedling state to its ultimate maturation.

As for my longtime editor and friend, Kate Medina, no paean of praise seems sufficient to describe her patience, tact, intelligence, and skill. Kate is simply one of the most creative and gifted practitioners of her craft that an author could ever imagine. I have collaborated with her on all of my books, and have been impressed by her careful attention to every detail. However, *this time* she has worked like a sculptor, scrutinizing every aspect of the raw first draft and indicating innovative ways of fashioning the material and shaping it into its present form. Kate is always tactful, always aware of a writer's sensitivities; and while I have found that our interaction is invariably an educational and deeply gratifying experience, it's only lately that I've come to realize that she is nothing other than a genius at what she does.

Finally, when it comes to expressing my thanks to the many, many individuals who volunteered to be interviewed on the subject of "secrets and lies," I hardly know where or how to begin. All that I can put into words is that I am profoundly grateful to you for your courage, your forthrightness, your willingness to open the most secret, often shameful parts of your lives to my gaze. I have thought about my conversations with you incessantly, wondered about you, worried about you, admired you; above all, *learned* from you—and in the course of the process have found myself becoming someone different, someone far more open to the world around me and more willing to be open with myself.

Maggie Scarf
Jonathan Edwards College, Yale

Author's Note

THE INDIVIDUALS WHOSE INTERVIEWS HAVE BEEN USED IN these pages have agreed to let their stories be told, with minor changes as far as identifying details are concerned (name, names of family members, profession, geographical location in some cases, etc.). The secret stories described here are therefore factual, aside from the omission or change of such unnecessarily specific and revealing information.

Contents

Preface

—

WHAT THE BODY KNOWS

"IF YOU WERE GOING TO TELL OR WRITE THE STORY OF your life—which would, of course, begin when you were a small infant in your own family—what would the first sentence of your autobiography sound like?" Some years ago, while I was doing research for a book about families (*Intimate Worlds*), I routinely posed this question to every member of a family I was interviewing—anyone who seemed old enough and willing to try to answer it.

I would watch as people struggled to formulate their replies—many of which were weird, extraordinary, completely surprising. But nobody ever challenged me to respond in kind, to reveal what my *own* answer to that question might be. Nevertheless, it always popped into awareness, stood out so clearly against the background of my mind's horizon: "I was born, and nobody noticed."

But how could this possibly be an elemental truth of my life, the actual starting point of my own autobiography, when I remembered my mother as the most caring, gentle, generous of persons? This was a question I always seemed to sidestep, never confront head-on. It was so much at variance with my vivid memories of my mother, with that sense of loving and being loved that—whatever else was happening in the desperate household in which I grew up—I'd always believed had filled up my psychic fuel tank for a lifetime.

Even in the middle of my life, when I was married, a mother, and long gone from my original family, I kept encountering "hard evidence" of my mother's caring and her love for me. For instance, once, while gathering material for a *New York Times* article on sleep disorders, I learned how to self-induce body muscle relaxation with the aid of a biofeedback device. What this device was used for was "feeding back" to the sleep patient ongoing information about the state of his or her own muscular tension. Nothing, I soon found, could slow the sounds so effectively as imagining myself as a small infant, lying on a table, kicking my legs, "talking" to my mother, and laughing.

Beforehand, I'd been ushered into a soundproof room, asked to lie down upon a comfortable sofa with a set of earphones over my ears and electrodes pasted on the mobile, reactive muscles of my forehead; this enabled me to "hear" my facial musculature clenching each time I thought about something that made me feel taut and anxious. The biofeedback mechanism translated the electrical charge of the muscles into sounds: What I heard first was a rapid barrage of *click-click-click*s.

It didn't take me long to discover that certain kinds of thoughts evoked an avalanche of sounds. Thinking about how to write the sleep article for the *Times*, for instance, evoked an auditory bombardment. But other thoughts tended to slow down the barrage of noises. When I set myself to focusing upon *those* thoughts, I was rewarded by hearing a widely spaced *click . . . click . . . click . . . click*. The image of my mother, whenever I brought it into sharp focus—complete with the image of her smiling and leaning over me—actually brought about extended periods of time during which I heard no clicks at all. How could this powerful, revealing experience compute with that recurring first sentence of my life's narrative: "I was born, and nobody noticed"? If this message, so discordant with anything I consciously believed about my past, was coming to me from within my body, a part of me didn't really want to decode it.

This book is about the ways in which the body remembers, and may be expressing symptomatically, not only those secrets we may be keeping from others, but those we are keeping from ourselves. For in the course of my studies I was to confront the shocking realization that my deep love for my mother was the motivation for my "stuffing down" certain hurtful thoughts and memories of her that I couldn't bear to acknowledge consciously. Nevertheless, what *my body knew* was being expressed via a bodily symptom—that of tension in my jaw, which would tingle painfully at times or grow rigid, even frozen.

One morning—had I had a nightmare?—I'd even woken up and found my jaw so locked that I had trouble opening my mouth to brush my teeth. But until I became involved in the research for this book, it hadn't ever occurred to me that there might be some link between this occasional mysterious symptom—tension in the jaw—and lingering memories, stored in my body, of certain distressing life experiences.

Ultimately, this book is about the secrets and lies we may tell to others, or to ourselves, about the actual truths of our lives—about those painful or shameful or wounding experiences of the past or the present that we may strive to ignore or may simply forget, but which *our bodies hold and remember*. Our bodies not only remember, but frequently "speak up" about these truths in the form of isolated symptoms (back or jaw tension), or of certain disorders (depression, alcoholism), or of repetitively problematic patterns of positioning ourselves in our most intimate relationships. However, it is only recently—due to astonishing advances in brain research and the study of human memory systems—that we have been learning how to listen to what the body has to tell us and to *use* what we are learning therapeutically.

It is now widely recognized that the body stores memories of intensely stressful experiences, particularly in certain regions at the core of the brain (the limbic system, which is the seat of our emotions). We may not care to speak of these events to anyone, but memories of them—whether vividly recalled or lost to awareness—color many aspects of our daily existence, often without our conscious realization.

The Body's Reactions to High Stress: Hyperarousal and Numbing Out

As the daughter of a messianic, irrational father—a man who was prone to unpredictable, inexplicable rages—I grew up with a sense that anything could happen at any moment. Everyone in the household, including my docile mother, was afraid of my father—and we children knew that she was powerless to protect us from him. Growing up, as I did, in an atmosphere of unknown but palpable dangers had instilled in me an ingrained sense of readiness to meet a threat—a threat that could come from anywhere, at any time, without explanation.

However, it was only in the course of working on this book that I came to learn that this state of bodily hyperarousal and hypervigilance is one of the two major reactions to events that are experienced as overwhelming.

The body's other mode of responding is the diametrically opposite one—it is shutting down, distancing emotionally, feeling numb, "spacing out."

These two bodily reactions have a very different outward appearance, but internally, similar things are happening. In both instances, the body's "emergency alarm system" has been switched on and an instantaneous physiological readiness to meet the threat has come into play: the well-known "fight or flight" (or "freeze" if there's no way out) response.

This lightning-swift neurobiological reaction to situations of danger, which involves an elaborate, integrated set of bodily and psychological changes, is actually a survival mechanism—one that has served our species well over time and which we share with all other mammals. The downside, however, is that a complex, highly developed memory network enables us to keep certain experiences alive within us. A person's body may, therefore, remain in a state of high arousal and preparedness to meet a threat long after the danger itself is in the past. The body "remembers" what once happened—and at times neutral, even benign, occurrences can trigger similar kinds of biologically based, internal alarms.

In any case, as my intensive reading and my interviews with secret holders and with a host of varying experts proceeded, I came to the realization that I was not only *discerning* a picture emerging from the research for this book; I myself was a part of the picture that was emerging. Before this time, I'd never taken special note of the pervasive feelings of wariness, of worried expectation, that were held by me *within my body*—never thought these might be an expression of unresolved, unintegrated memories that were held within my nervous circuitry but not within my conscious thought processes.

Quite the contrary: I'd always viewed my sense of physical high alert, of vigilance, as something that was simply "me"—simply who I was, a part of the way I was constructed. I'd never even considered the odd notion that how a person's body felt *inside* at the present moment might be integrally linked to the things that had happened in his or her life, even long ago—linked, that is, to events that had once felt overwhelming and to their often disturbing, long-abiding aftereffects.

Secrets, Lies, Betrayals

At a more superficial level, the question of what first kindled my interest in the powerful, often subterranean effects of secrets, lies, and betrayals is an easy one to answer. At the twenty-ninth annual conference of the New York Society for Clinical Social Work, where I was the designated honoree, I attended a series of talks on the topic *Secrets and Lies: Intrapsychic and Interpersonal Dimensions,* and the repercussions of this conference were to remain with me for months and then for years to come. For that day's events seemed to affect me like a tuning fork, whose vibrations began resonating with a hitherto silent part of my internal world.

During the afternoon sessions, I heard presentations with such titles as "Living Everyday Lies," "Sex, Lies, and Infidelity," "Seeing Is Not Believing," and "Transgenerational Family Secrets"—and the sessions didn't disappoint. The more I listened to these narratives of marital affairs, wife battering, traumatic bonding, unspoken family shame, hidden food-related maladies, verbal/emotional abuse, and alcohol and drug disorders, the more fascinated I became; and I decided to undertake some further study of the subject of secrets and lies on my own. And, as the work progressed, I came to appreciate how closely related to bodily symptoms and repetitive problems with relationships (to spouses, lovers, colleagues, friends) these subjects actually were.

I had thought that the idea of talking about secrets and lies would make it hard to find a list of people who would be willing to be interviewed for the project, but I could not have been more mistaken: Volunteers came to me from a number of sources, including audiences at lectures I was giving at the time. It didn't take long—a mere matter of months—before I'd amassed a freightload of highly privileged secrets and confidential, personal data. And at the same time, quite unexpectedly, I'd found that a strong, even inexorable current was carrying me toward the fascinating research on traumatic experience and the lingering effects that certain long-past events could exert upon the body, the brain, and ongoing behavior in the present.

In retrospect, the reason I became so captivated by this work seems to me both logical and obvious. For what could be more secret, more mortifying and shame-ridden, than those painful, somctimes overwhelming remembrances of the past that most of us don't want to examine candidly, even think about, much less reveal to other people? In any event, what the trauma literature—and the research on the brain and on human memory systems as well—was telling me was that the body has a way of remembering those things that we may most wish to forget.

Shame-Related Secrets

Not surprisingly, in the course of the interviews, I found myself encountering a dizzying *variety* of secrets; I also discerned in people a broad range of motivations for keeping the information under lock and seal. But some motivations for secret keeping did, I noticed, recur with great frequency, and for that reason they stood out from all the rest.

One virtually omnipresent reason was *shame*—about those aspects of a person's early or present-day life that had to be disclaimed and disavowed. A parent's mental illness or alcoholism, or the fact that a family member had gone to prison, or the existence of emotional maltreatment or physical violence in the family of origin, might be the matter that had to be hidden. In other cases, the confidential narrative I was hearing had to do with neglect or the terrible invalidation that a person had experienced as a child—people are often deeply *ashamed* of having been victimized. On yet other occasions the secret had to do with worse cruelties, such as interpersonal abuse that was ongoing at the time of the interviews but being kept under wraps in order to keep up a presentable social facade. These abusive relationships often bore an uncanny resemblance to "familiar" situations—situations that one or both partners had encountered in their family of origin.

Another conspicuous motivation for keeping secrets was *fear*—and the most frequently encountered fears were those revolving around the threat of rejection and abandonment. Here, the individual's deepest certainty was that if the real truth about him or her were known—about an abortion, a period of promiscuity, a drug habit, the kind of family he or she came from—the secret holder would be revealed as unworthy or contemptible, someone whose past history or behavior was so unsavory that he or she deserved to be cast off, deserted.

For example, a deep-seated fear that her new bridegroom would *leave* the relationship precipitously if he ever learned the full truth about her past was the rationale for Claudia Martinelli's ongoing lies and deceptions about her past. So, too, were a poisonous admixture of shame, guilt, and a deep belief in her own *badness* that had been with her since earliest childhood. Such ingrained beliefs were reflected in her body, which was in a state of constant, tense hyperarousal.

Claudia Martinelli, whose story is woven throughout part 1, seemed to be responding to a blaring internal alarm that was sounding off within her, one that made a state of calm and relaxation impossible. This clamorous alarm—a "fight or flight" response that kept her body on continual high alert—was actually drowning out the more subtle communiqués that our bodies send to us on a routine basis. For this reason, Claudia couldn't hear the less strident warning signals from within that our bodies routinely dispatch to us and that might have guided her behavior—messages such as "Something doesn't feel quite right here," or "There's a problem," or "Can I trust this person to be on my side?"

Claudia's story is at once her own—unique—and also illustrative of many of the other life narratives that I heard in the course of my interviews for this book. Her state of high arousal and mistrustful vigilance, which kept her anxiously patrolling the outer walls of her world—fully expecting an attack from without—led to an incapacity to be *fully present inside her body* and therefore able to be responsive to the important messages being beamed to her from within. This deafness to the body's internal stream of informational signals is a well-recognized, often long-lived aftereffect of disturbing events that were once experienced as overwhelming.

At the level of conscious awareness, Claudia Martinelli was out of touch with her body. And because she had never been able to integrate what was happening inside her body with what was going on in her mind, she had no understanding of *why* she was doing the things she was doing.

Instead, she seemed to be drawn toward continually reenacting and reexperiencing, *in her life*, the familiar distressing feelings. These bodily feelings and sensations were her baseline, her accustomed way of being.

People with a history like Claudia's—which is to say, those who have been witness to, or the target of, early trauma such as emotional neglect or abuse or physical violence—have a tendency to become involved in restaging strangely similar events in later adulthood. By getting into the same or a very similar situation, they return to a world with which they are familiar, one that *feels consonant with what is happening inside their bodies*—with the high arousal, shame, and fear they're experiencing. So Claudia's love choices kept re-creating, in the present, the secrecy, lies, hypocrisy, and abuse that she'd witnessed in her own original family. (See chapter 5, "Behavioral Reenactments: Was Claudia Martinelli in an Emotionally Abusive Relationship? What *Is* an Emotionally Abusive Relationship?")

Secrets Motivated by Love and Loyalty

Yet another oft encountered rationale for secret holding was *loyalty—the need, engendered by loving feelings, to keep someone else's secret or, alternatively, to protect that someone from learning information that would cause terrible pain*. Most commonplace among those secrets motivated by love and loyalty were, in my experience, secrets of a sexual nature—for example, a situation in which a person has grown up knowing of one parent's infidelity and yet has felt impelled to keep the secret from the other.

"My father was a serial adulterer, and he made *me* his confidante," an elegant woman in her late thirties told me. "I don't know why he did that—I think we'd call it sexual abuse nowadays—but I was only about thirteen or fourteen years old at the time. So his bringing all that stuff to me was terribly confusing. . . . The message I was getting was that *I* was his real intimate, and my mom was just the workhorse, there to run the house."

Worst of all, she said, was her dad's putting her into a painful triangle that involved keeping secrets from her mother—she'd felt so consumed with guilt, so helpless, so caught in the middle of that unhappy situation. "Somewhere around that time, I got something that was diagnosed as migraine syndrome—I would get these dizzy feelings, see bouncing lights, feel sick to my stomach. My mouth would go numb, too." Metaphorically speaking, her lips had frozen; it was as if her body were telling her to keep her mouth shut.

Secrets Being Kept from the Self

All in all, the most curious kinds of secrets that emerged in these interviews were those that could be called "secrets being kept from the self." In these instances, it often seemed as though one part of the individual's brain were resisting knowledge of an event or experience that was so startling, so overwhelming, so unthinkable, that it couldn't be integrated into the person's conscious awareness. The memory of the event had simply fragmented, dropped out of the individual's mind, even though his or her *body* or behavior often bore witness to the episode's existence.

There are many situations, which frequently go unseen for what they are, in which our bodies "talk" about hurtful, frightening, but seemingly forgotten events that we're loath to "know about" and acknowledge. They may do so in the guise of feelings of numbness and deadness, including sexual apathy, *or* in the form of high arousal, irritability, and unending tension. Yet again, they may "speak" about a person's pain and grief in the form of somatic reactions, appearing as "physical" problems—for example, severe headaches, perpetual stomach distress, irritable bowel syndrome, eating or sleep problems, painful muscular tension of the back, neck, or jaw.

The body's "memories" may, on the other hand, make their appearance in the form of some apparently inexplicable kind of behavior, such as Beverly Scanlon's panicky reaction when she'd been given the mundane task of overseeing the changing of the locks in the academic department that she usually ran with such admirable efficiency. (See chapter 12, "Secrets from the Self: Beverly Changes the Locks.")

Secrets of this sort are usually connected to experiences of painful, even traumatic significance to the individual involved. And as the interviews continued, I was coming to realize that a great many—though not *all*—of the secrets being told to me bore some connection to traumas, past and present, large and small.

Daddy

Although my father had had four wives by the time he died in his nineties, he didn't much like women, and he liked children even less. I can't remember ever having an actual conversation with my father, but I do remember those angry-sounding conversations—they sometimes rose to a shout—that he used to have with himself. He was talking to an unseen being—was it God?—but he wasn't to be interrupted. I would watch him apprehensively as he marched up and down the dining room, presumably at his morning prayers but sounding as if he were infuriated.

What were those angry colloquies about? It was impossible to decipher what he was carrying on about, why he sometimes sounded so enraged. You could never know what my father was thinking, surely not what might make him happy or please him—I try hard to remember him smiling—but most dangerously of all, you never knew what would set him off.

I can remember an incident that I tried hard to make sense of, something that happened when I was about twelve or thirteen years old. I was staying home from school with some symptoms of a flu, running a low fever, and feeling thoroughly contented with a book I was reading and our new kitty—an endearing, furry little ball of excitement who was bounding back and forth across the bedspread.

I did hear my father's heavy tread on the staircase but felt no alarm until I saw him standing in the doorway as if dumbstruck by the scene before him—myself, under the covers, the book, the little gray-and-white kitten. He was scowling at me, horrified, his entire body puffing up with outrage until it seemed to fill the entire door frame. I felt my heart pounding in my chest, looked around me swiftly. What was happening—what had I *done* that was wrong?

He didn't say a word, simply stalked into the room and grabbed me by one skinny shoulder. Then he brought his face down close to mine, his eyes glittering with outrage. "What are you *doing*?" he demanded, giving my shoulder a rough shake.

"I'm sick, I have a fever, Daddy," I blurted quickly. "Mommy said I should stay in bed." But his accusatory gaze remained fixed upon me, and he shook my shoulder again. I was staring up at him, and I can still recall the sensation, the feeling that the whole world had narrowed down so that it consisted of this one threatening being looming over me. I waited, frozen.

It took a long time for him to find the words, but at last he said furiously, saliva forming around the edges of his lips, "*You* say you're sick! And you're lying here playing with the *cat*! What kind of *sick* is this, playing with the *cat*!" With that, he gave the kitty a rough swipe with his large hand, so that she mewed loudly as she careened off the bed and onto the floor.

"Well, you're not getting away with *this*." He let go of my shoulder with a last, abrupt shove backward against the bed pillows, then turned on his heel. "I'm going down, and I'm going to call the school, the principal! And I'm going to tell him! She's lying in bed *pretending* to be sick, but she's playing with the cat in her bed!"

I lay there rigidly, too petrified to move, hearing the door bang at the bottom of the stair hallway. My heart was slamming hard, yet I was confused: What was so wrong with being sick and having a cat playing on your bedspread? I didn't understand, it made no sense. Would it make sense to the principal or the teachers? What would they think when they got that call? Would they believe I was *bad*—that I'd been pretending, not sick at all, not running any fever—and that having the kitty on the bed proved this to be so?

It didn't seem rational to me, but then my father was hard to fathom—and I was only about twelve-plus years old. Perhaps the people in the school office would think I was faking, as my father said—or maybe they would think *he* was crazy. Then again, if they thought the latter, what did that make me . . . the daughter of a crazy parent? I wouldn't want my classmates to think so, to have that kind of word get around.

At the age of twelve, a young person wants nothing other than to be a clone of everyone else; being singled out for negative attention is humiliating. So, when I returned to school, I felt terrified of being "outed"—known as someone who must be *weird* because she came from a family that was so strange and so bizarre. I remember waiting breathlessly to be summoned to the principal's office—knots in my stomach, tightness in my chest—but I spoke to no one else about my awful fear that I was going to be pulled out of class summarily. It was one of the most interminable days of my life, but although I expected to be called to the gallows momentarily, nothing further ever happened.

Later, I wondered if my father had ever called. And if so, had the principal simply recognized the strangeness of the situation and decided not to pursue it any further? Whatever the reasons, the incident was dropped, and I was able to go on with my daily struggle to look like a normal girl from a normal family. But of course, *I* knew the truth to be otherwise.

Being Familiarly Uncomfortable: What Is Written in the Body's Physiology

This episode was, however, paradigmatic of the many damaging experiences of childhood that my interviewees spoke about with me—experiences that often are taken inside and interwoven with a person's identity and personality. Certainly my own sense that "anything can happen at any moment"—that I had to be in a bodily state of readiness to meet a threat—had been reinforced by the fact that I'd been lying peacefully in bed, reading a book and playing with my kitten, when suddenly the walls of my world—in the person of my father—had come crashing in upon me.

Events of this sort are, of course, not the kind we usually think of as traumatic, in the sense of a highly dramatic, catastrophic occurrence—for instance, the murder of a sibling (see chapter 15, "Reenactments of the Past: The Barrys and the Freeds"), being sexually assaulted, getting caught in a fire, or losing a loved one in a terrorist attack. Still, frightening, stressful experiences, such as that mystifying encounter with my father, have a way of becoming situated in a person's body in such a way that they feel completely familiar.

I don't mean to say that they feel comfortable, only that they feel *familiar*—that is, *familiarly uncomfortable*—for they have become written into the body's physiology. And, as a result, it becomes difficult for a person to conceive of an interior world that feels profoundly *different*—that is, a body that is not hyperaroused, that feels relaxed and safe inside.

Big-T and Little-t Trauma

Let me hasten to say that the incident with my father and the kitty, searing though it had been to me, would never rise to the level of major trauma as defined in the standard psychiatric reference book, *The Diagnostic and Statistical Manual of Mental Disorders*. According to the manual, only certain *kinds* of experiences can surmount the bar when it comes to diagnosing post-traumatic stress disorder, and they are those that involve staring death in the face. These would be along the lines of military combat, violent personal assault, natural or man-made disasters, severe automobile accidents, learning of a potentially fatal illness, and events of this life-threatening dimension. Moreover, the diagnosis requires that the person experiencing the trauma must have responded with "intense fear, helplessness or horror. . . ."

There is ongoing controversy about this strict definition of what is meant by "trauma," for in clinical practice, many people respond to much less apocalyptic stressors with clear-cut post-traumatic reactions. To take an example, when Karen Barry-Freed's husband announced abruptly that their marriage was over, and that he had another woman, and that she should get herself a lawyer (see chapter 13, "The World Turned Upside Down: Extramarital Affairs"), this elicited a classic traumatic response. Karen reacted with shock and dissociation—she "numbed out," which is the body's other major behavioral reaction to events that are experienced as overwhelming.

For many months after this occurrence, Karen had felt spacey, disconnected, as if injected with an emotional anesthetic—although clearly, no confrontation with mortality was involved. This kind of frozen immobility (the rabbit in the headlights) is a *classic bodily response to situations of extreme danger* and is often seen in the aftermath of traumatic experiences—those that leave a person feeling devastated, damaged, unable to function normally, due to her or his "intense fear, helplessness or horror."

A person in Karen's situation may not have undergone the kind of horrific event or series of events that clearly merit a diagnosis of post-traumatic stress disorder, but may nevertheless be exhibiting some or all of the bodily signs and symptoms of a severe stress response syndrome—in this instance, a sense of emotional deadness and a host of physical symptoms, such as migraines, stomach distress, nausea, and other somatic complaints. Karen Barry-Freed's story, which is told throughout part 3 of this book, is illustrative not only of the second mode of responding to terrible events—that is, "zoning out," turning off the feelings spigot entirely; her story also illustrates how devastating experiences can remain *in the body*—and then suddenly jump out like a bogeyman, long after a person's difficulties appear to be completely resolved and in the past.

I should add that in some situations a person will seem to alternate between states of numbness and deadness and states of high emotional reactivity. But in any case, the overriding point to be made here is that the fine line differentiating "big-T trauma" (post-traumatic stress disorder) and "little-t trauma" (post-traumatic stress) remains somewhat blurry, indeterminate. Therefore, let me be clear about the fact that the word *trauma,* as I use it in this book, will *not* for the most part refer to big-T trauma—catastrophic happenings such as hurricanes, floods, fires, rape, and other events of a potentially fatal nature. My book's focus will be upon little-t trauma—those less obviously cataclysmic but nevertheless damaging experiences that are widespread and are at present widely underdiagnosed.

Perhaps this happens because exposures to trauma are considered to be rare, even though the statistics indicate otherwise. For example, a recent government study involving some fifty-nine thousand respondents found that "events and experiences that qualified as traumas" had been experienced by *60 percent of the adult men* and *51 percent of the adult women* interviewed.

Interestingly enough, the social scientists running this study never used the word *trauma* in the course of their interviews; each person in the sample was simply asked, "Has such-and-such an event ever happened to you?" When it was concluded, the results of this large-scale investigation surprised even the researchers themselves, for their findings demonstrated that exposures to traumatic stress are actually astonishingly commonplace.

Nevertheless, there does exist a widespread reluctance to think in terms of trauma—the word itself sounds so ominous—absent an out-and-out calamity. This, in turn, has created a situation in which the symptomatic aftereffects of profoundly disturbing experiences often go unrecognized as what they are—which is to say, the body's reactions to overwhelming stress.

New Findings, Powerful Therapies

For most of medical history, it has been taken for granted that the human brain, sequestered behind the hard, bony structure of the skull, was an inviolate "black box"—a marvelously complex yet totally sealed-off organ that could never be looked at directly, much less studied, while it was in action. Then, starting in the mid-1980s, an increasingly sophisticated battery of brain-imaging techniques made it possible to observe the functioning—that is, *thinking, feeling, remembering*—brain of a living, communicating person. Scientists could, for example, *look at* what changes in cerebral blood flow took place deep within the "old," emotional regions of the brain while a person was recollecting and describing an intensely anxiety-producing, stressful experience.

This fascinating work (which is described in chapter 4, "The Body Remembers") is part of an ever growing body of work that has served to highlight the neurobiological—that is, fleshly—roots of our mental existence. So, too, has the explosively expanding literature on human memory systems. The current understanding is not only that our memories exist at an impalpable, psychological level, but that they also have a *physical, corporeal* existence within the body's nervous circuitry. We now know that there are many situations in which we are having powerful somatic reactions to experiences that may have long since slipped beneath the surface of awareness.

Why and how does it happen that our brains and bodies can hold the knowledge of situations and events that we ourselves may have put aside or forgotten completely? Again, the answer, supported by the most recent scientific work on memory, is that while we usually think of our emotional lives as being immaterial in nature, they are in fact *deeply rooted in our bodily experiences* of emotionally charged events that are currently happening or that have happened in the past. (See chapter 3, "Physioneurosis: The Body Keeps the Score.")

What, then, can be done about disturbing memories—most especially strongly encoded *early* memories—that we are out of touch with, but which may be affecting areas of our work lives and close relationships? Are there ways to "cure" a difficult experience in the past that lives on, in the most literal, *physical sense*, within our body's nervous circuitry? Can words alone—that is, the more conventional, "talking alone" forms of psychotherapy—ever suffice, given our growing understanding of traumatic stressors, of the complexities of memory and the neurophysiology of the brain? And how, practically speaking, can one take advantage of the great smorgasbord of recent scientific findings in ways that might improve one's physical and emotional well-being?

One interesting development—and thus far the best answer to this question—has been the emergence of a group of relatively new therapeutic methods and procedures that rely heavily upon "somatic memory"—that is, upon what the body knows. These body-oriented approaches to the treatment of intense suffering vary widely and can *look* very different; still, they do have a crucial feature in common. That is, they are all geared toward targeting and then integrating scattered bits of data stored within the patient's *physical* as well as psychological self.

Moreover, all of them seek to promote a state of heightened bodily awareness by actively summoning up the person's feelings, emotions, and sensations—for example, what was seen, touched, smelled, heard, during certain critical events or time periods. The body's "memory" is thus put into play as a way of gaining access to regions deep within the brain where hugely oversensitized networks of reacting have been established. I should mention that in the course of researching this book, I myself sampled several of these "power therapies," so named because they often prove effective with such rapidity, especially when compared with the far slower-paced, traditional verbal methods of treatment. And, to my own amazement, in the course of this "research," I came to understand why I'd answered that question—"What would the first sentence of your autobiography be?"—in such a seemingly incomprehensible fashion. Around that same time, the tension in my jaw vanished completely, and it has never returned.

What follows, then, is an exploration not only of the ways in which the body holds the secrets of a life, but of the ways in which one might go about unlocking them and freeing the self from their power. This book is, too, a meditation upon memory, upon matters such as why certain memories are particularly long-lasting while others fade very quickly. I have also written about trust, sexuality, the recognition of emotional abuse, the reenactment of the past in the present, the latest scientific findings on severe stress and the brain, and a variety of kindred topics. My research has taken me to places that I could not previously have imagined and has actually transformed my thinking about the body, the mind, and the nonexistent division between them.

Part One

KEEPING SECRETS

THE HYPERAROUSED BODY

BEHAVIORAL REENACTMENTS

CLAUDIA MARTINELLI'S DILEMMA

Chapter One

—

IS IT FAIR TO GO AHEAD WITH THIS WEDDING?

It's still not clear how or why that strange misunderstanding occurred. The plan we'd made was pretty straightforward: Claudia Martinelli and I were to meet each other in the lobby of the Yale Club, which is just across the street from Grand Central Terminal. That waiting area isn't large, so it never occurred to me that we needed to describe ourselves, put carnations in our lapels, do anything of that sort.

When I arrived, ten minutes late, out of breath, the lobby was unusually crowded and noisy. Clusters of people stood around talking, laughing; their high-pitched voices echoed off the marble walls, muffling phrases of the familiar carols being piped in from unseen speakers. The whole lobby was dressed up for the Christmas holiday: Huge red velvet bows festooned the high archways leading to the elevators on the right side of the lobby; and on the opposite side, the same red velvet bows graced the handrails of the wide stairway leading up to the cocktail lounge on the mezzanine. The sounds of a loud party floated down from up there. I looked around but didn't see the woman I was expecting.

Very few people were actually sitting in the club's waiting section, which consists of several dark blue sofas and blue, comfortable-looking chairs arranged in an elongated oval. There *was* one person, actually, a strikingly attractive woman sitting by herself; but she surely didn't correspond to my image of the person I was meeting. Anyhow, this woman didn't seem to be on the lookout for *me*; her gaze slid right past without a flicker of interest and remained fixed upon the revolving door at the entrance.

She's waiting for a date, I thought. Someone important to her, for she was sitting forward on her seat intently. At her feet was a striped pale green shopping bag that bore the label Emporio Armani.

Behind me the front door went on swishing steadily, letting in blasts of cold air and new arrivals. I stood there, uncertain, feeling guilty about my perennial tardiness. The tall grandfather clock, which had been decorated with fragrant Christmas greens, suddenly emitted a loud, single chime. For a moment all the cheerful hubbub halted. It was actually six-fifteen, not ten after, so I'd arrived even later than I'd thought.

Was it possible that my interviewee had gotten here on the dot of six, waited briefly, and then left because I was nowhere to be seen? Or was this a plain and simple no-show? Claudia Martinelli had sounded pretty agitated during our several preliminary phone calls; she might have gotten confused about the plans, which had been changed a couple of times, or even decided against participating in this project—an exploration of secrets and lies and how they affect us mentally and physically. Had *I* said anything that might have sounded overly intrusive or alarming?

I sank into one of the deep armchairs with my back to the revolving door and soon found myself gazing covertly at the handsome woman sitting across from me. She had wide, pale blue eyes, fringed with black, unblinking as a bird's and focused on the entryway in back of me. Her hair was light colored—masses of curls, which looked carefully disarranged—and she wore a very short dark wool dress, clockworked stockings, and polished boots with heels so tall and narrow that the whole effect was faintly pornographic. She wasn't merely good-looking, as I'd first thought; she was *beautiful*—the kind of woman whose mere existence eclipses every female around her.

It was six twenty-five, and whoever she was meeting still hadn't arrived. In the meantime, a smattering of other people sitting in the area had linked up with their friends, and some new personnel had come to take up places on the dark blue patterned sofas. I was growing ever more certain that Claudia Martinelli wasn't going to show up and feeling responsible for whatever might have gone wrong. I had been too casual in making arrangements for this meeting. I had come too late, and she'd gone before

I got here. I'd made some ill-advised remark that had disturbed her, and she'd decided not to be interviewed.

I began to console myself with the fact that I had a goodly number of *other* volunteers for the research I was engaged in—a project that had begun as a straightforward study of secrets and lies, but then expanded as I'd reflected upon the narratives I was gathering. For as I'd moved from interview to interview, it had become ever clearer to me that there was so often a mysterious link between the secrets a person holds and painful events of the past—including painful events that he or she believes to have been fully dealt with and resolved. There was, too, a link between things that were happening in the person's current-day life and those same toxic experiences—which may have happened recently or so long ago that they'd become lost to everyday, conscious awareness.

But whether they're "forgotten" or present in the here and now, highly stressful events—by which I mean experiences that felt and still *feel* harsh, overwhelming, traumatic—can leave in their wake a sense of inner chaos, of being helpless, disorganized, unable to cope or self-soothe and calm oneself down. Traumatic situations leave their symptomatic calling cards, and while the story of what originally happened may go underground in the form of a closely held secret, the body "remembers" what occurred, for it remains stored within the neural circuitry. Not only does the body remember, but the original story goes on being told and retold in disguised form—often as incomprehensibly powerful emotional and physical reactions or as inexplicable, self-damaging, repetitive patterns of behavior.

Those symptoms that are carried in the body may emerge in subtle or in strikingly clear-cut ways. For example, they can show up as muscle tension, hyperarousal, stomachaches, headaches, anxiety, changes in sleep patterns, depressed mood, fatigue, colitis, irritable bowel syndrome, or an enhanced vulnerability to colds and other illnesses. The aftereffects of such experiences may also be expressed in the form of behavior, such as becoming involved in relationships that are hurtful and demeaning or in dangerous kinds of acting out, including wild sexual escapades, compulsive gambling, or addictions to drugs, alcohol, or food.

Less obviously, a trauma of some kind may leave a permanent mark upon a person's view of the self and of his or her world. Some fall into a way of being best described as a kind of "learned voicelessness," a peculiar talent for getting into depriving relationships. Such relationships foster a state of emotional numbness, a pervading silence about the individual's own desires and preferences; and in such situations, the voiceless partner's needs and wishes go unheard; they almost seem to have no existence.

This is by no means disconnected from the common observation that severely stressful events can leave an individual with a sense of not being fully present in his or her life, of being "out of it" somehow. The person is eminently capable of going through all the right motions yet lacks a real sense of being fully embodied in the here and now of the present moment.

It's now well recognized that traumatic events leave their neural imprint upon what is called the "old," emotional brain, and that even small reminders of the trauma can immediately activate the body's survival alarm system. This is the renowned "fight-or-flight response"—an instantaneous, physiological reaction to danger that has served our species well over aeons of evolutionary time. The only drawback to this wonderfully automatic, self-defensive reaction is that after the challenge, when all threat is long past, some people cannot calm their minds and their bodies down again. They remain battle-ready, sometimes for years—on the alert for fresh danger, mistrustful of others, prone to feelings of shame, anger, and apprehension.

Just recently, in the course of several long telephone conversations with Claudia Martinelli, it had seemed to me that I was hearing this kind of gut-level agitation and alarm in her fearful, pressured tone of voice.

To be sure, when it came to secrets and lies, Claudia was dealing with some very big ones; her current situation was distressing enough to get anyone upset. Still, as I sat there waiting, I found myself speculating about whether or not there had been earlier events in her life, some profoundly disturbing experiences, that had set the stage for her becoming embroiled in her current situation. For as I'd already come to realize in the course of my interviews, the secrets people keep, and the lies they tell, frequently stem from odd acts of loyalty and protection.

Those matters that we choose to censor or completely conceal from the world (and, in some instances, even from ourselves) often have to do with painful memories involving those we have loved, and may remain deeply loyal to, even though their behavior toward us or their heedless neglect of our needs once caused us great harm. So you had to wonder: Was something from the past driving Claudia's wildly mistrustful behavior, making her feel that the very notion of confiding in the person closest to her, her new husband, was completely out of the question—that simply being herself would drive him away? Moreover, what (if any) signals was her body sending her whenever she contemplated opening up and telling him the truth?

As Claudia was to tell me later on, the mere thought of doing so always set off some frantic reactions in her body—most prominently, feelings of constriction in her throat, as if she couldn't catch her breath, and a wildly thumping heartbeat. She took these to be urgent communiqués of alarm that translated into "Don't even think of it!"

Claudia Martinelli was behaving as if her life's experience had taught her, and taught her well, that trust and openness were simply *not* among the options to be considered in an intimate situation. Deeply ingrained within her physical being, as well as her belief system, seemed to be the basic assumption that lies and falsifications about who she really was, and what had actually happened in her past, were her only means of staying safe, if not to say surviving.

He Doesn't Know Who I Really Am

Before making plans to meet her in person, I'd gained some preliminary understanding of the difficult and potentially disastrous circumstances in which Claudia Martinelli had recently found herself. As she'd described recent events in her life, she had gone to see a psychotherapist two weeks in advance of her second marriage, which had taken place some eight months earlier. At that point in time, elaborate arrangements for her wedding ceremony and reception—flowers, music, caterers—had been made and were all set to go, but she'd had an agonizing problem on her mind.

The dilemma that had suddenly sprung to front and center at that time had to do with everything about herself that she *hadn't* told the man she was on the verge of marrying. For insofar as outward appearances were concerned, Claudia Martinelli was an attractive, stable, and reputable woman in her mid-thirties, who was on the fast track upward in the management hierarchy of an elegant Manhattan department store. However, unknown to Paul Novak, her bridegroom-to-be, there had been a period in her life—it was after the breakup of her first marriage—when she'd been partying uproariously, drinking too much, snorting cocaine, on the loose, living a wanton, promiscuous existence.

She'd said not a word about this to her future husband, even though she knew that Paul had been through a similar "crazy time" himself, after the bitter ending of his own first marriage. He'd gone through a period of living the same frenetic, drinking and drugging, dissolute life on the edge. He'd been a high-risk gambler for a while, too. The cardinal difference between them was that he had told her all about his past, while she'd held back about her own history and her reckless, extravagant experiences.

Why, I wondered, hadn't she told him her story early on, during the highly romantic and potentially more forgiving period when they were just becoming involved? It would have been far easier at that point, but she had been afraid to take the risk. She'd probably been frightened that he would look down upon her as a wanton woman and lose respect for her, perhaps end the relationship on the spot. That would have been *hard*, for he'd been so kind and caring then; she hadn't wanted to take the chance of spoiling things.

The truth was that this relationship had felt so *right* to her, and Claudia had been very tired of living on her own; she'd wanted to settle down, have a child or children, a real home. Moreover, as I was to learn, keeping secrets had been a way of life in the household in which she'd grown up. So she'd postponed making any revelations while events kept moving along, from courtship to an engagement to the plans for the wedding; and it wasn't until just before her marriage that she began to panic about the secrets she was holding.

At that penultimate moment, she'd needed to consult someone outside the situation (not a close friend, not a relative, not anyone who knew her) about the pressing question she was asking herself over and over: Is it fair to go ahead with this wedding when the man I'm marrying doesn't actually know who I am or the truth about my past? She was feeling beset by strong urges to unburden herself and just *tell* Paul about that period of her life; but each time she came close to doing so, those frantic warnings from within began prompting her to consider the probable consequences.

She seemed to know enough about her future spouse to realize that forgiveness wouldn't come to him easily. In truth, her fears about the potential magnitude of his reaction always drew her up short, horrified. With the wedding arrangements all in place, and so many acceptances in, how could she spring this information on him from out of nowhere? Besides, wasn't there a realistic danger that Paul would be so infuriated that he'd decide to call the whole thing off? If something like that did happen, she would be shamed and humiliated in front of all her and his family members and their entire circle of friends. Yet if she *didn't* talk to him until after the wedding, there was the very real threat that her new husband would feel cheated and manipulated—as if he'd been hoodwinked into marrying a woman who wasn't what she had appeared to be and who was, in fact, damaged goods.

Eleventh-Hour Wedding Jitters

I wondered what had really sparked those eleventh-hour wedding jitters and sent Claudia scurrying to seek a therapist's advice with virtually no time in which to consider her options and make a well-examined choice. Was it possible that her upsurge of anxiety had less to do with "being fair to Paul" than it did with her own doubts about the viability of the relationship—about how she really *felt* when she was with him? Did she go to that clinician because she herself, at some level, wanted to call the marriage off? It seemed quite plausible that she'd never been forthright with him about her own past because she knew, *in her gut*, that she couldn't trust him to hear her in a spirit of compassionate acceptance.

Indeed, she could have had her doubts about whether she really loved Paul—at least not for himself. But then, why had she chosen him? Maybe the underlying agenda that had pushed things this far had to do with her being a woman who was moving into her upper thirties and was eager to start a family before her biological clock ran out of time. Consulting a therapist might have represented the other side of a deep ambivalence (marrying a man she was coming to know as critical and judgmental versus giving up on ever having a child).

As I saw it, getting married with a secret of this sort on your conscience would be like getting married with a time bomb in your pocket; honest and open communication between the members of the couple would be impossible. However, the psychologist Claudia met with in that eleventh-hour consultation suggested a different, and in its own way reasonable-sounding, way to look at the situation on the ground.

That therapist had taken the position that the details of Claudia's past were her own "private information"—information that she could share or *not* share with her husband-to-be, just as she chose. Her biographical data belonged to *her* and to her alone. She could choose to hold on to it herself or not, but it existed on a completely different moral plane from any current-day secrets affecting their own relationship that she might be keeping from her prospective bridegroom.

This rational (you could say rationalized) perspective on the dilemma had sounded levelheaded enough to Claudia and enabled her to feel sufficiently comfortable to go ahead with the ceremony. But in my own view, she'd been withholding information that she knew to be highly pertinent to her partner and to the relationship. Did this fall into the domain of "maintaining privacy," or was it more on the order of "keeping secrets"—entering the marriage feeling that she'd offered only an airbrushed version of herself? In any case, in the months following the marriage—not too surprisingly—the time bomb had gone off. Paul began questioning her about her past.

Why in the world hadn't he done so earlier? They'd been engaged for over a year, and during that time her bridegroom-to-be had asked Claudia relatively little about what her life had been like after the ending of her first marriage or about the nature of her more recent relationships. You had to wonder why he hadn't discussed these matters with her during that prolonged, rose-tinted period of their courtship, when he had talked so much about his own past.

Was it possible that Claudia had been responding to *Paul's* signals by not telling him outright what he clearly hadn't wanted to hear (otherwise, he could have asked)? Perhaps he did suspect her, in a sub-rosa fashion; but there was a sense in which the two of them had been honoring a silent pact. Her past was to be a taboo subject, at least for the time being.

It wasn't until after they were man and wife that those concealed parts of her history began to emerge and affect the couple's relationship in profoundly damaging, destructive ways. For only then did Paul's curiosity about the details of her recent past—most particularly, the saga of her sexual adventures—begin to make its appearance and thereafter continue to escalate steadily. By the time of our interviews—which got under way about eight months after the marriage—Claudia was sounding as if she'd been taken hostage. Her husband was now interrogating her, demanding that she fill in the blank spaces, complete with all the distressing, upsetting details—things he'd never asked about before.

Who were the men she had gone out with, and which ones had she been to bed with? he wanted to know. What kinds of sexual activities had she engaged in? Had she ever been involved with a certain mutual acquaintance (a high executive in the firm for which she now worked) whose erotic exploits were legendary? Perhaps most heinous of all, had she, a religious Catholic woman, ever had an abortion? Paul was badgering her continually, trying to get her to say that she *had* done so.

She felt isolated, full of self-blame, so worthless and unsafe. Such feelings, it should be said, are fairly commonplace among people who have experienced acute stress at some period of their lives, particularly during early childhood; and this did prove to be relevant in Claudia's case. But for now she insisted that no matter what else happened, or how scared or bad she felt, being open with her husband was an option that was off the table, totally out of the question. He would "torture" her; she would never hear the end of it.

Actually, he was "torturing" her at this moment. The pair seemed to be locked in a marriage of mutual projections: She carried all the "badness" in the relationship, while Paul had assumed the robes of righteousness and represented morality, truth, and "goodness." Did this domestic scenario—a flagrant distortion of reality, in which she was the base, humiliated, powerless one and he was the fierce, upright, and judgmental one—have an air of familiarity to both of them? In the course of our conversations, I'd begun to wonder whether Claudia Martinelli had placed herself in a relational position that she knew well and that felt deeply *fitting* to her, even though it kept her in a state of distress and high bodily arousal.

Keeping Secrets

I suppose I'd fallen into a kind of reverie, for when the chimes of the grandfather clock pealed for a second time, they caught me by surprise. My thoughts had wandered afield, and I'd begun musing about the high costs of keeping secrets, especially secrets from a person with whom you share an intimate relationship. Holding out on undesirable, embarrassing information can turn you into a kind of undercover agent, someone who must be on guard constantly lest the dangerous truths about your character and history emerge. You can't be open about certain important matters that are really on your mind, and the upshot is that you move into a position of isolation—the secret is your closest companion.

This state of affairs generates great tension within a person and in a relationship, not only in yourself as secret holder, but in those close to you, who become confused, uneasy, mystified. The partner (or close friend or family member) has a sense of being shut out—unable to connect with you and understand what is happening in your life. And while, at the outset, maintaining silence may have presented itself as the simplest, easiest, most sensible way of preserving an appealing exterior or persona, in reality this kind of "solution" exists only at the problem's surface: The secret itself doesn't go away.

Instead, what is untold and feels as if it *cannot* be spoken of (in part because one *hasn't* ever spoken about it) seems to inflate in the dark, as if its forbidden nature has endowed it with a yeastlike quality. The hidden truth takes on more and more power and dimension, silently increasing the emotional space between the secret keeper and the unaware other, thus rendering trustworthiness and clear communication between the self and the partner impossible. And inevitably, that sequestered material assumes a menacing importance that it might never have had if it hadn't been thrust out of sight. For not only the secret itself, but the series of lies, omissions, and/or cover-ups that have been utilized to maintain it have a poisonous effect upon the secret holder's most needed, valued relationships—upon friendships and family ties as well as the emotional attachment to a mate.

Why, then, does keeping secrets strike so many people as the most efficient way of dealing with those awkward, uncomfortable facts about ourselves or our family members that we wish would go away? Many secrets are created because it seems much simpler to suppress certain less than flattering data—to "stuff it," whisk it out of awareness, never speak about matters that might place us in a vulnerable or embarrassing light. Who needs to know about your parent's alcoholism; a brother's mental illness;

an illegitimate half-sibling; your level of income; the true nature of your inner feelings; the pornographic films you sent away for; the psychoactive medications you're taking or once took; an extramarital affair; or the relationship struggles you and your partner were involved in or are involved in at the moment?

According to most marital and family experts, the primary underlying motive for secret keeping has to do with shame. Secrets are founded upon the belief that if certain aspects of your life and history were to see daylight, you would not be regarded as an acceptable human being; you would be seen, and see yourself, as outside the pale of decency, the shameful violator of some kind of taboo. When it comes to holding back or opening up, fears of spoiling other people's images of you or of disrupting important relationships are always being weighed in the balance against the heavy psychological and interpersonal burdens of living alone with the information.

Also, it hardly needs saying that there are many situations in which, practically speaking, it seems wiser and more judicious to remain silent. For even though the suppressed information may weigh heavily on the secret keeper's spirit, daring to reveal it can generate brutal counterattacks.

One woman I interviewed in the course of this work had had an incestuous relationship with her father during her late adolescence. Much later on, when she wrote about her experiences in an exquisitely poetic and painful book, many people were scandalized. A number of reviewers attacked her for not having kept quiet about what had occurred. As she later said wryly, no one appeared to be bothered by the fact that these things *had* happened to her; they were far more outraged by her daring to discuss them openly! Societal pressures had been brought to bear to keep a secret out of sight—to suppress the ugly truth that such episodes do occur, to simply live with it, never speak of it aloud, move on, and pretend it never happened.

The reasons for maintaining silence are not only shame and self-protection, but family loyalty as well—an entire kinship network often depends upon the secret keeper's silence. When I asked this woman how she had managed to endure the consequences attendant upon her public truth telling, she responded by saying that difficult as it had been—and it had been *hard*—she had no regrets about having done it.

"I was living a life that felt completely fraudulent, because no one knew who I really was. Now I don't have to pretend to be anyone but who I am. I am *myself,* the person who underwent those experiences," she told me. Her strong motivation, which had been more powerful than the need for self-protection, the feelings of shame, or the pull of family loyalty, had been to get to a place where she could live a life that *felt real* to her; a life in which she felt like a real person. My own thought was that it takes tremendous courage to open up a raw and explosive family secret of this sort—to face the barrage of flak that's sure to follow and get to a place where moving on becomes possible.

Just recently, a friend's loyalty to her family of origin had been the major underlying factor in a secret that was being kept from me. The truth had tumbled out in the midst of a seemingly desultory conversation I was having with this friend, with whom I've shared a close, confiding relationship for many years. I knew that her older sister had died some six months earlier, but suddenly, with no preamble, she told me that her sister's death had come about largely as the result of years of domestic violence: Her husband had been a wife beater.

I'd found this revelation startling. Why hadn't my friend ever talked with me about this while her sister was still alive? Given that this sibling lived across the country in San Francisco, there wasn't the remotest chance of any untoward consequences. Nevertheless, despite our longtime attachment, my friend hadn't even mentioned what had been happening until many months after her sister's death. It was as if she'd been loyally guarding this secret all the while, protecting her sister's ugly story from an outside world, which included me, a close friend.

At one level, I could understand why my friend had done so; it is *hard* to speak of sorely painful, hidden matters that place members of our families (and, by extension, ourselves) in an ignoble light. Also, I was well aware that almost everybody keeps secrets and tells lies on occasion: I knew that when a nationwide poll on truth telling was carried out in the 1990s, a full *90 percent* of the respondents had acknowledged having been deceitful (and who can say whether or not the other 10 percent were being perfectly aboveboard?). Keeping secrets appears to be fairly normative in the general population.

Nevertheless, on another level, my friend's revelation about her sister left me feeling cut off and frustrated: If my friend had ever talked with me about this situation while it was occurring, I might have offered her my comfort and support, perhaps even suggested options that hadn't been thought of or considered before. Secrets do erect barriers that shut other people out, closing off possible sources of emotional supply and help—this was something I surely knew from my own life.

A Loyal Liar

Shame, loyalty, protection: All of these had motivated my steadfast keeping of the big family secret that had preoccupied much of my adolescence. "Don't ever tell people your parents are divorced, or they won't respect you," my mother had counseled me in the most ominous, fiercely cautionary tone of voice.

How young and how credulous I'd been—it was almost endearing—but I'd believed her, oh, I'd believed her. It all seemed so screwy now, this so-called momentous family secret with which my own adolescent years had been burdened. She and my father had parted for good when I was fourteen.

My mother. Her warnings came from a world she knew, but it was the old world, another world; she was walking around with a tiny nineteenth-century village inside her head. I embraced the truth of everything she'd told me, but how does a fourteen-year-old girl keep a secret like *that* one?

I did it, somehow. I did it for her, and for me. I did it to fend off the never specified but clearly terrible consequences that would surely follow upon any foolishly candid revelation. It meant that I couldn't let anyone get too close to my real life, not so close that they were in danger of knowing who was in my family and how we actually lived. Even years later, when one of my college suite-mates complained continually about her *own* parents' divorce, I followed my mother's stricture and kept the monstrous secret of my family's breakup.

But simply saying nothing in that kind of situation can make you feel like a fraud and a liar. You feel disconnected, watchful, haunted by the thought: He or she wouldn't like or respect me if the shameful truth were to come out. Inevitably, I developed well-defended, sealed-off compartments within my head. In one such compartment my suite-mate was perfectly entitled to talk about her parents' "disgusting" split-up, and in another compartment was the forbidden knowledge of my own parents' divorce. *That* could never be divulged lest I be sunk in degradation, become the object of everyone's scorn. Worst of all would be the sin of disloyalty—betraying my mother's edict and her confidence, the shameful knowledge that had been left in my keeping.

The imposing clock nearby emitted a sonorous single *bong!*, snapping me back again into the present. Another fifteen minutes had gone by: Strange how the memory of that onerous secret could still affect me, so many years later. My cheeks were feeling hot and flushed, and I could hear the tom-tom of my speeded-up heartbeat reverberating within my chest. I'd been reflecting upon matters that belonged in the long-ago past, yet my body was reacting as if this whole dilemma existed in the "real time" of the present moment.

A quick glance at my watch told me that it was now six forty-five—time to give up on this appointment. The glamorous woman (was she a model?) sitting across from me seemed to be coming to the same conclusion; I noticed that she'd gotten up and was standing there, frowning, looking uncertain. Then she strode across the lobby to talk to the bedazzled young Hispanic clerk at the front desk.

I stood up, too, crossed to the other side of the seating area, and plumped myself on a sofa near where she'd been sitting. I wanted to spend a last few minutes keeping my eye on the front door. But there was a lull, nobody seemed to be arriving or leaving; this interview wasn't going to happen.

I'd begun gathering my things together and was just buttoning up my coat when the woman who'd been sitting across the way came back, approached me, and said hesitantly, "You aren't . . . by any chance . . . Maggie?" I must have looked startled—and I think I startled her, too—for she took a small step backward.

I stood up immediately and then just stared at her, as dumbfounded as if a statue had suddenly sprung to life and spoken to me. "Are you *Claudia?*" I asked incredulously. The two of us gazed at each other, open-mouthed, and then just burst out laughing; the ridiculousness of the situation had struck us both immediately. Here we were, the only two women sitting alone in the lobby—and we'd sat there without either one making a move to identify herself! It was as though we'd each decided, on the spot, that the other *couldn't* be the right person!

Even now, as I think back upon that curious episode, I'm hard put to come up with some explanation about why neither one of us stepped forward. As far as my own part in that strange scenario is concerned, however, I have several alternative theories. My best guess is that I saw the woman in the Yale Club lobby area as too flawless, too well organized, too in charge and in control, to be the distraught person I'd spoken to on the telephone. I'd been completely misled by an outward presentation of self that was so utterly at odds with everything about this woman that I believed I'd already learned—a potent reminder that many people are marvelously skilled in showing to the outside world those parts of themselves that they want the outside world to see.

The Filtering Lens of the Past

Claudia and I went up to the fourth-floor library, but we couldn't find a completely private place to talk. The best we could do was to settle in a small, book-lined room just off the main reading room; but we had to talk to each other in quiet voices. Someone else was present, a woman curled up in a leather chair, riffling through a stack of magazines. She was sitting on the far side of this cozily shabby, enclosed little area.

The two of us pulled a couple of library chairs up to an old, round lamp table, and I put my tape recorder upon it, midway between the two of us. Then I opened my large drawing pad, leafing through it till I came to an empty page. I began the interview in my customary fashion, which is by quickly sketching in the most significant facts of Claudia Martinelli's life history, as it had commenced in her family of origin and as she'd lived it out thus far.

In so doing, I made use of a favorite clinical device known as a "family genogram." The genogram is the shortest, safest, most efficient way of gathering an overview of a person's emotional and relational biography—his or her family's narrative and its major themes. The method is so simple that it almost borders on the silly, for it consists of nothing more than a series of straightforward, mundane questions—questions such as: What is your mother's first name? Is she living? Did she work while you were growing up? Is she retired now, or is she still working? Can you give me a few adjectives that would describe her, generally speaking, such as "warm" or "stern"or "tender" or "reserved"?

Dry and factual as these questions may sound, they are always strongly evocative, for the answers to them are inevitably laden with rich associations—associations that begin spilling out in the course of the discussion. As the person being interviewed talks about each individual parent and about what their marriage was like; as she gives the names of her siblings and perhaps talks about other relatives (such as grandparents) who were important in the family's life; as she describes her present partner, her ex-partner (or partners), and her children (if there are any)—something both remarkable and totally predictable occurs. Even as she focuses intently upon the past, and the tenor of life in her family of origin, the particular words she chooses and the associations she makes create an uncannily accurate overview of the structure of her present-day consciousness.

Why and how does this happen? Because there are reliable continuities between *what is now* and our stored remembrances of *what has gone before*; the past becomes incorporated in our psyches and our bodies. The basic components of consciousness itself—our ways of perceiving ourselves, others, and the world around us; our emotional reactions to those perceptions; and the ways of thinking that accompany those perceptions —are powerfully defined by the framework for living with which our embedded memories have provided us. We are always experiencing the present moment stereoscopically, seeing it through the filtering lens of what has happened to us earlier.

Thus, the very act of *seeing*, in the immediacy of the here and now, is to some considerable degree an act of remembering—remembering from a certain perspective. "While sifting through the sensory present, the brain triggers prior knowledge patterns, whose suddenly reanimated vigor ricochets throughout the [neural] network. Old information comes alive, and a person then *knows* what he used to know," as memory researchers Thomas Lewis, Fari Amini, and Richard Lannon have written. In brief, the brain is constantly responding to experiences in the present by linking them to associated experiences in the past.

And in some instances the past is exerting such spellbinding power that an individual behaves, all unwittingly, as if compelled to continually play out a familiar role in a well-known script or family libretto. It is almost as if this role has become the individual's single option for being, the behavior software of the self; it's deeply lodged within his or her body and psyche. Typically, however, when the connection between *what used to be* and *what is right now* is recognized, it is experienced as a shocking revelation. It is the hardest thing in the world to *know* this about the self.

The realization that a forgotten but eerily familiar family theme is being re-created in one's present-day existence usually comes as a sobering, eye-opening experience—yet it can be a liberating and life-enriching experience as well. This is especially true in those frequent instances in which there's been a disconnect between certain body-based emotional states—for instance, pervasive feelings of anxiety, anger, or grief—and the network of subliminal thoughts and associations that have given rise to them.

What the body remembers has been encoded and stored within the central nervous system's vast internal filing system. And often it is only when these bodily data have been summoned forth and integrated with an understanding of the milieu in which certain destructive patterns of being have emerged that *something new can happen*. Later on in this book, I will be describing some of the ingenious, relatively new therapies that are oriented toward freeing the body from the hurtful memories it may hold and achieving a kind of body/mind integration—that is, toward accessing and resolving the past as it exists within our mental and physical beings, simultaneously.

Core Schemas and Dynamic Themes

Not only is it true that there are strong continuities between our past histories in our families of origin and the basic organization of our present-day consciousness; there are also continuities between what *used to* be, what is now, and what *will be* in the future. For our expectations of what *is likely* to happen to us are strongly predicated upon what *did* happen: The fundamental truths that our life's experiences have already taught us seem to move us in the direction of making those familiar things occur once again—though frequently, at a conscious level, we really don't want that to be so.

In brief, we often operate in ways that will result in our inner expectations—good and bad—being fulfilled. Our most basic perceptions of the world around us are always being selected and shaped by an internalized blueprint for living that we've developed over time. This "framework for living" contains the core schemas and dynamic themes—the images of who we are and what we will be—that shape our perceptions of the past and understanding of what lies in the future. At an unconscious level, our personal blueprint underlies the well-known "self-fulfilling prophecy," which is to say that what we believe in our hearts—that is, our bodies as well as our minds—about "the way things are" tends to become true in reality. In some subtle fashion, one that's usually not within reach of conscious awareness, we shape the way the narrative of our life develops.

A Carousel of Slides

As Yale psychologists Jefferson Singer and Peter Salovey observe in *The Remembered Self,* "Imagine that each individual carries inside his or her head a carousel of slides of life's most important memories. These slides have been carefully selected to represent the major emotionally evocative experiences that the person has ever had. . . . Although memory is perpetually taking snapshots of each and every experience that we encounter, there always emerges a core of slides to which we return repeatedly. This dog-eared bunch of slightly obscured or distorted images comes to form the central concerns of our personality."

These are the very images that come to dominate our interactions with the world around us. They are the things we "know" and become—and because we know them so well, it's often difficult to see ourselves or our lives in other ways, to consider fresher, less familiar, perhaps healthier and more effective options for how to be and how to interact with those around us. Thus, reflecting again upon Claudia Martinelli's current marital situation, I couldn't help but wonder: Had she found herself hopelessly entangled in such no-win secrets before, a life where lies and subterfuges—and feelings of inner turbulence and hyperarousal—had become a deep-rooted part of her existence? And if so, what had her secrets been about?

Chapter Two

—

LAYER UPON LAYER OF SECRETS

On that evening of our first interview, Claudia Martinelli and I spent most of our time working on her family genogram. When I asked her for some adjectives that would describe her mother, Claudia responded with the following words and phrases: "blunt; smart; a good person; energetic; self-reliant; independent; she sometimes settles too easily." I wasn't sure what she meant by the last-named quality but later realized that she was referring to her mother's habit of backing down in any real confrontation, of constantly giving way to Claudia's dad.

At this point, however, I simply jotted down these mainly positive-sounding terms on the chart, just beneath the round circle designating "Sylvia, age 69." As I did so, I couldn't help but notice how nonmaternal her depiction of her mother sounded. I could probably be accused of gender stereotyping, but when I heard "blunt, smart, good, self-reliant," I couldn't help thinking of a guy. I didn't hear anything warm or womanly in that characterization, especially when it came to a daughter's description of her mom.

Still, Claudia's feelings about her mother were far more favorable than were her feelings about her father, Nick, who was just turning seventy. The words she used to describe Nick were "a hypocrite; inconsistent; moody; depressive; critical; judgmental; a tightwad." Her father was going to be a *priest* before he met her mother, she added, an expression of derision flickering across her features. "Which is so ironic, because he's a real holy roller—he goes to church every morning—but he doesn't practice, he can be a *mean* person."

She paused, then added in a clipped tone of voice, "That's a good adjective for him, hypocrite. My father *is* a hypocrite." My gaze slid downward to a section of the genogram I'd sketched in earlier. I was struck by the fact that when I'd asked Claudia for adjectives that would describe her new husband, Paul Novak, the responses she'd given without hesitating were "judgmental; controlling; inconsistent; generous to a fault." Clearly, there was some intergenerational continuity here.

Aside from the single discrepancy—her dad was a "tightwad" and Paul was "generous to a fault"—there was an overlap between many of her husband's and her father's outstanding qualities, at least in her own mind. I asked her then if the word *hypocrite* could apply to Paul as well.

Claudia shook her head and said it didn't; but then she paused. She drew in a deep breath, exhaled with a kind of sigh, and recanted: "Paul *is* Mr. Nice-Guy, too—on the outside, to everyone *else*, I mean. He'll help *anyone* with any kind of problem, but at home he's different, very critical. Which is just the way my dad was when we were growing up." Both men were given to presenting a hypocritically genial face to the world outside the family but were demeaning and judgmental within the household.

She folded her hands in her lap, stared down at them like a sullen schoolgirl, murmured almost inaudibly, "The way he *talks* to me . . ." Then she looked up, stared at me fixedly for a few moments, and said, "My husband is a very smart, quick-witted man. He's really *funny*, but he can cut you down in two seconds. And he's very sarcastic." I nodded, acknowledging how that could make a person feel: Sarcastic people can often misread the line between what is funny and what is cruel.

Claudia looked grim. Once again I had the thought that she and Paul had fallen into a pattern that involved his playing the part of the condemning, judgmental father/parent and her taking on the role of his blameworthy (secretive, sexual) adolescent daughter. But when I asked her directly if her husband tended to take on a faultfinding, "parental" role in his relationship to her, Claudia merely shrugged and said she couldn't answer that question—she thought he would have been equally controlling and critical with any other partner in any kind of circumstance.

She thought it was "the way he was," and to some extent this was obviously so. For while it might seem that all the anguish in the relationship was being created by her secrets—that the relationship itself was *defined* by her secrets—Paul was surely reacting to a script of his own. Indeed, like many troubled couples, both partners seemed to be involved in reenacting a highly patterned minidrama over and over again. *His* script had to do with projecting all the blaming and the badness outward, away from himself, and seeing it as existing in the "immoral" Claudia. *She* was reacting to a guilt-ridden, shame-filled script of her own—a script that interfaced with her husband's all too well and left her in a continual state of fear, wariness, and high arousal.

At this moment the major area of discord between the partners had to do with Paul's stance in the relationship, which was that of the prosecutor, the paramount authority, the one who is always in the right and has all the forces of moral law and rectitude behind him. He was constantly hounding Claudia for information, pummeling her with questions that she felt far too intimidated to answer in an honest way. There were so many things about her past that made her feel tarnished and stigmatized, secrets she couldn't even dream of telling him.

Abortion was one such taboo topic—the real truth was that she'd had not one but two of them and had never said a word about them to anyone (though she believed an older sibling had her suspicions). I paused momentarily on hearing this, for it signaled the fact that holding on to secret information was nothing new in Claudia's life. Her way of dealing with the less palatable aspects of her reality seemed to be to maintain sole control of all potentially damaging information and to trust nobody—even those closest to her, who might otherwise have been sources of comfort and support. Clearly she had adopted this lonely, emotionally distant strategy in that "basic training camp for later living" that is the family of origin.

In any event, information that's suppressed and "disappeared" doesn't truly vanish or diminish in intensity: Even in situations where a person dissociates and puts the matter out of mind entirely, the body holds the knowledge of what has happened. In this instance, Claudia's feelings about those abortions *seemed* to have been resolved and faded; but suddenly, perhaps due to the harsh questioning she was undergoing, she'd found herself filled with grief and ruminating about them all the time.

Thought of those abortions preyed on her, she said, making her feel ashamed, guilty, and sick at heart. Claudia placed one hand on her abdomen, the other on her breast, and said that these thoughts often gave rise to woozy, lurching sensations in her stomach and feelings of tightness in her chest. Then she stopped speaking; tears were brimming in her eyes, and she paused to take a tissue from her purse. But she merely began wringing it in her hand without wiping away the plump, glistening tear that was sliding down her cheek.

"I'm sorry, it gets me so upset to think about it," she said in a low, muffled tone of voice. Then she added with a small, hopeless shrug that talking with Paul about these matters that so weighed upon her was completely out of the question. "He would feel *totally betrayed*, because he's asked me any number of times, 'Have you ever had an abortion?' and I've always said that I haven't." She knew he didn't believe her; and in fact he was pressing her harder and harder on this subject.

Why had this issue suddenly taken on such importance to him? Had the question of abortion played a role in some episode earlier in Paul's own life? Or had Claudia's reactions been such that he'd realized "abortion" was an agonizing issue for her and therefore a winning card in the fierce win-all or lose-all marital game the pair seemed to be playing? Was there a level at which this sense of embattlement felt uncomfortable, but *familiarly uncomfortable*, to both of them—the way a marital relationship ought to be? One couldn't know, but just recently Paul had begun upping the ante on this inquisition and subjecting her to ever fiercer cross-examinations.

"He will hammer at me, 'You *did* have an abortion, right? Tell me the truth! You *did*.'" She would try to deny it, but Paul would come back at her immediately, "You did; come on, you *did*. I think you did, right? *Tell me!*" Even as she said these words, Claudia and I were both startled by a sudden *thump!* It was the sound of a book dropping on the floor. The woman at the other end of the room, whose existence had disappeared from our mutual consciousness, had gotten up and was shrugging into her overcoat. She stooped over to pick up the book, then stood again and couldn't resist a curious look in our direction.

We turned back to our conversation, for she was clearly at too great a distance to have heard what we'd been saying. The next time I looked around, she was gone. We were alone, and the two of us had fallen silent. Claudia's eyes were fixed upon me, her expression taut, the portrait of vulnerability and fear. I met her gaze with compassion but was wondering how and why she'd managed to box herself into so untenable a position . . . and why she was allowing this state of affairs, with its obvious impact upon her highly aroused physical and mental state, to continue.

How Can I Trust Him?

Claudia was acting as if she lived in a one-option world, one in which there was no method of responding other than to stick adamantly to the original version of her story. And even though this basically unworkable strategy was requiring that she pile lie upon lie—to the point where the relationship threatened to buckle under the strain—she was behaving like the proverbial horse who *knows* his way back to the barn and cannot deviate one step or conceive of any other means of getting there. Why was it so hard for her to envisage any of the possible alternatives when it came to coping with this impasse—ways of proceeding that might serve to lower the tension level without setting off an explosion?

One such strategy might be for her to go to Paul and say directly, "You know, by putting me through these constant inquisitions, you're destroying our relationship. These grilling sessions make me feel as if you're searching for some terrible wrongs that I committed earlier in my life, and I'm not sure why you're doing this. Where is all of this heading? Are you looking for a full confession, so you can give me absolution and we can go on? Or are you just looking for reasons to be upset and angry, so that we have to dredge up things that happened in the past—things that can't be changed at this point in time? If so, I don't want to continue doing this."

A statement such as the above would serve to let him know that she had her limits, and he had reached them: that she would no longer enact the role of the bad, immoral victim as his counterpart, so that he could play the role of her indignant, righteous denouncer. And if she were able to maintain this posture, it would also stop the cycle of aggressive accusations and disbelieved, discounted denials.

Yet another, fairly similar approach to the situation might be for her to say to Paul, "I know I haven't lived a perfect life—you haven't, either—but do you think it's going to be helpful to continue going back there, when neither one of us can undo our own history? Can't you accept me as I am, at this moment in time, so that the two of us can go on from here? You yourself must realize that these inquisitions are making us both miserable and destroying the good things we had together. So for the meanwhile, for both our sakes, *I'm not going to respond to any of these questions anymore.*"

Of course, availing herself of an option of this sort would require a level of inner fortitude, entitlement, and healthy self-regard on Claudia's part—and Paul's interrogations put her on the defensive so quickly, made her feel so demeaned, guilty, and frightened. As I contemplated her situation, it seemed to me that in the process of withholding information in order to keep the relationship going, she had backed herself into an existential corner. As matters now stood, Claudia felt she had no choice but to go on lying to her husband about her past—her personal history might once have been her "private information," to be revealed at her own discretion, but in this relationship it had assumed a fissile potential that was akin to TNT.

In a strictly operational sense, that psychotherapist's carefully reasoned statement *hadn't* proven true: Claudia's past didn't seem to belong to her, despite the fact that it predated that period of her life when she and her husband had become involved. And at present Paul wasn't behaving only like a prosecutor, he was also like a hanging judge, harassing her for the very information that would condemn her in his eyes. It was as if he had *chosen* her so that she could play out this role in his internal drama. And she herself was in a no-win situation, for the very things she needed desperately to talk over with a loving, supportive partner were the things she couldn't dream of telling him—despite his own flamboyant past, he was fiercely critical and judgmental of other people, especially his wife.

"He would *use* this stuff against me, as my first husband and my father always did," Claudia said, looking terrified.

I paused, thinking about this statement: It was clear that this situation was deeply familiar to Claudia in many respects, a situation she'd found herself in before. This suggested that she might be involved in an unconsciously staged reenactment of a long past relationship, one involving a man who is critical, judgmental, and in a state of chronic anger and a woman who is subservient, "settles" (gives way, as her mother did) all the time, and feels culpable and frightened. Was Claudia reliving, as many people do, charged aspects of an unintegrated, unresolved past—one deriving from an old family pattern—in the context of this present-day relationship?

One could only speculate about that possibility at this point: Far more pressing and starkly obvious was that the existence of so much secret information was making it impossible for this couple to get on with their lives, to bond with each other and create any sense of mutual closeness.

"If I can't feel comfortable talking about these things with Paul, how can I *trust* him?" she now demanded, then didn't pause to hear an answer. "And why should he trust *me*, if I'm holding back on him?" Prior experience seemed to have taught Claudia Martinelli that being open and honest with the men in her life was neither safe nor advisable; and her current-day experience was confirming—underlining—what she'd already known beforehand.

She leaned toward me expectantly, looking hopeful, as if she thought I might come up with her answers in some magical fashion. I looked at her sympathetically but said nothing—given her agitated, hyperaroused state, there didn't seem to be any calmly reasoned, carefully worked-out solutions to the dilemma in which she'd found herself. But as we sat there, I found myself speculating about those wedding jitters and that desperate, last-minute trip to the therapist. Had that eleventh-hour request for help actually represented her wish and her hope that *this* relationship might be better, more open, and more honest than any of the ones she'd been involved in earlier?

One couldn't know, for by now it wasn't only her past that was causing their fierce, ongoing arguments. They were fighting about all sorts of *other* issues, too, most especially about the handling of money and her style of interacting with Paul's adolescent children by his first marriage. These items were both hot topics, which frequently led to ugly, unresolvable conflicts, fights that always ended in his triumphant rightness and her being in the wrong—and wanting to leap out of her own skin, unable to soothe herself or to calm down. Claudia was feeling desperately afraid that this new marriage—her "second chance at happiness"—was doomed and might not even make it through the coming year to the time of their first anniversary.

I glanced down at her partially completed family genogram. She was essentially giving this marriage no more than a year, and I noticed that her first marriage had actually lasted much longer—she'd been married for five years, having wed at twenty-six and divorced at thirty-one. Gazing down at that five-year time span—designated by a slashed line on her chart, indicating the marriage and the breakup—I couldn't help but speculate about how and why *that* relationship had ended. Had her first husband been as angrily "critical" and "judgmental" as the other males in Claudia Martinelli's life always seemed to be or to become? And had she been in the one-down position in that relationship as well?

I paused, inhaled, and exhaled deeply before resuming; the magnitude of her emotion was such that it seemed to have leapt the arc between her body and my own. As if by means of some communicative miracle, I'd started feeling that I wasn't merely listening to her talk about her fears, I was feeling her tension and anxiety *inside* my body as well.

Chapter Three

PHYSIONEUROSIS: THE BODY KEEPS THE SCORE

INEVITABLY, IN THE COURSE OF THE RESEARCH, I BEGAN looking backward in time and wondering whether something in my own life had kindled this interest in secrets, lies, and traumatic experience. Had I myself ever felt overwhelmed by severe early stresses? In terms of life's potential catastrophes—earthquakes, floods, rapes, childhood sexual exploitation, being threatened with death, or witnessing a homicide—I was surely not a "trauma survivor." There had been no alcoholism, incest, drug abuse, or wife battering in the household in which I grew up.

Nevertheless, as I talked with various women, including Claudia Martinelli, about their relationships with their fathers, I found myself thinking hard about my relationship with my own—or, more accurately, about the void that had always been "Daddy." Our household had always been filled with his silences, with closed doors and unfathomable events. Daddy almost never spoke, either to me or to anyone else in the family; he was a cold, simmeringly angry, unapproachable human being, and everyone in the household, including my beloved mother, was afraid of him.

I have such graphic memories of his staring, expressionless gray eyes, not meeting anyone's gaze but forever looking beyond, as if searching out new grounds for his ever seething indignation. But does spending your young years in a domestic police state constitute "developmental trauma"? The question of what actually *constitutes* a traumatic experience remains unsettled, a subject of ongoing controversy, while newer definitions continue to be proffered. For example, a task force of the American Psychological Association has recently defined a traumatic stressor as "an event or process that leads to the disorganization of a core sense of self and safety in the world and leaves an indelible mark on one's world view."

What is meant by a "traumatic stressor" would obviously never be in doubt in certain instances—for example, a serious car accident that proves fatal to a family member riding in the car or, more globally, the cataclysmic attacks upon the World Trade Center. Those brutal attacks involved civilian losses never seen before; and for those who made their terrified way out of the collapsing towers as well as those who lost fathers, mothers, sons, daughters, sisters, brothers, and/or friends in that morning of catastrophe, the world will never look the same again. Altogether shattered were their basic assumptions about their own personal safety, and they were left with a haunting sense of personal vulnerability with which most Americans had been unacquainted before.

Could growing up in an atmosphere of chronically oppressive threat be compared in any way to such hugely calamitous sorts of events? I couldn't point to any clear-cut trauma that was making me feel vulnerable and scared; still, as I reflected on that long-ago time, I stumbled upon so many shut doors, so many unknowns in my family of origin—mysterious fragments of distant events that could emerge at the surface and then vanish again, unexplained. There was the visit of an "uncle"—his name was Albert—who came to see my father on one occasion. He never returned, and in the prevailing silence of my childhood home, he seemed to have disappeared as abruptly as he had materialized. He was a jack-in-the box uncle, who'd bobbed up and then disappeared without anyone's ever alluding to him again. It wasn't until many years later that I learned that "Uncle Albert" was actually my half-sibling. He was my father's grown son by a second marriage (my mother was his third wife, and another wife was to follow).

An Economic Slave

When I think about my childhood, my most vivid memories are always of my mother. I worshipped her, yet even so, the immediacy with which that little-girl ardor sprang into being during that sleep clinic biofeedback session amazed me. It was as if my feelings about my mother were as present as ever, fully intact within my very brain cells; and those feelings had the capacity, at the deepest levels of my being, to relax me and make me happy. Beneath all later misadventures and setbacks there still existed that central and fundamental image, described in the preface, myself as the baby of my mommy. When it came to self-inducing a state of calm and contentment, no other imagined scene had the same ability to cut off those clicking sounds of tension so completely.

An early, very strong aspiration—the fiercest goal of my girlhood and what I wanted more than anything else—was for my mother to be happy. "You *will* be happy someday, Mommy," I, her impassioned confidante, would assure her. I willed it to be so and believed that it *would* be so, in the brighter, more fulfilling future that awaited her. But unless there are aspects of my mother's life of which I know nothing, that brighter day never did come.

These days, an early photograph of my parents sits on an antique cherrywood bureau in the bedroom. It must have been taken around the time of their marriage. She looks so limpid, so wide-eyed, tentative; she can't be more than eighteen or nineteen. He was almost fifty, twice married when they wed, and his jaw juts out sternly, as though he's her irritated parent. His image is sharp edged, hers hazier, as though each stood in a separate light. She is all softness, soft dark hair, a dark V-necked blouse. Lining the V is a long strand of pearls, and even they are not well defined, but glimmering vaguely. She tried to leave my father, she told me, when my oldest sister, Norma, was still a tiny baby.

"What could I do, though? Where could I go?" She always sighed when she got to that point in the story. She couldn't have survived with a small child, in a strange land whose language was not her own. Why had she ever agreed to come here, to marry him? I wanted to know. She explained that her own father, whom she'd loved dearly, had died young; he'd left a widow, five children, and a Warsaw dry goods store that soon began failing miserably. My grandmother, a less sympathetic-seeming character—she sounded to my childish ears like the Old Woman Who Lived in a Shoe—had ultimately told my eighteen-year-old mother that she was literally unable to keep her.

The upshot was that my mother had been contracted to go to America as the bride of the aging ogre who was to become my father. The brutal, economic truth of the matter was that she'd been condemned to a form of domestic slavery, and over time she'd been forced to bend to the yoke of that marriage.

I think, every once in a while, of a certain contest that I, as a young schoolgirl, entered and reentered time and again. The contestant completed an endorsement of a certain product "in twenty-five words or less," and the winner's prize was a genuine diamond ring. I can bring to mind so readily the fantasies with which I indulged myself: joyful scenarios in which I sprang that genuine diamond ring upon my astonished and ecstatic mother. I would have done anything to make her life better.

There are other scenes, real-life scenes, remembrances of sitting alone with my mother. I was a little older then, and I watched her as she shoveled coal into our basement furnace. Her face was beautiful in the flickers of light as she talked about her girlhood, her own mother, and the good-looking captain of the boat that had brought her to America. He had really *admired* her, she recalled; but she was already promised—on her way to be married. I was so filled with sorrow and regret about that lost possibility, that romance that had never come into being.

"You'll be happy someday, Mommy, you'll see," I assured her passionately. If only I could have changed her history, willed her elopement with that unknown captain! She must have believed it, too, because she often sang or hummed her favorite song, "Bluebird of Happiness" ("Be like I, Hold your head up high / . . . Somewhere there's a bluebird of happiness . . ."). Besides, there was the Gypsy's prophecy. On the eve of her departure from Warsaw, my mother had consulted an ancient Gypsy woman, who'd read her palm and foretold her future.

The Gypsy had predicted that my mother's forthcoming marriage would produce four children (it did; I was the third) and that it would be an unhappy union. The fortune-teller also said that the marriage would end in the middle of my mother's life (this proved true as well; my parents divorced when I was fourteen years old). On a more positive note, the Gypsy had told my mother that she would eventually marry again and that this second marriage would prove a very different one—one in which she'd find the peace and happiness she had been seeking throughout many long years. In the wake of my parents' separation and divorce, when so much family ugliness of all kinds erupted, I know I hung on to that bright prophecy like a lifeline.

Another Kind of News Flash

Obviously, that consistently repeating first sentence of my life's narrative, discussed in the preface—"I was born, and nobody noticed"—was at variance with such passionate, loving memories as those just described. I was my mother's adorer, her oh-so-willing vassal, and I'd listened to her, empathized with her, and worshipped her as long as I could remember. My very consciousness—who I was, and the person I became—took shape within the cradle of this initial, magical attachment. Yet from somewhere deep within my being came this other kind of news flash, this piece of information I didn't want to contemplate or even register.

For the statement's obviously painful translation was this: While I'd always listened to my mother well and willingly, my own normal child needs for attention and affirmation had gone unheard. The first sentence of my story was about a little girl who had emerged into consciousness in an environment that contained barely enough emotional nutrients for any family member's survival. It was about a young child who'd found her own special niche in a depriving world by listening scrupulously and barely realizing that no one was listening to her in return.

I know that I felt sorrier for my mother than I ever felt for myself. I loved her so unreservedly, so indebtedly, that it took me more than half a lifetime to recognize how profoundly neglected a child I'd been. Of course, denial and excuses on her behalf were always readily available. She had lost her adored father as a young girl and then been delivered into economic slavery in her adolescent years. If these terrible blows had left her with what E. M. Forster called "the undeveloped heart"—by which he meant the ability to *care enough* about another human being—the reasons why were all too apparent.

I knew that I'd been a shabby, ill-kempt child—there were never any clean clothes in my bureau drawer. At times I'd even arrived at school with my hair uncombed, and I recall one humiliating occasion when the teacher chewed me out in front of the entire class, then sent me to the girls' bathroom to make myself presentable. The trouble was that I didn't have a comb with me. I remember being unable to admit this when I was exiled from the classroom, and I remember trying to comb my curly hair with my fingers in front of the bathroom mirror.

Why was it, then, that the opening sentence of my autobiography—"I was born, and nobody noticed"—ultimately burst upon me as a shocking realization, one that turned all prior understandings upside down? I suppose that this disconcerting knowledge had been contained within me for a lifetime, for that first sentence of my life's narrative had popped up so briskly and so immediately. From the point of view of empathy, validation, and affirmation, it was clear that I had been my mother's mother. In this magical first love attachment of human existence, the normal caring-parent/dependent-child roles had been reversed.

How did that scene at the school bathroom mirror end? I have a shadowy notion that an older girl came in, took pity on my situation, and let me use her comb; but I don't really know whether such a thing actually happened. The still vivid, emotion-packed parts of the episode are like a reel of film that ends abruptly at that moment of panic: I am standing there trying to comb through the tangles in my hair with my fingers.

And even many years later, the evocation of that scene could pack a wallop, one I felt in my rigid jaw, and the cavity in the pit of my stomach. Its message was that even if my own legitimate growing needs had gone unnoticed at an explicit, conscious level (by myself as well as anyone else), those unmet needs had, at another, more subterranean level, been silently encoded. At the silent, wordless level of the brain and the peripheral nervous system, my body had always kept the score.

Highly Arousing Events

There is now a large body of preclinical (which is to say, animal) literature—and some fascinating evidence from clinical research involving human subjects as well—indicating that the brain has a way of specially bookmarking highly arousing events. What we remember with the greatest clarity are the things that happened when we were very happy, very sad, very angry, or very frightened. We remember these happenings well, and for extensive periods of time, because of the intense, immediate, bodywide reactions they evoked—and often *continue* to evoke, despite the passage of years and what may be the vastly changed circumstances of a person's life.

Seen from a purely biological vantage point, it is well known that bodily states of emotional stress—for example, those associated with feelings of intense fear—trigger a panoply of psychophysiological responses. In a situation of threat, activating biochemicals, such as the hormone cortisol (which is manufactured in the tiny adrenal glands, above the kidneys), are immediately pressed into states of high activity. So, too, is the neurotransmitter norepinephrine, a chemical substance that ferries electrical impulses across the tiny gaps, or synapses, that separate neighboring nerve cells in the brain.

These rapidly circulating neural "messengers" serve to augment vigilance and sharpen the focus of the individual's attention upon the danger at hand. They promote a sense of being fully in the moment, and of perfect clarity, as if all of one's perceptions had been fine-tuned instantaneously. Such reactions are, of course, a part of the immediate, bodywide reaction that many experts view as evolution's gift to us—the instantaneous "fight or flight" response—which prepares us to stand and do battle or to flee the alarming situation as quickly as possible.

What is most arresting, however, is that this cascade of brain chemicals not only prepares us for emergencies, it enhances the retention of memories as well. In other words, what becomes quintessentially *memorable* appears to have its all-too-fleshly roots in the underlying neurochemistry of the body during states of emotional arousal.

Emotion and Remembering

One of the most ingenious demonstrations of this biological reality is a study carried out by neuroscientist Larry Cahill and his colleagues at the University of California at Irvine. In the first phase of this remarkable research, two groups of college students were asked to view a set of slides. One group heard a dramatic and upsetting voice-over narrative during the viewing—a story that commences with a mother and son leaving home, after which the boy gets caught in a terrible accident while crossing the road, receives critical injuries during the fray, and then is rushed to the hospital. The other group of subjects was told a completely different story about what was happening during their separate viewing of the same slides—a rather bland version in which a mother and her son are leaving home; they cross the road, and along the way, the boy sees some wrecked cars in a junkyard. Then they go to visit the boy's father, who works at a hospital. In this more benign version of the tale, nothing much happens.

One week later the students returned and were given a surprise memory test. Those who'd heard the traumatic version of the narrative recalled the story far better and in much greater detail. The Cahill researchers then hypothesized that a surge in the brain hormone norepinephrine had enhanced and sharpened those subjects' ability to remember. So in the second phase of the study, they recruited two different groups of students and had them look at the same slides with their differing accompanying stories.

In this second go-round, however, the scientists had previously injected a beta-blocker (propranolol, which would block the upsurge of the neurotransmitter norepinephrine) into half their subjects about an hour before the viewing. The remaining volunteers were also given an injection at that time, but theirs was an inert substance, a placebo. The two groups were then mixed together into one larger group, and then the original experiment was repeated. That is, the students were once again divided into two sections and asked to view the same set of slides while the varying versions of the narrative were told to them.

Then, as in the previous go-round, the students were summoned back for surprise memory testing one week later. In this case, the participants who'd heard the upsetting narrative and received propranolol—which of course blocked the actions of the brain hormone norepinephrine—could not recall the slides any better than those who'd listened to the neutral voice-over. But those who'd received the placebo *and* heard the upsetting story were well able to recall the slides; they remembered them much more clearly than did those who'd listened to the mundane narrative. The highly galvanizing neural hormone norepinephrine clearly played a critical role in human memory retention.

Physioneurosis

As recent experimental work with a variety of mammals—cats, rats, monkeys, and human beings—has compellingly shown, memory preservation occurs in what might best be described as the shape of an upside-down or inverted U. If you're in a situation in which the levels of your stress-related brain biochemicals happen to be low—say, out to lunch with a friend—you're likely to focus less intently on the experience and to forget the details of the lunch conversation later on. You can think of low levels of these "fight or flight" hormones (such as norepinephrine, also called adrenaline) as existing at one end of our envisaged upside-down U. At this peaceful, nonthreatening side of the U, the details of the luncheon, perhaps even the memory of the event itself, are likely to fade fairly soon.

But if on that occasion you should hear some personally threatening news—your friend thinks you should know that your son's been getting plastered at recent high school parties; or your job promotion is being challenged by a recently hired competitor; or your husband has been spotted in some highly questionable circumstances—the levels of your stress-induced, circulating neurotransmitters will surely rise abruptly. As they do, the memory of this occasion will be highlighted internally: That remembrance will be highly likely to become preserved within your body's neural circuitry, as will the strong emotions that attended it.

The basic principle here is that higher levels of fight-or-flight-related brain biochemicals equal better memory—*but only until the summit of that inverted U has been reached.* Then the opposite effect begins to emerge, and as the outpouring of fight-or-flight substances continues, the quality of remembering declines. At dramatically heightened levels of stress, memory becomes disrupted and fragmented, and in some cases an experience may be so shocking that all (or parts) of it is deleted from conscious awareness. This occurs, of course, in cases of amnesia.

There are countless examples of this phenomenon cited in the animal literature. To take a very simple one: A rat that's learned a maze, and immediately upon completing the learning task has been given an arousal-inducing norepinephrine injection, will typically traverse that maze more efficiently the next time around. The injected rat will perform this task much *better* than will a noninjected peer, who has forgotten the "neutral," unexciting experience shortly afterward.

But—and this is an important "but"—if the injected rat's norepinephrine levels are then augmented by further doses of this potent neurochemical, there will come a point at which there's a conspicuous *decline* in the animal's performance. The rat will run the maze far more haphazardly, because too much of the stress-related norepinephrine affects memory as adversely as does too little.

Actually, when you think of this from the point of view of species survival, it does make overall good sense. It makes *sense* to mark well those situations that have ignited feelings of alarm and anxiety, so that they're held firmly in mind and avoided in the future. Such memories, with their strong component of powerful emotion, would clearly be of crucial importance in terms of living long enough to mate, reproduce, and pass on one's genes—which is always the bottom line, biologically speaking.

During the human species's extended prehistory in the natural habitat, this highly italicized kind of remembering was probably programmed into the human genome. For chances were that if an individual didn't remember *keenly* those situations that felt threatening, he or she might not live long enough to be threatened again. It goes without saying that things have changed over the aeons of intervening evolutionary time, so that the nature of "what is dangerous" looks very different—the psychological and physical threats that we face in a modern-day industrial environment are vastly different, and infused with far more complexity, than simply managing to not get eaten by a hungry saber-toothed tiger or lion!

Still, when it comes to human coping mechanisms, our brains and our nervous systems haven't changed significantly since the relatively recent (in terms of evolutionary time) period when large predators roamed and ruled the earth. Nowadays it may be your explosive, abusive, short-tempered parent or stepparent who threatens you, rather than a charging animal; but memories of situations that *have once been experienced as highly dangerous* still tend to be what experts call "overencoded" or "overlearned"—that is, etched deeply into our cerebral wiring.

Aversive, distressing memories of this sort appear to be concentrated, and perhaps stored as well, in a tiny brain structure, the "amygdala." Within this diminutive, nut-shaped structure, potent memories of danger and threat can abide for days, months, or even years after the crisis situation itself has ended. Even in instances where a person realizes, at a rational and intellectual level, that a position of safety has long since been attained, his or her nervous circuitry can nevertheless remain fixed in a state of high tension, supervigilance, and hyperarousal.

This state of internal affairs makes it impossible to relax completely, to feel calm within, to trust, to truly let down one's guard; there is always that pervasive sense of the danger hovering around the corner. One of the pioneer trauma theorists, Abram Kardiner, called this sort of human plight a "physioneurosis"—an affliction that is neither purely physical nor purely psychological in nature, but a combination of both.

Chapter Four

THE BODY REMEMBERS

WHY AND HOW DOES IT HAPPEN THAT OUR BODIES CAN hold the knowledge of situations and events that we ourselves have forgotten? The answer is that while we usually think of our emotional lives as being psychological in nature, they are in fact *deeply rooted in our bodily experiences* of charged events that are occurring or have occurred in the past.

The human brain, with its hundred billion nerve cells and its million billion connections, holds boundless numbers of impressions, some briefly and for a passing moment, some throughout an entire lifetime. These are our memories, which not only exist at an impalpable, psychological or "mental" level, but also have a corporeal existence within the body's nervous system.

To be sure, we are far from being able to point to a particular location within the dynamically active brain where a distinctive memory resides. However, we do know that thoughts pertaining to that memory can give rise to *body-based emotions* and that there are many situations in which we are having powerful somatic reactions to experiences that may have long since slipped beneath the surface of awareness.

To take an example: Suppose it was late at night and you were driving through a dangerous-looking area. Having found yourself feeling thoroughly disoriented and in need of directions, you might be thinking, I'm afraid of this strange neighborhood, and I think I'm lost. You might even be on the verge of panic but still feel too frightened to roll down your window and ask a questionable-looking passerby for directions. The main thing to realize about this experience of fear is that although it *feels* as if it's happening at a cognitive, "thinking" level, it is actually being accompanied by an instantaneous cascade of internal, neurobiologically driven bodily reactions and responses.

You might experience these internal responses as a speeded-up heartbeat, a shallowness of your breathing, gooseflesh on your skin, a trembling of your lips and hands, or a tight feeling in the pit of your stomach; but the important point to be made is that this fear experience is occurring *in your body and your mind simultaneously*. And even if no outright harm actually arises in the course of this episode—aside from a storefront gang screaming sexually loaded comments at you and banging on the car's window—it might well happen that long after the memory of this incident has become hazy or faded from your thoughts entirely, the mere suggestion of a night drive in an unfamiliar neighborhood makes you (that is, *your body*) feel agitated and queasy.

The body remembers. Curiously enough, however, this widely acknowledged biological truth—that our memories are *physically* as well as mentally present within us—is one that's often overlooked by practitioners of the more traditional forms of verbal ("talking") psychotherapy. This is regrettable, because there do exist many situations in which all the discussion, understanding, and insight in the world never succeeds in dispelling the painful images, reactions, and somatic aftereffects (such as hypervigilance, jumpiness, or a depressed mood state) of events that were once experienced as horribly out of control or overwhelming.

According to world-renowned trauma expert Bessel van der Kolk, M.D., numerous treatment impasses occur because "top down" brain processing—cerebral processing that proceeds downward from the neocortical, "thinking" areas of the brain, where language and higher reasoning processes are represented—cannot fully access and effect changes in the deeper, wordless regions of the midbrain, where the engines of anxiety and hyperarousal are churning.

An afflicted person may, therefore, reach an exquisite intellectual and emotional understanding in regard to some of the painful events she or he has been through yet remain in a *bodily* state of apprehension—perennially jammed on high alert, internally mobilized for a danger that has long ceased to exist in reality. In these not uncommon cases, the reasons for the fear are past—and may have been thoroughly analyzed and interpreted—but the sense of dread and foreboding persists at a visceral, bodily level.

This happens because our conventional therapies tend to rely upon what psychiatrist van der Kolk calls "the tyranny of language." In clinical practice, he asserts, it often proves difficult, if not downright impossible, to alter an individual's underlying *physiological* state even when the person is making giant strides in terms of his or her psychological understanding and self-awareness.

Achieving insight about a chronically neglectful or emotionally abusive history, or a loss or fearful incident of some other kind, doesn't necessarily succeed in changing certain *bioemotional* reactions and responses. Very often the body is still reacting to the past as though it were the present; and even though the person may have made sense of and seemingly resolved painful bygone problems, the relief is only partial—the body holds the memory of what has happened, even at a cellular level.

Inside the "Black Box" of the Brain: Trauma

Until relatively recently, most neurological researchers took it as a given that the functioning—thinking, feeling, remembering—brain of a living human being would never be accessible to scientific observation. For the brain, solidly sequestered behind the hard, bony structure of the skull, seemed to be an inviolate "black box"—a marvelously intricate, yet totally sealed-off organ that could never be looked at directly, much less studied while it was in action.

Then, starting in the mid-1980s, an increasingly sophisticated array of computerized brain-imaging techniques—among them functional magnetic resonance imaging (fMRI) and positive emission topography (PET)—came into being. These new technologies enabled researchers to look directly at the brain's interior regions and *observe what things happened* when a person was responding to memories of an emotional nature—for instance, recollecting an intensely stressful, fearful experience.

At the present time this neuroimaging research is, relatively speaking, still in its infancy, but it has already yielded some remarkable results. One fascinating study, undertaken in the mid-1990s by Bessel van der Kolk and a group of Harvard colleagues, involved carrying out PET scans of the brains of trauma survivors at the same time as they were reminiscing about the terrifying experiences they had undergone. In other words, these scientists *took a series of photographs of the brain's interior* while memories of the trauma were on the individuals' minds.

To their surprise, the researchers found that in terms of oxygen flow, there was clear-cut *increased* activity in the right hemisphere of the brain, which appears to be more associated with states of emotion and bodily arousal. At the same time, there was a marked *decrease* in oxygen utilization in a brain region in the left hemisphere known as "Broca's area," which is known to be responsible for putting words to internal experience.

These results raised an intriguing question: Could this shutdown of the language-related Broca's area, in conjunction with a surge of activity in the "emotional" right hemisphere of the brain, be the cerebral model for a state of speechless terror? If such a link existed, it could explain why some people find it impossible to put their feelings into words and instead express those feelings in the guise of symptoms or as repetitions of self-defeating behaviors.

A Difference in the Brain: The Hippocampus

We now know, due to our newfound technological capacities, that the brains of adults who underwent chronic physical or sexual abuse during childhood tend to look somewhat *different* from the brains of people who experienced no such early mistreatment. The particular region of the brain in which this difference shows up is called the "hippocampus"—a name that derives from the Greek and means "horse-shaped sea monster," for this small, lobelike structure does resemble a sea horse when viewed in cross section. To be more precise, the hippocampus actually consists of *two* small lobes, one on each side of the brain, but it is generally referred to in the singular.

The hippocampus is situated deep within the brain's unconscious core, the midbrain—also known as the "old" or "mammalian" brain because in evolutionary terms it is believed to have first emerged in mammals. While much about this structure remains unknown, it is now widely recognized that it is crucial to the processing and retention of short-term memory—it can, indeed, be thought of as "short-term memory central."

The hippocampus is responsible for the ongoing sorting and organizing of the steadily arriving streams of sensory data that we are constantly receiving; in other words, it functions as a kind of high-speed, superefficient reception center where newly incoming information (for instance, sensory data, such as what is being seen, felt, heard, and so forth) is instantaneously sorted, cataloged, and held in short-term memory for an unspecified period of time. Short-term memory is also known as "working memory," for its primary focus is upon recognition and processing of what's happening in the present.

Some of this incoming data may fall into the realm of the familiar—information that's been encountered earlier—and therefore be speedily identified, categorized, and preserved provisionally for possible long-term retention. Or the arriving information may be surprising, novel, unfamiliar—and therefore be responded to with an enhanced degree of emotionality before being passed upward to the topmost, outer "thinking" areas of the human brain (the "neocortex") for further assessment. What is unknown and unfamiliar requires *attention* and may possibly demand some kind of defensive response on the part of the individual.

Brain Cells and High Stress

In the late 1990s, three different brain-imaging studies, all focusing on the hippocampus, produced the same remarkable findings. Two of these research investigations demonstrated that people who'd undergone traumatic stress during childhood—chronic physical or sexual abuse—tended to have *smaller* hippocampi than did a group of "controls" (non–severely stressed individuals). The third research study involved war veterans who were suffering from lingering symptoms of trauma; and in this case, too, that same strange hippocampal shrinkage was prominent among the volunteers.

Why should severe stress lead to shrinkage of the hippocampus, and what might be the meaning of these findings? Well, one clear inference flowing from the results was that individuals who had been subjected to chronic, bruising stress tended to experience cell loss in this vital brain area that is so critically important when it comes to the temporary storage of short-term memories. Could this be a *physically* based reflection of the common clinical observation that people who have been exposed to traumatic experiences often have great difficulty integrating certain fragments of memory into a coherent autobiographical past that makes sense?

Moreover, could this reduction in hippocampal volume explain why such individuals often find it difficult to experience the past as something *that is over* and often feel that what happened *then* is continuing to happen in the here and now? It is known that the hippocampus is where aspects of personal history (so-called episodic memories) are put into their proper context of space and time. These memories are organized along the lines of what happened, and where it happened, and when (for example, "I went to the park; met my friend; stopped and had a coffee with her; left her at the corner; promised to call tomorrow").

The experience I've just described has a neutral, benign quality and is therefore likely to be retained for a while and then eventually fade. However, if that coffee shop were robbed during this outing, and my friend and I were in fear for our lives, that memory would be extremely emotionally charged. Furthermore, if I were someone whose short-term memory had been impaired by awful stresses earlier in my life, I might have extraordinary difficulties when it came to sorting, processing, metabolizing, and digesting this traumatic experience. Then, instead of moving along into long-term memory retention and becoming part of my past, this terrifying episode might exist only in splintered form, and remain stuck in short-term memory—that is, in the here and now of an unending present, neither fading away nor undergoing further processing.

Response Readiness: The Amygdala

Close by the hippocampus and located just above it is another important brain structure, the amygdala. The word *amygdala* means "almond" in Greek, and this part of the brain has been so named because of its small size and nutlike shape; again, though it's referred to in the singular, there are duplicate amygdalae, one in each cerebral hemisphere. Both the hippocampus and the amygdala are part of an intricate, varied group of modules that make up the brain's *limbic system*, that cerebral area where our emotions and emotional responses are thought to be generated.

The limbic system is responsible for a host of functions related to survival, including monitoring of the organism's internal state (body temperature, rest/activity cycles) and its instantaneous physiological reactions to situations of fear and danger. The latter, of course, is the fight-or-flight response, to which must be added the "freezing" or "numbing out" response in situations where battle or escape is completely impossible. This body-wide crisis response is mediated by the amygdala—often called the brain's "emergency alarm system"—for it is within this tiny knob of nervous tissue that information about a potential threat is received and powerful emotions such as anger, fear, and rage are generated.

Due to the work of neuroscientist Joseph LeDoux, whose careful studies have traced the neural pathways of fear in an animal model (the rat), we now know that the amygdala can rapidly traverse what LeDoux terms a "quick and dirty" shortcut to another limbic system structure called the hypothalamus. On receiving the amygdala's signal, the hypothalamus initiates a series of bodily reactions that puts the threatened organism into a state of immediate readiness to meet the stressful challenge—sometimes even before the conscious mind has fully grasped the presence of any menace or peril. In other words, via this newly detected cerebral pathway, our "emotional brains" can be recognizing and responding to an imminent threat before we ourselves—our thinking, evaluating selves—have even appreciated the fact that it's present.

In any event, whether we are or are not consciously aware of a looming danger (which may indeed have arisen from within, in the form of a terrifying memory), our innate fight-or-flight emergency reaction will automatically switch to "on." This body-rooted emotional response, which has evolved to aid survival under conditions of peril, involves a vast array of physiological changes throughout our bodies and our brains.

These include an elevation in heart rate and blood pressure as more blood flows to the muscles of the arms and legs (to promote running or fighting) and a rise in oxygen consumption as bodily metabolism moves into high gear to meet the emergency. Also evident is the stepped-up secretion of neurohormones such as norepinephrine (aka adrenaline) to help mobilize a host of other "crisis" resources. For example, the spurt of norepinephrine entering the bloodstream causes the pupils of the eyes to dilate; an individual can literally see better when under stress. In short, this resultant surge in physical energy and mental acuity, brought about by means of sympathetic nervous system arousal, is elicited with lightning speed by situations that are seen as menacing to the organism's integrity.

The good news is that the body's resources are rapidly mobilized to meet the danger or to contain and control it as much as possible. However, the bad news is that there are many instances in which the emergency itself is over—and perhaps has been for many years—but the brain's survival alarm system hasn't been fully turned off. The threatening situation may be part of the long-ago past, but it feels as if it's free-floating in time, with you at every moment.

In the wake of overwhelming stress, which has never been fully metabolized and integrated, a person is likely to feel profoundly unsafe and to see dangers and difficulties lurking everywhere. Curiously enough, though, that same person is often credulous and unseeing when it comes to recognizing and identifying the realistic threats that do exist in his or her life. It's as if the noise level generated by the predominant warning system is so compelling and attention demanding that myriad smaller, yet utterly essential warnings are being drowned out.

Chapter Five

BEHAVIORAL REENACTMENTS: WAS CLAUDIA MARTINELLI IN AN EMOTIONALLY ABUSIVE RELATIONSHIP? WHAT IS AN EMOTIONALLY ABUSIVE RELATIONSHIP?

SO MANY TERMS IN DAILY USE ARE BANDIED ABOUT WITHout anyone being certain of their exact meaning, and the phrase *emotional abuse* is surely prominent among them. For even though many people think they're quite clear about what is meant by this expression, if asked to define it precisely, they'll hesitate and their faces will turn blank.

Then, after a long pause, one person may characterize emotional abuse as verbal bullying: one partner constantly storming and shouting at the other, who then exists in a cowering state of fear. Someone else may define it as having to do with expressing dislike and icily ignoring or neglecting the other's needs and requests—an example that comes to mind is that of an interviewee of mine who had developed a breast lump, but whose husband never talked with her about what was happening or showed any interest or concern as she underwent the frightening process of diagnosis. Still another person may conceive of emotional abuse as an ongoing series of put-downs—one mate's continual undermining and devaluing of the other's intelligence, competence, and basic worth as a human being.

Actually, all of the above contain a piece of the truth, for "emotional abuse" covers a vast expanse of ambiguous and often elusive territory. A very broad definition of the term, suggested by expert Marti Tamm Loring, is that it is "an ongoing process in which one individual systematically diminishes and destroys the inner self of another. The essential ideas, feelings, perceptions, and personality characteristics of the victim are constantly belittled."

A core element of both emotionally and physically abusive relationships is that there is a power imbalance between a controlling tyrant and his or her oppressed partner; this was surely the case in Claudia Martinelli's marital relationship. In such instances, where the aggression is only on a psychological level, the partner under attack—typically, though not invariably, the female member of the pair—is often completely unaware that she's involved in an emotionally abusive relationship. This is because nonphysical violence leaves no black eyes, bruises, or broken arms and is often occurring at a subtle level in some quite innocent-appearing situations. An additional reason why the victim of abuse fails to recognize what's actually happening is that she is often someone who feels that whatever is going wrong is her own fault: Again, this was true of Claudia, who felt deeply responsible for her mate's behavior and as if she actually deserved it.

This assumption of blame feels natural to the abused partner, who has typically grown up in a situation where—owing to a child's magical sense of being at the center of the universe—she has taken on all the responsibility and blame for everything that is going wrong in her world. For such feelings of omnipotence, a normal aspect of early childhood, lead many a youngster to feel personally at fault for a parent's bad or frankly outrageous behavior, or even the adult couple's decision to divorce. Here, the child's thinking is, If only *I* were better, the *right* kind of person, my mother or father would be different, and this sweeping sense of guilt and failed responsibility has often been carried into adulthood.

The target of emotional abuse, therefore, is often someone who (despite the fact that she's being undermined, scorned, trivialized, and misunderstood in her most intimate relationship) has found herself living in a tense domestic atmosphere with which she is deeply *familiar.* For as author Loring and other workers in the field have noted, *there is a recurrent relationship between early trauma and psychologically abusive attachments later on in adulthood.*

This is because, in Loring's view, emotionally victimized women often remain oblivious to the fact of their abuse. "For them, emotional violence has become a way of life. As the experience of being emotionally mistreated often begins early in childhood, the victim cannot conceive that another, entirely different kind of relationship is possible. Yet although they have become accustomed to emotional violence, they never cease to feel its pain. Each new wound is as devastating as the preceding demeaning assault."

Clearly, the defining difference between physical and nonphysical abuse is that the victim of wife battering *knows* that someone is periodically attacking and hurting her—she has the bruises to prove it. The victim of psychological aggression, on the other hand, is often in a state of internal chaos, confusion, and uncertainty about what is, or is not, taking place. This is why it is so important for individuals of *both* sexes, who want to maintain healthy partnerships, to identify and familiarize themselves with the multiple forms in which this type of emotional violation can occur.

An extremely illuminating list of behaviors that fall under the rubric of emotional abuse—you might call it an early warning list, setting forth the most significant features of this form of interpersonal aggression—will be presented further along in this chapter. But first I'd like to talk about abusive attachments more generally—about why some people are drawn into these relationships and why they so frequently remain in them while their confidence and sense of security are slowly drained away.

Overt and Covert Abuse

As the poet Yehuda Amichai has written, "The past throws stones at the future / And all of them fall on the present." In the course of our second interview, Claudia Martinelli described a recent quarrel with her husband that had erupted like a geyser the previous Saturday night. It had gotten so out of hand that, as she put it, "I was ready to put on my sneakers and *run* for it. My gut feeling was just *that*—I'm out of here! I'm out! I don't have to be treated like this! It isn't *right*; I'm being abused!"

Still, by the time of our meeting, that particular argument had been settled and Claudia didn't appear to be taking the idea that she was "being abused" too seriously. Hers was, of course, a characteristic kind of reaction; the last thing that she or any other successful, seemingly independent woman ever wants to fully confront is the fact that she's become marooned in a devaluing, emotionally injurious relationship.

But although such situations can't be easily identified and tallied up in terms of incidence within the general population, most clinicians believe emotionally abusive attachments to be extremely pervasive. As psychologist Joan Lachkar points out in *The Many Faces of Abuse: Treating the Emotional Abuse of High-Functioning Women*, a surprisingly large number of individuals who (like Claudia) are competent, attractive, and successful players in the career marketplace—lawyers, executives, physicians, and the like—come home in the evenings to endlessly belittling, frustrating, ego-draining relationships with their intimate partners. And only slowly, if ever, do they come to recognize their close attachments as being "abusive" in any way, shape, or form.

There is simply huge inner resistance to doing so. For among the many other reasons for "not knowing" what is happening, there is the victim's effort to maintain some inner sense and outward image of her personal dignity. This is why it is only with the greatest of reluctant foot-dragging that a woman who has earned the respect of the world around her becomes willing to recognize that an unsavory word like "abuse" has anything to do with a process happening in her own life.

Moreover, there are many kinds of emotional aggression that are difficult to detect. *Overt* abuses (derisive put-downs, constant criticisms) are obviously easier to recognize, but there are a great number of *covert* forms of attack that are insidious, confusing, and extremely hard to discern clearly. For example, a seemingly loving, well-disposed partner may always be in "objective" agreement with anyone who states an opinion or position that is at variance with that of his mate: It is as if the game that he's playing is always on the side of the net that is opposite to his partner's, and she is being consistently invalidated and belittled.

Behavioral Reenactments

Claudia Martinelli was an adult, experienced woman at the time of her second marriage, not a starry-eyed, unformed teenager. So I couldn't help but speculate about whether the "stones of the past" had fallen into her present-day existence. Had she walked into—even helped to construct—an intimate relationship in which she would be periodically attacked and castigated; and had she done so because such experiences had become (in Loring's phrase) "a way of life" much earlier in her own personal history?

Claudia's track record through adulthood (at least what I knew of it thus far) surely did bespeak an individual who feels profoundly *bad* about herself; she'd been involved in so many self-damaging behaviors—drinking, drugging, emotionally uninvolved sex—that had left her feeling empty, degraded, and worthless. People who are filled with negative feelings about themselves will frequently "act out" in this way, do things that will make them feel ashamed and guilty, thereby confirming their ingrained views about their basic worthlessness and unacceptability.

As many trauma experts have observed, such people seem to be under the sway of strong internal forces to re-create, in their present-day relationships, certain core experiences of early life that once terrified and overwhelmed them. This reliving of certain problematic or downright menacing aspects of the past is known as a "behavioral reenactment"—which is to say, an unconscious drive to replay the devastating experience(s), either just as it, or they, occurred or in some slightly disguised version.

It was Sigmund Freud who first drew attention to this curious tendency and called it the "repetition compulsion." Freud was struck, as have been many subsequent clinicians, by the frequency with which people behaved as if they were under some curious pressure to stage reenactments of painful early dilemmas. It was, observed Freud, as if the individual's "way of remembering" the past was to restage the problem in the present—to keep getting into strangely repetitive revivals of traumas that had never become integrated, resolved, and part of a time that was *over*.

There are, not surprisingly, important sex differences when it comes to reenacting, in adult life, overwhelming stresses that were experienced during childhood. As psychiatrist Bessel van der Kolk observes, in an important article entitled "The Compulsion to Repeat the Trauma," a number of research studies indicate that "abused men and boys tend to identify with the aggressor and later victimize others whereas abused women are prone to become attached to abusive men and allow themselves and their offspring to be victimized further."

Efforts to Master and Resolve Unfinished Business

Most modern-day therapists view the tendency to stage reenactments of painful aspects of the past as driven by unconscious efforts at mastery—that is, the deeply cherished hope that by resurrecting the traumatic experience(s), one can try again to work it through and resolve it. This "unfinished business" kind of explanation certainly did strike me as one of the more plausible reasons why a woman like Claudia Martinelli—highly attractive, successful—would have walked into a marriage with so critical and ferociously blaming a partner, someone whom she dared not be honest with because she was sure any efforts at openness on her part would be greeted with contempt and rejection on his.

In any case, it was reflections such as these that made me wonder whether Claudia's parents—whom she'd dryly dubbed "the Bickersons" because they quarreled all the time—had done more than merely bicker. Had there been more serious physical or emotional aggression in her home, aggression that was currently being resurrected and relived in her relationship to Paul? If Claudia was in fact involved in a behavioral reenactment—one that might have to do with a hypocritical, hostile, tyrannical man and a devalued, invalidated woman—then it was clear that her irate, verbally abusive mate was in some ways the perfect partner in a script that felt all too familiar.

Traumatic Bonding: Why She Stays

Why would anyone stay in an intimate relationship where one partner—the powerful one—is periodically trivializing, deriding, harassing, threatening, intimidating, or even physically attacking his disempowered mate? One important factor in such situations is a phenomenon psychologists have termed "traumatic bonding." Traumatically bonded relationships are characterized by what is known as "intermittent reinforcement"—in plain words, alternating intervals of reward (lovingness and warmth) and punishment (psychological or physical abuse).

It has been well established that relationships of this kind—that is, those that fluctuate between outbursts of aggression and times of loving tenderness—create emotional attachments that are far *stronger* than attachments that proceed on a steadier, more even keel. The paradoxical truth is that this mode of inconsistent, unpredictable relating creates a gluelike connection between the oppressor and his oppressed, always apprehensive partner. This is why, as painful and damaging as these fear-ridden relationships may be, they are extremely hard to sever.

Why should this be so? According to Dr. Janet Geller, who works with couples in emotionally and physically abusive relationships, most individuals living with an assaultive partner can recall an earlier time when the relationship felt safe and secure and the mate's behavior was far more caring and affectionate. "Things were *good* at one time," Geller told me, "and maybe they still *are* good from time to time, especially in the wake of an outburst, when the partners are in the making-up phase. So the abused person in this situation hangs in, waiting for the rewarding part; she's always trying to get the relationship back to the way it was in the beginning. This makes it very hard for her to extricate herself."

In addition, the fact that the submissive partner's efforts *are* thus rewarded from time to time provides her with even more of an incentive to stay. For what learning theorists call an "intermittent reinforcement schedule" of this kind serves to keep the victim in a state of anxious anticipation. She is always holding fast to the hope that she will get it *right* eventually—that whatever she does that keeps making him turn surly and aggressive will be clarified and worked out, and the relationship will proceed much more smoothly in the future.

Her dilemma is that, being human, her natural impulse is to run for comfort to the person closest to her—her partner—when she is feeling endangered. But this dilemma is complicated by the fact that she is in need of comfort and soothing from the very person who is *causing* the fear and trepidation that she's feeling. Furthermore, in the course of the couple's ongoing interaction, he is becoming ever more empowered as she becomes more and more unsure about who she is as a person. Over time, the abuse she's been absorbing has inevitably begun to affect her sense of her adequacy, self-worth, and basic lovability, while her psychological dependence upon her domineering, controlling mate's acceptance and approval has continued to increase.

This unstable, confusing state of affairs is rendered ever more bewildering by those periodic glimpses of the *good* parts of the relationship—the way things were at the beginning and the way she thought they would always remain. This periodic positive reinforcement serves to keep her hopes alive, and during those times when things are going well, she will often indulge in the fantasy that their problems have been settled and the rewarding parts of the attachment are here to stay. This fond belief is especially bolstered by his changed behavior during the couple's making-up phases, for at these times he may show some remorse and be far more understanding, friendly, and affectionate. He is on his best behavior, and this calms her down; she experiences a huge, if temporary, sense of relief.

This sense of relief is not only mental; it exists at a *physical* level as well, for her bodily reaction to the partner's attack has been to switch into an instantaneous readiness (fight, flight, or freeze) to meet the threat that confronts her. Thus, whether or not she recognizes the mate's aggression for what it is—that is, whether it is overt and blatant, or covert and subtly demeaning—the victim's *internal being* is in a highly agitated state of heightened arousal. Indeed, some experts believe that the reason traumatic bonds are far stronger and more difficult to sever than are healthier bonds is that they are forged in an atmosphere of such high intensity—an atmosphere in which deep-seated bodily fears and alarms alternate with the release of disagreeable mental and physical tension during times of relative tranquillity.

The traumatic bonds that are formed in emotionally and physically abusive relationships are, it should be said, not dissimilar from other strong emotional attachments formed between a periodically attacking, dominant person and someone who perceives him- or herself to be hopelessly subjugated. The famous Stockholm syndrome was one such instance, in which, during the course of their captivity, some female flight personnel fell in love with the terrorists who had taken them hostage. Other such intermittently terrifying/loving relationships that one might think of are those that can spring up between master and slave or between the maltreated child and his or her tyrannizing parent. In this regard, it is well known that children who have been abused by hostile or severely neglectful caretakers still love their parents passionately and resist being made to leave their homes.

Recognizing Psychological Abuse

What are the specific behaviors that *constitute* emotional abuse? One of the most illuminating answers to this question, at least in my opinion, is that provided by a Boston-based human rights organization called Peace at Home, Inc. In the comprehensive Warning List that this group has drawn up, a particular cluster of behaviors is identified as abusive—behaviors seen in situations where ongoing psychological assaults on the mate, but not necessarily any physical attacks, are taking place.

Again, it should be emphasized that in the majority of cases the victim has no conscious knowledge that anything "abusive" is actually happening; far more often she is blaming herself and her own failings for the fact that the relationship feels so flawed and ungratifying. For, over time, the abuser's sense of his own legitimate power, control, and essential "rightness" has continued to expand, while his partner's sense of her self-esteem and competence has undergone a process of attrition. She may be feeling bad, lost, guilty, isolated, and despairing; she may be suffering from fierce headaches, painful stomach troubles, a sense of constant tension, heart palpitations, fatigue, or back or neck problems; but all too rarely will she make the connection between her mental and bodily state of being and anything so alien sounding as "emotional maltreatment."

*The Peace at Home, Inc., Warning List**

1. *Destructive Criticism/Verbal Abuse:* Name-calling; mocking; accusing; blaming; swearing; making humiliating remarks or gestures.

* The list may be subject to future fine-tuning, but I consider it an excellent overview of what is meant when we talk about emotionally abusive behavior.

2. *Abusing Authority:* Always claiming to be right (insisting statements are "the truth"); telling you what to do; making big decisions without consultation; using "logic."
3. *Disrespect:* Interrupting; changing topics; not listening or responding; twisting your words; putting you down in front of other people; saying bad things about your friends and family.
4. *Abusing Trust:* Lying; withholding information; cheating on you; being overly jealous.
5. *Emotional Withholding:* Not expressing feelings; not giving support, attention, or compliments; not respecting feelings, rights, or opinions.
6. *Breaking Promises:* Not following through on agreements; not taking a fair share of responsibility; refusing to help with child care and housework.
7. *Minimizing, Denying, and Blaming:* Making light of disturbing behavior and not taking your concerns about it seriously; saying the abuse didn't happen; shifting responsibility for abusive behavior; saying you caused it.
8. *Pressure Tactics:* Rushing you to make decisions through "guilt tripping"; sulking; threatening to withhold money; manipulating the children; telling you what you must do.
9. *Intimidation:* Making angry or threatening gestures; use of physical size to intimidate; standing in doorway during arguments (as if to block the way out); outshouting you; driving recklessly (to scare the partner, even put her in fear for her life).
10. *Destruction:* Destroying your possessions (such as furniture); throwing and/or breaking things.
11. *Threats:* Making threats to hurt you or others.

Friendly Advice and Constructive Criticisms

The most clear-cut distinction between emotional violence and abuse of a physical nature is that an attack on someone's body is a tangible *event*—one that's likely to leave evidence, in the form of bruises and scars. Psychological mistreatment, on the other hand, usually involves an indirect, far more bewildering kind of process: Disgusted looks, muttered insults, and mocking jokes about a person's adequacy, intelligence, appearance, integrity, or moral value leave no injuries that can be seen or photographed, and to my knowledge no one has ever called 911 because a partner was assaulting her sense of self-worth.

Furthermore, hurtful and invidious comments are frequently couched in the wrappings of "friendly advice" offered by a concerned and well-meaning partner. As one female attorney, now separated from her husband, said to me, "Nothing I did was ever *right*; I was always off the mark, somehow. I can't tell you how many times, after we'd been out for an evening, my husband had some 'constructive criticisms' to offer.

"Maybe it was about something I'd worn that night, or about some 'ridiculously naive' remark that I'd made. Maybe I'd just been talking too much, or too loudly, or on the other hand looking spacey, seeming zoned out. . . . *Or* my laughter was so shrill, and you could hear me all the way across the room! God, that man could just slice me right down the middle! And I'll have to admit it, he was *good*, it was like radar! He had a way of being 'helpful' that could lock right on to my worst insecurities."

If, in this instance, the partner tries to defend herself and resists the emotional abuser's condescending judgments, an epic confrontation may ensue. Or if she is silent and just "takes it"—even accepts his denigrating comments as the impartial truth—her sense of selfhood will undergo a process of steady erosion. She will feel more and more defined by his negative appraisals and confused about who she really is, while he will emerge as the ever stronger, more powerful member of the pair. The abusive partner sups grandly on his mate's feelings of self-esteem, competence, and dignity in order to augment his own uncertain sense of efficacy, mastery, and control.

Shocks and Ambushes

While some interpersonal attacks are relatively explicit—that is, above the waterline of the victim's awareness—there are, as mentioned earlier, a variety of subtler forms of psychological aggression. One such tactic is that of habitually disparaging the partner's views, beliefs, ideas, and opinions.

A fine example of this undermining ploy was told to me by an editorial assistant in her late twenties, Carole, who said that almost *any* expression of her own independent point of view was likely to elicit dryly invalidating statements from her lover, such as "You can't possibly *think* that," or "You know nothing about the subject," or simply "That's completely *mistaken*."

If her partner spoke to her in this way when the two were in a social situation, which *did* happen from time to time, everyone present seemed to stop listening to anything else that she had to say. It was as if they'd taken their cue from him—she was a birdbrain, who had no idea what she was talking about—and after that, they ignored her. But instead of blaming her lover, who was a divorced senior executive within her firm, Carole absorbed the blame herself. She internalized his derogatory estimates of her; and came to believe that she was ill informed, not sufficiently quick-witted, and by no means up to his high intellectual standards. She often came home from such evenings out feeling thoroughly discredited, humbled, and in a numbed state of disbelief.

What seemed most peculiar to her, in retrospect, was the fact that each time her partner demeaned her publicly in this way, she'd felt as shocked and ambushed as if it hadn't ever happened earlier. This kind of bewildered, incredulous reaction to an abuser's sudden onslaughts isn't at all unusual. For as author Joan Lachkar has written, "The intimate partner who is abusive is the same one who provides hope, love, caring, validation, and intimacy." What could be more impossible, more unreal and confusing, than this sort of open derision and disrespect emerging in what is supposedly a trusting, nurturing relationship?

It is quite understandable that in such cases the wish to preserve the loving parts of the bond (and, often, to gain a sense of mastery over a depriving past) renders the victim resistant to recognizing the mate's cruelty for what it is in the here and now. And as a result, she often begins to inhabit a dual reality. In one small corner of her mind she *does* know what is really going on; but on a more global level, she remains unaware. She cannot confront the painful knowledge face-on and develops a kind of self-protective obliviousness. This involves making light of each hurtful incident, viewing it as an aberrant, exceptional occurrence in an otherwise caring, committed relationship.

Still, this sort of personal betrayal often *feels* nothing short of catastrophic, and over time, it can lead to those omnipresent feelings of terror, insecurity, and dread (When will the next assault come?) that are ordinarily associated with post-traumatic stress. The emotionally abused individual's reactions may then materialize in the form of extreme hyperarousal, bodily tension, hypervigilance, and generalized anxiety. Alternatively, the person may respond by shutting down emotionally, which is the body's other typical reaction to shocking, dismaying experiences. This kind of response involves numbing and constriction, inactivity, self-blame, an aching self, and a stark, boundless sense of deadness and helplessness.

Nevertheless, despite the fact that both her body and mind are being profoundly affected, the clear link between the state of the victim's relationship and the state of her mental and physical being is likely to remain unnoticed. There are so many ways in which she depends upon her mate and values the *good* parts of the attachment—those times of warmth and closeness—that she simply cannot allow her thoughts to go to certain places. Over time, her judgment becomes more clouded, and she is less and less sure that she is thinking correctly.

Her body may be sending her messages about her misery—in the form of ongoing agitation and hyperarousal or in the guise of a "numbed out" sense of paralysis—but at the level of awareness, she is deeply committed to *not* comprehending them.

Intimate Sabotage

The myriad ways in which a psychologically abusive mate can sabotage his partner's confidence and self-respect can't be definitively cataloged, but I'll describe a few more of the well-documented maneuvers here. He can, for starters, simply ignore or override the majority of her requests, needs, and wishes by behaving as if her input is irrelevant and, in any event, not nearly as important as his. He can behave as if she's the last person on his mind, and certainly no one with any power or rights that need to be respected.

Or he can make slyly invidious, undermining comments, then resist taking responsibility for them by either denying or contradicting what he just said; he can at times "not remember" having made any such comments, even if he made them thirty seconds earlier! Then again, he can deftly switch the topic of a discussion that's not going his way and do it so adroitly that she hardly realizes what's happening at the time. She may not even realize it afterward—all she knows is that she's feeling disoriented, stranded, and bewildered. This tactic is somewhat similar to a basketball play, for the attachment abuser has suddenly grabbed the conversational ball and dribbled it swiftly to the other end of the court.

On the other hand—staying with the basketball metaphor—the abusive partner can simply *drop* the conversational ball unceremoniously by not even troubling himself to answer when she addresses him. This is a passively aggressive way of saying, "I don't think what you said merits any feedback, so I'll just make that remark go away." If, then, she tries to confront him about his subversive nonresponsiveness, the partner may fob her off with further double-talk, such as "Oh, I didn't quite hear what you were was saying" or "I didn't understand what you were talking about." She is then left to wonder what happened, why he'd simply dismissed the matter so unceremoniously. Why didn't he question her further if he didn't hear or understand what she'd been trying to tell him?

Still another disconcerting conversational gambit that crops up in emotionally abusive relationships is a highly confusing kind of patter that might justly be called "fuddle speak." This is basically a meaning-mashing kind of blather that decimates all coherence and scuttles any chance the pair might have of focusing upon a real issue or misunderstanding. Fuddle speak is just plain goofy talk, a mode of interacting with the partner in ways that are intended to mislead and disorient her.

For example, an interviewee of mine, Carla, told me that she and her husband had attended a revival of a Broadway musical being staged at a country playhouse. During the intermission, the pair turned to each other and agreed that they were disappointed; it was a poor performance, which neither one of them was enjoying at all. Carla then went to the women's room and stood in line for so long that when she came out her husband was already reseated. He then turned to her and said enthusiastically, "Isn't this a *wonderful* treat?"

She was startled and asked him what had happened during the intermission that could possibly have changed his mind. He insisted that he hadn't changed his mind at all; he'd been enjoying the show all along.

"Then why did you say otherwise?" she demanded. He in turn reacted indignantly and asked her what *her* problem was and why she was trying to start a quarrel. She could not calm down throughout the rest of the show, and the couple got into a furious, thoroughly incoherent argument as they drove home.

What had caused his strange turnabout? When I asked her, Carla said she could think of no explanation. She did recall that during the intermission he had chatted with two senior partners from his architectural firm; they and their wives were enjoying the presentation enormously. One hypothesis she had was that *their* judgment had overridden his own, and he hadn't wanted to admit it, even to himself—it would make him seem too much like a wimp, someone without a mind of his own. So he'd insisted on pretending that he'd been pleased with the performance from the outset, then been provoked when she hadn't been pliantly accepting and simply gone along.

This was, Carla hastened to add, her guess, but not a certainty. In any event, this kind of incident, which occurred from time to time, left her feeling as if the very earth were moving beneath her. Fuddle speak does do that: It serves to shift the solid ground of rational thought right out from under its hapless victim, leaving her in a tension-filled state of uncertainty and hyperarousal. She is trying to maintain a relationship in an interpersonal realm permeated by absurdity and shifting understandings—one in which real engagement and rapport are being avoided as the oppressing partner maintains his strict control over "what is real" and what has actually occurred.

Anxious and agitated, his bewildered victim flip-flops from one possible "reasonable explanation" of what's really going on to the next one. *Her* struggle is not only with the emotional abuse she is absorbing—which she's typically highly reluctant to recognize for what it is—but with a lack of any outside validation that her own perceptions, thoughts, and feelings are actually the result of genuine provocations. It is only her internal, physiological state—what is happening inside her body—that accurately reflects the true nature of her situation, for so often the body knows what the person herself, intent upon preserving the intimate relationship, is steadfastly refusing to realize.

And in Carla's case, an important piece of personal history had sent her body's emergency alarm system into a state of high alert, for she happened to be the daughter of a binge-drinking father, whose occasionally irrational behavior had terrified her as a child. "As we were driving home from that night, the weather was stifling, and my chest felt so tight; I was even having trouble breathing," she told me. "I was holding a flashlight on the map, and my hand was shaking so hard that I couldn't read it."

As trauma expert Bessel van der Kolk has observed, both *internal* experiences, such as particular states of feeling, and *external* events that are reminiscent of earlier trauma can trigger a return to a sense of being in the original overwhelming situation. For Carla, a fear-ridden past and an alarming present had converged; she'd found herself striving desperately to make sense of a loved and needed male's inexplicable, illogical behavior. And while she herself, at a conscious level, was unaware of the scope of what had happened, she'd been unable to calm herself down for some days afterward, for her body *was* remembering and was keeping the score.

Cutting Off

Perhaps the most wrenching of all abusive tactics is the dominant mate's steely withdrawal and communicational shutdown when he is registering his disapproval or simply in a bad mood about matters in his own life that have nothing at all to do with her. So much of the subjugated partner's selfhood is being abraded over time that this sudden cutoff is terrifying and leaves her feeling beached, forsaken, unsure about whether or not she'll be able to survive on her own emotional supplies. So frightening does she find this minidesertion that it invariably serves to bolster *his* sense of ascendancy and leaves her in a state of fear and abject confusion.

Because she has become so psychologically dependent upon him for whatever degree of approval and validation she receives, she cannot gain enough distance from the relationship to think independently and validate herself. Thus she finds the threat of emotional abandonment so upsetting that she cannot focus on the real truth, in terms of what's going on in their lives together. What was it that *did* trigger that most recent, intense two-day argument? She's unable to piece together who said what to whom, and when and how the whole thing got started. Is her partner arrogantly deriding and discounting her feelings and perceptions, or is she herself overresponding?

Inevitably, as time passes, the subordinate partner surrenders more and more of her unique personhood—*who she was before becoming involved in this relationship*. And as she does so, the intimacy abuser encroaches ever further as the owner and interpreter of her subjective experience. It is he who, in the role of the superior, knowledgeable partner, lets her know *what is real and what actually matters*. His interpretations, however, are always framed (whether consciously or unconsciously) in ways that will fortify his own sense of superiority and advantage. Her internal world has become occupied territory—occupied by him and by his self-promoting views about the sort of person each of them is.

The Knower of Truth

One striking instance of the kind of situation in which the dominant partner makes himself the infallible "knower of the truth"—the supreme judge of what is true and real—was recounted to me by Anna Jellinek, a graphic arts designer in her early forties. Some five years earlier, the Jellineks had hired a Norwegian exchange student to come in every afternoon and help out with the family chores.

"At first, we thought the whole arrangement was delightful," Anna told me in the course of an interview. "This young woman, whose name was Karin, was in the grad school at Columbia, where my husband, David, teaches. She watched the kids two days a week while I went to the office, and she also cooked the family dinner on those evenings. As it happened, she was an exceptional cook; and the twins, who were three years old at the time, just *loved* her. It was great, it couldn't have been more perfect!"

After a while, though, certain small items started disappearing. They were inconsequential things, most of which belonged to Anna—a special hairbrush, a blue silk blouse, a pair of brown suede boots she hadn't worn for a while. It was certainly possible that the brush and the boots had been misplaced and that the shirt had disappeared at the cleaners. Nevertheless she began feeling mildly alarmed—"You could say my yellow light was on," she told me—and she talked with David about what was happening.

In *his* view, Anna was imagining things, and he dismissed his wife's suspicions out of hand. David even seemed to view her misgivings as personally offensive; he couldn't understand how she could *entertain* such ugly, unfounded ideas! As he saw it, Anna's apprehensions had an overly suspicious flavor, for she'd probably misplaced those unimportant items herself. Moreover, he thought his wife was curiously ready to pick on the au pair for reasons that weren't completely clear to him—in any case, what did a hairbrush, a blouse, and some worn boots *matter*? These comments were not made to Anna as if they were merely her husband's opinions; they were made to her as declarations about reality itself.

He was sure that the friendly, capable, good-natured Karin couldn't possibly be a thief, and he surely hoped Anna wasn't going to make unfounded accusations and upset what was obviously a splendid arrangement. "David managed, somehow, to enforce a code of silence around the whole issue," she told me, her eyes widening like an animal's caught in the headlights.

Throughout the following months this series of petty thefts had continued, but her husband continued to make light of this as a real problem. "It got to the point where I could feel my stomach lurch every time I opened a bureau drawer. Sometimes I'd know that something was different—*gone*—but I couldn't figure out what it was. . . . One of my silk scarves? It could even be my underwear! The pile would look a little lower, but of course I didn't have the whole inventory in my head."

She inhaled deeply, let the breath out, then said, "It was never anything *valuable*. No jewelry—nothing that wouldn't have sounded ridiculous if I'd ever gotten up the nerve to confront her! It started making me feel like a—I don't know—a nutcase. And the worst of it was the way David would roll his eyes and look pissed off every time I tried to talk about what was happening. He was acting as if *I* were the crazy one, as if *I* were the one making trouble!"

It was his certainty that had made her doubt herself. An expression of chagrin crossed Anna's face, and she said in a voice of apology, "I know this all sounds absurd, but I was really suffering. It was *painful*."

I nodded my understanding, for this sounded like a prime example of "gaslighting"—a term now in clinical use but derived from the classic film *Gaslight*. The film is about a woman whose perceptions of reality are being systematically invalidated by her seemingly devoted mate. For example, the husband hides his wife's possessions and then convinces her that she's misplaced them herself. He takes a cherished painting off the wall and then insists that it was *she* who removed it. His efforts are methodically destroying the heroine's trust in her experience of reality, and at the climax of the drama there's a moment when she's certain that she's going insane.

In the movie, in the service of her love for her new spouse, this wife is losing faith in herself, her own thoughts, senses, memory, and judgment —slowly coming to agree with him and their housekeeper, who is colluding with him, when they keep insisting, "You didn't *have* that experience. You don't really know what you believe you know. Nothing ever did happen, or *is* happening, in the ways that you think." This nullification of a person's basic experiences constitutes a major assault upon the self, an undermining of her very sense of inhabiting a world that is safe and predictable.

I suppose it was these reflections on "gaslighting" that made me wonder why, in this instance, Anna's husband had taken such a decisive stance against her. Why had he landed on the side of the issue that was so antithetical to *her* interests and her fundamental sense of security and comfort in their own home? Had it been because he couldn't bear to think that the young and cheerful Karin was robbing them, which would have been a betrayal not only of his wife, but of him and the entire family?

When I questioned Anna about this—not directly, but in a roundabout manner—her only reply was a brief shrug. Then, after a prolonged silence, she gave me an approximation of an answer. In a hushed, almost guilty-sounding tone of voice, she admitted that even now—years after Karin's ultimate dismissal—she found it hard to focus upon the question of David's unfeeling behavior.

Why had he downplayed and even derided her legitimate anxieties over such an extended period of time? Had he simply not wanted to be hassled by any issues that might lead to an outright confrontation? David was not an assertive person and would typically do anything to avoid a conflict, even in situations where conflict could legitimately have been called for. Also, when she'd first come to them, the au pair's enthusiastic employment reference had been from a departmental colleague at Columbia whom David valued greatly and with whom he was on close and friendly terms.

All in all, Karin had been with the Jellineks over two years, during which Anna's husband had insisted that he *knew what was true*; it was Anna herself who was confused and mistaken. He'd been so sure there was no real problem—that amid the hurly-burly of their hectic work and family lives, Anna was routinely misplacing things, then entertaining suspicions about poor Karin.

Eventually, however, their young helper's petty thieveries began to escalate—she almost seemed to want to be caught. It slowly became clear to *both* members of the couple that she was in fact stealing things and had been doing so all along. But for the sake of the kids, the parents decided not to confront Karin openly; instead, they let go of her quietly, and the entire sorry episode had ended there, with very little discussion of what had happened.

Nevertheless, even now—it was some five years later that Anna recounted these events to me—there was a look of alarm on her face as she talked about this phase of her life. She was still unable to think back upon that time without being assailed by memories of her utter helplessness and a sense of mortification about the way she'd let herself be victimized by this form of intimate treason.

These days, she and David never referred to the matter—it had migrated into the area of the taboo—but the whole experiencc was one that had never been resolved in her own mind. Why had he, her life's partner, summarily rejected—even refused to consider—her own version of what was happening? Why had he opted so confidently for the model of reality that left *him* feeling most at ease and untroubled—even though it meant leaving *her* hanging out to dry?

By completely denying (to himself as well as to her) that anything untoward was actually occurring in their home, he'd managed to avoid the kind of open hostility that she knew he feared and deplored. But in so doing, he'd made himself remarkably impervious to *her* suffering, *her* mystification, the constant state of agitation—both psychological and in her body—that she'd experienced throughout. She still couldn't comprehend that, at least not completely. Why had he taken her well-being so lightly?

And why, I wondered, had she been so excessively dependent on her husband's approval that she hadn't defended herself and simply given the au pair her walking papers early on? Anna had behaved as if remaining in lockstep agreement with her unempathetic, unconcerned spouse—which meant accepting *his* version of the truth—was far more important to her than was her own sense of herself as a rational, sane human being.

Symptoms as Witnesses

In retrospect, would Anna Jellinek have labeled her husband's behavior as "emotionally abusive"? I didn't think so. Would she view the long, painful episode with Karin, and her own frozen, paralyzed reaction to it, as having anything to do with trauma, past or present? I doubted it. For even though abuse of this kind can produce a variety of post-traumatic stress symptoms, it is, as mentioned earlier, both difficult to identify and something that the victim is usually loath to recognize clearly.

Many individuals would rather endure real psychic suffering—feel "crazy" and suffused with tension as Anna had, over such a long period of time—than recognize the source of their suffering as problems emanating from a vitally important and needed other, in an intimate relationship. This is why the psychological assaults a person may be experiencing will often find expression in one or more of an array of seemingly unrelated bodily and/or psychological symptoms.

The Body Speaks: Physical and Psychological Symptoms of Abusive Situations

What sorts of symptoms are prone to emerge in these abusive situations? The list of unpleasant possibilities is a long one. At a predominantly mental and behavioral level, the problems may include chronic anxiety, agitation, social withdrawal, feelings of emptiness, persistent melancholy, reveries about suicide, emotional numbness, persistent nightmares, and a sense that the world and the self are not actually real (in technical language, "derealization").

At a purely *physical* level, the target of abuse may manifest such symptoms as chronic headaches, stomach distress, life-draining fatigue, nausea, insomnia, dizziness, chest pain, muscular aches and joint pains, heartburn, and palpitations. Problems of this sort are often perceived and treated as strictly *medical* difficulties, and in some instances that may be what they are. But there are also many situations in which a person's bodily symptoms are actually a garbled SOS in need of translation. The body is bearing physical witness—in disguised form, but still the only witness that exists—to the battering of soul and spirit that's going on in an intimate relationship.

Nasty Quarrels Versus Emotional Abuse

Let me call a "time-out" at this juncture, for a vitally important caveat is in order here. We all know it to be true that many loving, caring, ordinarily supportive partners will sometimes treat each other in ways that are invalidating, unfeeling, unfairly critical, or otherwise "emotionally abusive." It's also true that most couples will become involved in an occasional nasty confrontation, during which regrettable, below-the-belt insults may be flung about.

Still, in the main, these partners feel reliably connected to and nourished, truly seen, and intimately known by the trusted and trustworthy other. They can be open about their most personal (even shameful and embarrassing) thoughts and feelings without fear of rejection, mockery, or misunderstanding. They are able to grasp and to respect the real differences that exist between them—to understand, accept, and even *cherish* the fact that their individual beliefs, preferences, and ways of looking at life are not always going to be in sync and may at times diverge radically.

Ultimately, however, these mates care about who the partner really *is* and how he or she really thinks and feels. They're not trying to impose upon each other their unique agendas about how the other *should think* or *should feel*. Moreover, the members of these couples are far less interested in vying with each other for power and control than they are in achieving a sense of "what's right," of fairness and mutual gratification.

Clearly, relationships of this sort are fundamentally different from those of mates who are involved in ongoing virulent struggles. In abusive kinds of attachments, the dominant mate is engaged in grinding down his partner's sense of selfhood, in order to maintain the illusion that he himself is independent, strong, and self-sufficient. In actuality, though, it's been well established that abusive males are anything *but* the above. A good deal of research with men who mistreat their partners has demonstrated very consistently that abusers are narcissistically vulnerable individuals who are struggling with acute feelings of weakness and dependency.

The term *narcissistic vulnerability,* clinically speaking, is a shorthand way of referring to people who have fundamental problems when it comes to maintaining a good internal image of themselves. Men who abuse harbor profoundly negative images of themselves—as inept, uncertain, unmasculine—and are operating not from a source of inner strength, but from a fear of further harm to their already damaged, brittle egos.

This kind of domineering, controlling partner relies very strongly on the primitive psychological defense mechanisms of *denial* and *projection.* That is, he has an unconscious but overriding need to *deny* all the weakness, ineptness, insecurity, and vulnerability that exist within himself, and he *projects* these intolerable aspects of his inner world onto someone close to him. That "close other" may be a child, or a boss, or some other person with whom he shares an intense relationship; but most frequently, the recipient of his projections will be she who is closest to him of all—that is, the intimate partner. He projects onto her, then perceives as *existing within her* all of the unacceptable attributes that he has so stoutly disowned as anything that is part of his own inner being.

Partner Abusers: Getting Rid of the Bad Stuff

By thus emptying himself of his own pervasive feelings of powerlessness and deficiency, the partner abuser can locate all of the shortcomings, faults, and failings as existing within the hopelessly defective mate. In other words, his way of dealing with his suppressed self-loathing is to project his intolerable feelings and thoughts about himself onto his unwitting partner, who is then disdained and criticized. He shields himself from his own ongoing stream of self-directed invective by externalizing the bad stuff; and he sees in her, and mercilessly attacks in her, those flaws and inadequacies that he cannot "own" and take responsibility for as existing inside himself.

Then he either denounces her for her failings or behaves in taunting ways that will inflame her into striking out at him. Whichever way the particular scenario plays itself out, though, she has been co-opted into holding *for him,* and is carrying *for him,* those aspects of his own inner world that he finds to be unbearable. The emotional abuser's partner thus serves as the psychic "container" for his most disavowed, unacceptable, self-hating thoughts and feelings.

For example, Paul's own "bad sexuality" was being denounced *in Claudia,* who was carrying all the guilt and blame in the relationship; by mutual, if unconscious, consent, *she* was being seen as the wanton, immoral member of the pair. Nevertheless, Paul's fulminating rage on the subject of abortion did make me wonder if someone in his own wild, boisterous past had actually *had* an abortion—one that was carried out at his behest.

According to psychologist David Curran, pathologically dominant, abusive, and controlling men are those who feel deeply unsure about whether they're good enough, strong enough, forceful enough, self-sufficient enough, independent enough—whether they are *real men,* in other words. These individuals are profoundly rejecting of their own gentler, more "feminine" feelings; they cannot, therefore, provide compassion, support, or empathy to their female partners.

The domineering male, writes Curran, "is unlikely to possess a capacity for honest introspection, self-appraisal or objectivity. His internal emotional life is incomprehensible to him. He will have minimal capacity for insight into and understanding of the internal feelings and thoughts of his female mate. He is uncomfortable with emotions and cannot identify any of them except anger."

While the external trappings of this person's existence may make him *appear* to be confident, self-assured, and in charge of his life, the abuser lives with a gnawing sense of his own inferiority and a fluctuating, sometimes wildly rocking, estimate of his own significance and status. Furthermore, because he feels so incomplete and basically unlovable, this kind of person fears that a highly confident mate, whose own sense of self-affirmation was intact, would be unlikely to hang around him for very long.

It is, therefore, in the interests of his own security that he needs to weaken her and to assume a watchful control over his partner—to intimidate her, chip away at her sense of self-worth, and curtail her capacity for independent thinking, living, being. In order for him to feel completely safe—and certain that she will stay—he must make sure that she is somewhat debilitated and helpless; and in fact, his episodic emotional assaults do keep her feeling fragmented, devitalized, dependent, unsure about what is really happening, and deeply unsure of herself.

The Three-Stage Cycle of Physical Violence

We all know that the physically bruising "sticks and stones" of partner violence do break real bones and sometimes cause serious injuries; nobody is disputing the fact that the batterer's blows can have a devastating impact upon his victim's entire existence. Still, many experts in the field of partner abuse have told me that assaults of a strictly verbal and emotional nature can have even more damaging, long-lasting effects.

Why should this be so? One hypothesis is that verbal assaults are much more unpredictable—they can blow up at any moment—while physical abuse usually follows a clearly recognizable, patterned course: This is the three-stage "cycle of violence" first outlined by researcher Lenore Walker in her celebrated book *The Battered Woman*.

According to Walker, stage 1 of a physically violent episode is characterized by a slow accretion of tension and resentment in the dominant member of the couple (statistically, the likelihood that this will be the male is about 95 percent). The attachment abuser's simmering bad feelings amplify until there comes a moment at which they can no longer be contained. Then there is a precipitant of some sort, one that may appear to be remarkably trivial—the mate delivers a snappy comeback or serves an overcooked steak, and he feels she is deliberately provoking him, willfully refusing to meet his needs (which may include reading his mind). This minor incident lights a fuse in the already tense domestic atmosphere, which then explodes into a chaotic, out-of-control, enraged attack upon the insufficiently "respectful," subservient mate.

This is stage 2 of the cycle of violence, and it can involve the indiscriminate punching, shoving, beating, choking, or sexual overpowering of a person who is typically much smaller in stature than is the batterer himself. Finally, when the abuser's fury is spent and he himself is exhausted (stage 3), he "comes to his senses." At this point, the cycle of violence has run its course and a period known as "the honeymoon" ensues.

Now, the intimacy abuser is filled with remorse, regret, and repentance. During this phase, he courts his injured partner, often bombards her with gifts, flowers, profuse apologies, and heartfelt promises that it will never, never happen again—and indeed, in the aftermath of the explosion, the domestic atmosphere may remain calm for a period of time.

Blaming the Mirror for What It Reflects

How long does it take to go through one full sequence of the cycle of violence, and how long does the ensuing "honeymoon" phase of relative peace and tranquillity persist? The answer is that it can be very different for different couples. Each pair seems to have their own time frame, and a single progression can take place over a period of days, weeks, months, or even years. Where partner battering is concerned, however, it's been well documented that over time, as the relationship continues, the severity of the abuse escalates and the honeymooning, "makeup" phase diminishes or disappears completely.

Much less is known about the typical course of events in abusive situations where *no* physical attacks occur, for emotional abuse is not a well-studied area. But experts in the field have told me that women who've experienced *both* kinds of assault will often state unequivocally that it's the incidents of emotional abuse that hurt the most and take the longest to heal.

Why should this be so? Some people believe it is because nonphysical abuse occurs so much more erratically than physical violence and doesn't follow the same fairly predictable "one, two, three, and it's over" sequence. On the basis of my own interviews, however, I'm not sure I'd agree: A number of my interviewees *have* in fact described an emotionally abusive sequence that closely resembles Walker's three-stage cycle of physical violence.

There is the same initial episode of pressure building, during which the dominant partner becomes ever more controlling, thin-skinned, and oppressive. For any of a variety of reasons, he is experiencing great tension.

His state of agitation could be due to some external rebuff, perhaps something that happened at the office; he could, on the other hand, be experiencing an upsurge of self-directed criticisms, about which she knows nothing whatsoever—and of which he himself may be oblivious, at the level of conscious awareness.

In any case, though, he is building up a head of steam, and the partners are heading for an emotional explosion—which again, when it erupts, will often be triggered by something remarkably unimportant. When it does erupt, the angry clash will not be initiated by real conflicts within the couple's relationship; the drama being enacted with the mate will have far more to do with the abusive spouse's own internal state. *His* basic predicament is that while he is filled with self-directed negativity and noxious sensations, no intelligible, coherent thoughts are attached to them. He is full of subliminal self-condemnation, which he's not only out of contact with but is unequipped to handle.

For he is a person who hasn't ever developed the capacity for focusing upon his own issues, getting them out on the table, and—with the help of his partner—perhaps succeeding in putting them to rest. In emotionally abusive situations, this healthier, more efficient way of being in a relationship simply doesn't exist. Instead, the dominant spouse's ever amplifying internal pressures build up until they eventually burst forth in an emotional onslaught against the mate—who hasn't got a clue about what's happening, because so often it has nothing to do with her.

The basic problem is that the attachment abuser has fallen prey to the total fallacy that he can hold the partner to account for his own mortifying feelings of deficiency, failure, and deep-dyed unlovability—in other words, as therapist Steven Stosny has observed, he is someone who "blame[s] the mirror for the reflection."

The Familiar Script

"What makes me angriest is the *instability* of the relationship, the inability to keep things on an even keel," Claudia said irately at some point midway through our interviews. She found herself vacillating continually between two varying images of herself—that of the attractive, highly competent career woman and that of the insecure, periodically subverted wife. She seemed unaware of the pattern of their marital imbroglios, which always moved through a familiar sequence. These episodes began with a period of nervous, edgy buildup on Paul's part, followed by an inevitable outburst, which eventually subsided into an apologetic, anxious-to-please, positively toned ending.

But Claudia never could tell, in the heat of the moment, what got the whole, draining process into motion; and she thought that Paul didn't know himself. He was always quick to anger at her (though he was a perennial "nice guy" with others), but he never seemed to have any insight into what, exactly, was ticking him off. At one point, at his wife's urging, the couple had consulted a clinician together, but Paul had failed to show up for any appointments after the initial one—as far as he was concerned, seeing a "shrink" was an unnecessary waste of his time and resources. So during those intervals when he was growing ever more tense and irritable, neither one of them could put a finger on exactly what was happening.

It was only later on, in the aftermath of a furious encounter, that Paul might talk about the fact that he was having trouble with a colleague at the large merchandising company he worked for, which was then undergoing a period of restructuring. Or it might be that he was having some financial difficulties with his ex-wife, Barbara, or problems with the children of that marriage, who made him feel so guilty because he was the parent who had walked out.

But early on in the cycle, instead of talking with Claudia about whatever might be the issue, he would withdraw from her abruptly—"shut down" and shut her out completely. She knew she should be used to this, but the suddenness and unexplained quality of the cutoff always left her feeling abandoned, frightened, in a state of what she called "agita," the Italian word for bodywide agitation and hyperarousal—a state of internal distress and discomfort with which, I believed, she was uncomfortably familiar.

To be sure, there were *other* times when this early, tension-building phase got under way differently. In these instances, when Paul was getting uptight he didn't walk away emotionally; instead, he turned increasingly sour, rigid, and authoritarian. If Claudia then asked what was bothering him, he became edgy and defensive. He heard her solicitous questions as criticisms and began insisting that she was attacking *him*; frequently she ended up losing patience and started acting as irritated as he'd accused her of being. In this kind of projective interaction, she was being subtly cued, goaded, and pressured into feeling and behaving in ways that were congruent with his fantasies about her as the "all bad," withholding, nagging, untrustworthy partner and himself as the highly moral, dependable, honorable, "all good" one whom she was always letting down.

Then, as the smoldering resentments in the atmosphere continued to escalate, Paul found more and more reasons for feeling furious. At this point, anything at all could set him off: Claudia's working hours, the clothes she wore, her lecherous colleagues, her independent ways, the dishes she'd left in the sink that morning. Once, he had even gone into a major burn because she'd packed away some old, cracked plastic tumblers that he'd kept from his college days, even though nobody ever used them; it was as if she'd invaded some territory that was supposed to be under *his* sole control.

This had occurred at a time when the emotionally abusive cycle was heading toward its crest—its middle "fighting phase"—and the inane, frenzied, and insoluble argument that would predictably erupt. This quarreling went on and on, until both of them were wrung out, after which Paul always did become calmer; the frantic exchange of insults had served to siphon off some of his inner turmoil. The argument had now served its unconscious purpose, which was to divert his own attention from the barrage of harsh, self-directed negativity he'd been experiencing.

In this third and final stage of the psychologically abusive cycle, Paul's agitation was subsiding. At this stage of the game, he usually became aware that he'd let things get out of hand; he was full of apologies and did try to set things right. Perhaps he felt pacified because Claudia and he were now in the same place emotionally—that is, because she now felt as upset and flooded with anxiety as he did. Now, however, it was she who wanted more distance in the relationship. She had withdrawn emotionally in order to protect herself, and it was Paul who became the ardent pursuer.

He could be so conciliatory and complimentary now, so much the giving, attentive person he'd seemed to be when they'd first begun going out. He behaved as if he were truly sorry about some of the harsh things he'd said to her and wanted to set things right. He knew he shouldn't talk to her in the ways that he did, but he maintained that *she* shouldn't provoke him so much, either. Nothing had actually been resolved when the depleting quarrel ended, but in its wake the couple did move into a honeymoon "riff" of smoother, calmer weather. The pair of them would feel relatively contented and relaxed for a while, for in situations of intermittent abuse, the sweeping sense of bodily and psychological relief that succeeds the periods of turbulence is rewarding in itself. The *good* parts of the relationship have returned, at least for the meanwhile.

Chapter Six

—

A WITNESS TO VIOLENCE

WHY HAD CLAUDIA MARTINELLI CHOSEN TO LINK UP WITH a partner like Paul? As a mature, polished, experienced adult woman, she'd certainly been sufficiently capable of assessing her future husband's character and attitudes to have known that she was walking into a potentially incendiary situation. So I couldn't help but wonder if her willingness to enter so punishing an attachment—one in which she had to keep secret the most basic aspects of who she really was—had been predicated on much earlier experiences of shame and guilt.

Was she in a situation that *felt* strangely right, because secret keeping and the uncomfortable bodily sensations that accompany shame and guilt were what she'd always been accustomed to feeling? Claudia had the air of someone whose feelings of deep unworthiness have never been resolved and are being recycled continually.

She and her husband remained deadlocked in a struggle, one that seemed to me to revolve around the basic issue of authenticity. At issue was the question of how she could ever be a whole, genuine person in this relationship, given the energy it took to keep on editing out important segments of her life's actual experiences and her husband's tendency to construe matters so that he was always the superior, "right" member of the pair.

Land Mines of Memory: The Scapegoat

In the course of our conversations, I asked Claudia whether or not the behaviors cited on the Peace at Home, Inc., Warning List ever occurred in her relationship with Paul or in relationships she'd been involved in earlier. As I read out each of the definitions, she paused, considered it briefly, and then nodded her recognition and assent. When I finished reading, she acknowledged that probably all of these things had happened at one time or another in her marriage to Paul, and some of them happened fairly often.

I looked at her reflectively, wondering if—as I suspected—keeping secrets about the self, telling the lies that were necessary to maintain them, and feeling shame and guilt about who she truly was were part of a pattern of being that stretched far backward in Claudia Martinelli's lifetime.

"This may be slightly off the track, Claudia," I said, "but there's something I'd like to ask you." I glanced down at the family genogram briefly, and when I raised my eyes, she met my gaze expectantly. I said, choosing my words carefully, "You know, of course, that in lots of families there are certain roles or 'parts' that people tend to fall into. For instance, there may be someone who's 'the optimist' and someone who's 'the pessimist,' someone who's 'the pretty one' and someone who's 'the clown.' If you had such a role or nickname, what would it be?"

She paused, then said with a bleak certitude in her voice, "I guess . . . I was 'the scapegoat.' . . ."

We sat there, saying nothing, until I asked Claudia if she could bring to mind some incident—an example of a time when she remembered being put in the role of the scapegoat. The question seemed to stump her.

There was another extended pause, after which she shook her head and said that even though she was searching through her memory, she actually couldn't come up with a single concrete instance. All she could produce was a vague comment to the effect that she'd been the one who was always being blamed for everything, including many things she hadn't done.

I prompted her a third time, but she still couldn't remember any scapegoating incident in particular. This was highly atypical: Most people who recall playing a role in the family have the "evidence" ready at hand. But here was Claudia, usually so articulate and forthcoming, acting as if she'd taken an eraser and run it over certain regions of her brain—those areas where you'd suppose the relevant memories and associations would be stored. And I couldn't help but wonder if she was "zoning out" in order to steer clear of certain experiences too distressing or overwhelming to think about or even remember.

Mind/body disconnections of this sort are often linked to severe early stress, as are the ongoing internal states of hypervigilance and hyperarousal that Claudia appeared to be experiencing. So, too, is the inability to tune in to the body's internal warning cues and signals—those gut-based kinds of intuitions ("Uh-oh, there's something wrong here!") that help to steer a person through the highly nuanced, convoluted shoals of adult life. This situation, in turn, feeds into an unfortunate propensity to make gross errors in judgment when getting into close relationships, for when it comes to making practical use of the body-based information normally flowing into conscious awareness, the hyperstressed individual's data receivers are jammed.

Then, added to these suggestions of unresolved injury and pain somewhere in her past, Claudia's period of wild drinking, wanton sexuality, and cocaine involvement was a further indication that she might have been self-medicating and acting out around an unprocessed history of trauma. Thus, I found myself puzzling over whether there were other, unknown matters in her earlier life—the life she'd lived in her original family—quite aside from the present-day secrets she was keeping from Paul. Were there land mines of memory buried in her neural circuitry—events long forgotten and never talked about or even *thought* about these days—which were nevertheless having a profound effect upon her and subtly acting to keep her stuck in her one-down, scapegoated position?

Seeing What Is Not Supposed to Be Seen

When we met again several weeks later, Claudia told me that she'd been giving a lot of thought to the issue of "scapegoating" that had arisen during our previous interview. She'd been thinking most of all about the fact that her parents were always at each other's throats, perpetually fighting about one unimportant issue or another. They'd been fighting like that—over everything and nothing—ever since she could remember. "That's why I nicknamed them 'the Bickersons,'" she reminded me with a sardonic smile.

That afternoon it was raining hard, and gusts of water were crashing against the glass windows of the living room in which we sat. We were in a small apartment/office that I'd sublet from a friend, but it felt as if we were inside a diving bell. Claudia's family genogram was on the table between us, and we both gazed down at it for a short while. She kicked off her high-heeled shoes, which were wet around the edges. Then she said, "So I've been wondering if maybe that's what the scapegoat feeling comes from. I mean, trying to help them settle their differences and taking the heat myself." Her intuition, a highly astute one, was that she might have been part of an emotional triangle—one consisting of her mother, her father, and herself as the "lightning rod," or third party who had absorbed all the excess heat of the couple's conflict-ridden, ungratifying relationship.

I shook my head and shrugged as if acknowledging that it was a good question but one to which there was no reply; its answer was lost in time. Claudia nodded. "I don't know, myself. I can't say for sure—I don't remember a lot from my childhood—I remember it in bits and pieces." She turned away, began staring fretfully out at the rain.

I looked at the marital line connecting Claudia's father, Nick, and her mother, Sylvia, on the genogram. Just above it I'd inscribed the notation "constant fighting," so I said, my voice carefully neutral, "It sounds as if there's been a continuing power struggle between your folks." Claudia turned back to me, fixed me with a look I found hard to read.

"I don't know if you could call it a *struggle*, not in the real sense of that word, because my mother never won," she said. "She lets things *go* a little too easily . . . she gives in . . . she *settles*." There was irritation, even a note of contempt, in her voice.

"You're saying that your mom doesn't have a real voice in the marriage?" I asked, and Claudia didn't miss a beat before responding tartly, "Oh, my mother has a voice! She definitely has a voice. But she doesn't get her way, ever . . . not really." I wondered whether Claudia herself, as the senior female in a row of five siblings, had taken on the job of referee or "therapist" in those ongoing parental quarrels. If so, such efforts were highly likely to have left her feeling both impotent and responsible.

In any case, it sounded as if her family's "rules," in terms of adult male and female relationships, had allowed for a woman to battle noisily for her rights and to voice her own point of view but never to gain access to real power, which is the power to be heard and to participate in making important decisions. But this could only be part of a longer story, or so I believed.

Claudia then said, out of nowhere, that she was "trying hard to accept responsibility" for some of the unhappiness and negativity that were going on in her marriage at this moment. I paused, stared at her. Was this an example of "the scapegoat" in action? I told Claudia that I wasn't completely sure what she meant.

She responded with nothing other than an enigmatic smile. Then she murmured something to the effect that she knew she had trouble "seeing things." This statement left me even more at sea.

"You have trouble seeing things?" I repeated.

She nodded, and then the two of us sat there for a few moments, simply looking at each other. I picked up my teacup, took a sip, put it back down. Then I took a flyer and said, "Claudia, you tell me you have trouble 'seeing things,' and it makes me wonder if there were things happening in your family that you weren't supposed to see."

She shot me a quick "aha!" look, that look of someone who feels well understood; but she didn't say anything aloud. So I went on and said in an even tone of voice that *lots* of families have secrets, of the small and large variety. Did she believe she knew the secrets that had existed in her own?

Claudia jumped slightly, as if suddenly recalling something. Then she looked down at the narrow gold watch on her wrist, and I thought she'd suddenly remembered that she had another appointment at this time and that this interview would be ending. I started to get up, expecting her to do so, too; but she didn't. Instead she leaned back in her chair and exhaled deeply. I did so as well.

"It wasn't so *much* of a secret, because my parents didn't try to keep it a secret. But one of my brothers, Nicky, was brain-damaged. The doctors called it a 'pervasive developmental disorder.'" I nodded; she had mentioned this impaired sibling, four years older than herself, early on in our work on her family genogram.

"He had seizures, too, and he definitely was a problem," she continued. "Nicky and my father never got along; they still don't. And the funny thing is that he's very *like* my father. They have similar attitudes, similar ways of dealing with things—like they'll both hold on to grudges. They're just *alike,* and there's always been a lot of fighting between the two of them—*physical* fighting—sometimes to the point where there'd be blood."

She paused, took a sip of tea, and the cup clattered against the saucer. "So you didn't want to bring your friends home," she said in a flat, tonelessly reportorial voice, "because you never knew what Nicky was going to do. You didn't know if he was even going to be *around,* because he started running away when he was in his teens. He finally went out to the Northwest—to Seattle—when he was seventeen. And upsetting as it was when he ran away like that, the house was really peaceful."

I noticed that red patches were appearing on Claudia's face and neck; they were like red flags of embarrassment and culpability being waved from within. "So then," I asked, "everyone must have been feeling relieved and a bit guilty at the same time?"

She nodded. "Right. But while it was happening we never spoke about it much. Outside the house, we kids *never* spoke about it; but inside, things were very chaotic and scary. Nicky was on major drugs for his seizures and for his retardation. He was on lots of barbiturates, too, like massive doses of phenobarbital to keep him calmed down.

"He eventually got into other drugs, too—a *bad* cocaine habit—though none of us realized it for a long time. He was stealing from my parents; he stole anything he could lay his hands on. So it wasn't safe. You had to keep all your stuff locked up." Her voice had taken on a throbbing undercurrent of alarm, and her arms were folded tightly across her chest once again.

I asked her if she could recall just when these pitched family brawls—especially the physical, sometimes bloody clashes between her brother and her dad—had gotten under way. "Oh, this stuff went on throughout my whole life," she answered tautly. "At least, until Nicky moved out of the house."

Chapter Seven

ATTACHMENT TRAUMA

MERELY WITNESSING, AS CLAUDIA HAD, THE CHRONIC violence being visited by your dad—an out-of-control adult—upon your sibling contained the elements of what Freud viewed as the essence of a traumatic experience, which is to say *a situation in which a person feels completely helpless and ineffective in the face of what is perceived to be overwhelming danger*. For what could this younger sister, or any of the other children, do without taking the chance of being drawn into the ongoing familial violence? If the children's mother wasn't able to stop the wild physical clashes between father and son, who else in the family could?

A Discontinuity in the Thread of the Self

Any startling, frightening, and inescapable situation has the potential to overwhelm a person, whether that person is a mature adult or a young child. However, as trauma experts Steven Marans and Anne Adelman have pointed out, a traumatic event will be experienced very differently depending upon the individual's age and stage of development. And obviously, a child's coping skills and self-protective capacities will be far more limited than the skills and capacities available to a grown-up.

"In the throes of the maturational process, children have fewer and more uneven psychological resources at their disposal; their developing defensive organization is acutely vulnerable to traumatic disruptions . . . from the environment," these clinicians write. As a consequence, the child's strategies for dealing with threatening experiences will be relatively weak and his defenses easily breached; he is, moreover, in a dependent situation, usually without any recourse in terms of finding shelter elsewhere.

In situations where neither of the well-known instinctive human reactions to danger (fighting or fleeing) is a viable option, that third, less familiar but similarly automatic reaction (freezing helplessly in place) is the usual outcome. In the instance of the young child, this is frequently the most adaptive response available, for in the midst of the traumatic event itself, many of his immature coping capacities will be effectively knocked out of commission.

What "coping capacities" am I referring to? Among others, the ability to differentiate what is real from what is fantasy; the ability to think clearly; and the ability to self-regulate bodily sensations. Given that dealing with the fearful situation *actively* is usually out of the question, the child's best (if not to say sole) response option is often that of spacing out—shutting down emotionally. This results in a feeling of being "not really here" despite the fact that one is physically present.

The resulting state of self-induced mental anesthesia—which is, of course, accompanied by a souped-up internal bodily state—is the human organism's way of distancing itself from the intolerable experience of feeling utterly helpless in an unavoidable predicament. It is like disengaging an inner steering wheel, even though the machine itself is in high gear. The upshot is that the whole body "knows," and expresses in its state of hyperexcitation, what the individual cannot bear to comprehend clearly at the level of conscious awareness.

This in turn creates what the great theorist D. W. Winnicott called a "discontinuity in the thread of the self." For while this zoning-out reaction does serve to mitigate the immediate impact of the overwhelming experience in the short run, in the longer run it produces its own set of consequences: As long as areas of the individual's internal being remain a vast terra incognita, the traumatizing experiences can never become processed, resolved, and integrated into an understanding of his own personal history.

Then, instead of dealing with what did happen once upon a time, the individual will be apt to avoid, minimize, or perhaps forget entirely the frightening events that actually did occur. Nevertheless, a bodywide physiological alarm reaction has been set off; and because the danger has never been recognized as belonging to the past, the body remains on chronic high alert to meet an unnamed threat that exists in an eternal time present.

A Boundary of Silence

Trauma exposes a child to his own absolute helplessness and lack of control of his world at the very time when he is struggling with the crucial developmental issues of competence and mastery. At the same time, traumatic experiences strike at the heart of a youngster's sense of self for a very different, somewhat paradoxical reason: Early in life, children are wonderfully grandiose and experience themselves as *central to* and the *cause of* anything and everything that occurs around them.

Therefore, when bad things happen in their worlds, they are prone to experience an exaggerated sense of responsibility for whatever is occurring—for example, many a youngster believes that his parents would not have divorced if he'd just been better behaved and brought home a perfect report card. Similarly a child who, like Claudia, has seen her brother being punched and pummeled to the point of bloodiness may have felt responsible in a variety of different ways. She may have thought she was bad because she *should* have spoken up and yet felt utterly without power because she was too frightened to do so. She may have believed she *could* have helped her brother if she herself had taken some of the heat, instead of trying to melt into the background when the fighting got ugly. She may have had such shame-inducing thoughts as "I'm glad he's the one who's getting it, and that it isn't me!"—and then felt guilty about seeing Nicky getting beaten up without anyone stepping in to stop what was happening. Or if she'd actually said or done something that had gotten her brother into trouble, she might have experienced herself as a vile, nasty human being who'd actually deserved that beating herself.

Shrouded as it was in family secrecy, this domestic situation had clearly created a boundary of silence around the household—one that could only amplify the sense of guilty secrecy, of stigma, shame, and embarrassment of everyone within it.

What had those bloody battles been about? As an adult, Claudia had little or no understanding. All that she could say about her father's periodic attacks upon the troubled, troublesome Nicky was that "while it was happening we never spoke about it much. Outside the house, we kids *never* spoke about it." I wondered if it had been talked about *within* the home, among the members of the family; I suspected that it had been talked about very little, if ever.

But now it seemed to me that Claudia's cryptic remark—"I have trouble seeing things"—had become more comprehensible. It made sense in the context of what had been going on during her childhood. She had, I thought, received intensive training in "not seeing" and "not knowing" too much in a household where violent, bloody outbursts were occurring.

To be sure, not knowing too much about what was happening had been highly adaptive *at that time*—for a dependent child, dissociating, spacing out, and not feeling too much would be the most natural ways of protecting the self from unbearable pain in situations where no action is possible. But in adulthood, "not seeing" and "not knowing" are extremely *maladaptive* ways of responding. Life is far too complex, and the choices to be made are too nuanced, for a grown-up person to be zoned out and functioning on autopilot.

Moreover, this kind of stark disconnection between *what the body knows* and what thoughts, feelings, and memories are available at the level of conscious awareness is probably what motivates the powerful urge to resurrect the unfinished business of the past in the real time of present-day existence. This did appear to be happening in Claudia's troubled relationship to Paul, for she was engaged in the re-creation of a theme that harked back to her earliest history: She had somehow "found herself" in a cowering, subordinate position in relation to a periodically eruptive, dominant male. Her husband (like her father) always presented himself to everyone outside the home as an affable nice guy, but in the privacy of their intimate relationship, Paul was projecting his simmering anger and his frustrations outward.

He was perceiving as existing *in Claudia*—the unforgivably defective, morally flawed member of the couple—everything that was bad and wrong about his own life, just as her father must have seen in his unforgivably imperfect son everything that was damaged and defective about himself.

Who Was the Scapegoat?

What I found surprising was the fact that Claudia had described her role as that of "scapegoat," when it surely could be said that her brother Nicky had been the chief contender for that hapless position. But when I asked her about this directly, she shot me a strange look. "Yes, I guess you're right there," she conceded after pondering the thought for a few moments.

Then she went on to say, in a glum, depressed tone of voice, that her brother now lived in the Northwest with his girlfriend and was not included in any of the family functions. He hadn't even been invited to her wedding to Paul, because her parents didn't want him there. "My mother *does* send him money that my father doesn't know about. And she says it's 'guilt money.'" Evidently her mother still had lingering qualms about her inability to protect her son and was secretly trying to make whatever small amends were possible.

Aside from that fragile and secretive connection, though, her brother had been dismissed from the family. He was among "the departed," though clandestinely alive, and as she explained this situation to me, Claudia's face took on a withdrawn, frozen expression. It occurred to me that not only her mother, but she herself was probably still carrying a burden of guilt and responsibility for Nicky's having been eliminated from the family portrait in this way. But she said nothing further, as if the family injunction to maintain silence on the subject of this brother had not been lifted to this day.

Claudia had speculated that her sense of herself as "the scapegoat" might have been caused by her trying to intervene in her parents' constant quarreling and ending up by taking the blame for things she hadn't actually done. Now, I reflected upon the meaning of the word *scapegoat* itself. And my thought was, Who *is* a scapegoat if not someone who's being held responsible—and perhaps *feeling* deeply at fault for—problems that she never caused and couldn't cure no matter how much of the family "heat" she tried to take upon herself?

Trauma: A Wound to the Self

In *The Random House Dictionary of the English Language*, the psychiatric meaning of "trauma" is given as "*a startling experience which has a lasting effect on mental life; a shock.*" The word itself derives from the Greek and means "wound." Some traumatic events, such as seeing your brother beaten bloody, may not be life threatening in the sense of your own physical survival; however, they can be nothing short of self-defining in terms of telling you who you are in the very dawn of your lifetime (helpless, powerless, scared, cowardly, bad, overwhelmed, out of control).

Such events are highly likely to leave you in a state of chronic bodily arousal, with a highly uncomfortable overreactivity to life's minor insults, threats, and dilemmas. This physiologically based state, a bodily condition of dysregulation, makes it very hard for a person to soothe herself, calm down, and regain stability in the wake of *any* negative event, even one that has nothing to do with the painful experiences of the past.

Perhaps most troublesome of all, however, is the subtle, devilish way in which shocking early experiences can lead a person into endless repetitions of the same unhappy situations she saw earlier in her life. The famed theorist Harry Guntrip once suggested that all of human pathology is in reality just "failed metabolism"—which is to say, the inability of the overwhelmed self to process and absorb indigestible hunks of intolerable experiences. In short, symptoms develop when aspects of a person's past history are so "stuck" in her body and her psyche that they become regurgitated endlessly into her current-day existence.

Attachment Trauma

It has now been over two decades since the American Psychiatric Association added a new classification to its official *Diagnostic and Statistical Manual of Mental Disorders* and called it "post-traumatic stress disorder" (PTSD for short). The *Diagnostic and Statistical Manual* then listed the particular symptoms that individuals are prone to develop in the aftermath of traumatic experiences—such as persistent agitation, intrusive thoughts, nightmares, flashbacks, and the compulsion to replay the traumatic event in some disguised form. It was also noted that such symptoms might emerge immediately or, in some cases, weeks, months, or even years afterward.

A widespread belief at that time, and indeed one that persists to this day, is that traumatic experiences are relatively rare happenings in the population at large—that they're limited to such things as having been in military combat or involved in a natural disaster, such as a flood, fire, or earthquake, and similar high-profile events. But as mentioned in the preface, a huge, government-sponsored study, led by sociologist Ronald C. Kessler, involved actually asking some fifty-nine thousand people about which "events and experiences that qualified as traumas" they had gone through. And to everyone's surprise, the researchers found that exposures to traumatic stress are not at all uncommon.

In fact, the Kessler team's findings indicated that *60 percent of the adult men* and *51 percent of the adult women* interviewed reported having experienced at least one—and sometimes more than one—of the adversities about which they were being systematically interviewed. All in all, the most frequently encountered traumas were found to be 1) witnessing someone being injured or killed; 2) being involved in a fire, flood, or natural disaster; and 3) being involved in a life-threatening accident.

A higher proportion of males in the study reported having been through one of these three experiences; also, many more males had been exposed to such events as physical attacks, involvement in military combat, being threatened with a weapon, and being held captive or kidnapped. By way of contrast, a significantly higher proportion of females reported having been raped, sexually molested, or subjected to parental neglect and physical abuse during their childhoods.

There were also clear-cut male/female differences when it came to what happened *in the wake* of a traumatic event. Here, it is important to realize that an event that clearly qualifies as traumatic does not necessarily produce a post-traumatic stress disorder in everyone exposed to it. Despite the widely held belief that dramatic symptoms are sure to follow in the wake of terrible experiences, the statistics tell us otherwise. Only a subset of trauma survivors actually go on to develop full-blown PTSD.

However, arrestingly enough, the results of the Kessler research indicated that in the aftermath of trauma, women were more likely—*more than twice as likely*—to develop post-traumatic stress disorders than were men. The figures themselves told an extraordinary story: In the wake of trauma, 20.4 percent of the women (some fifteen to twenty million) tended to become symptomatic, as contrasted with 8.2 percent of the men (roughly six to nine million). In discussing these findings, the researchers acknowledged that they could spin theories about—but not fully account for—the striking gender differences that had emerged from their results.

What this nationwide study did make very evident, however, was that exposure to trauma is omnipresent in the population—far more so than anyone had previously imagined. Still, because traumatic events are considered to be highly exceptional experiences, their profoundly distressing aftereffects—which can persist for years—all too often go unrecognized, undiagnosed, and untreated.

Big-T and Little-t Traumas

In the years since 1980, when PTSD first made its debut upon the psychiatric stage, the effort to hammer out a universally acceptable definition of what trauma actually *is* has proven extremely elusive. But in the most recent update of the *Diagnostic and Statistical Manual* (known as *DSM-IV*), trauma is defined not only as an event involving direct personal injury or the threat of injury to the self, but as the "*witnessing [of] an event that involves death, injury, or a threat to the physical integrity of another person. . . .*"

The italics are mine and are meant to emphasize the notion that you don't need to be the direct victim of an assault in order to be traumatized by it; you can be profoundly damaged simply by *being present when it's happening*. The phenomenon of witnessing, and later becoming symptomatic in some way, is known as "vicarious traumatization."

I should, however, underscore the fact that the word *trauma,* as I am using it here, doesn't for the most part refer to those hugely dramatic events such as hurricanes, floods, fires, serious auto accidents, incest, rape, and witnessing a homicide or other catastrophic occurrences that basically involve looking death in the face. My focus, in these pages, is upon those far less cataclysmic, but nevertheless damaging—sometimes life-changing—experiences that are often referred to as "traumas with a little 't.'"

Of course, the fine line differentiating little-t and big-T traumas will often be indistinct. For example, it's obvious that a sensational headline appearing in the morning's newspaper—GIRL, 10, WATCHES AS SISTER IS STABBED TO DEATH—falls into the big-T category. But where does a lifetime of watching sudden, unanticipated, sometimes bloody battles between your father and a sibling belong?

Seeing People You Love Hurt Each Other

You may well ask, Was Claudia Martinelli actually suffering from posttraumatic stress disorder—that is, big-T trauma—as formally defined in the psychiatric reference bible, the *DSM-IV*? She had surely not experienced a big-T event on the order of "military combat, violent personal assault (sexual assault, physical attack, robbery, mugging), being kidnapped, being taken hostage, terrorist attack, torture, incarceration as a prisoner of war or in a concentration camp, natural or man-made disasters, severe automobile accidents, or being diagnosed with a life-threatening illness."

Nor had she witnessed horrifying events such as "observing the serious injury or unnatural death of another person due to violent assault, accident, war, or disaster or unexpectedly witnessing a dead body or body parts," as described in *DSM-IV*. She wasn't having the emblematic "flashbacks"—those terrifying episodes of reexperiencing the trauma as if it weren't long over but were happening right here and right now. She didn't complain about intrusive, crazy, out-of-context thoughts that would pop into her mind as if from nowhere. Nor did she speak of difficulties in falling or staying asleep owing to persistent, terrifying nightmares.

Still, many clinicians who work with trauma patients believe that the current version of the *Diagnostic Manual* places too much emphasis on extraordinary and rare occurrences, such as earthquakes, floods, terrorist attacks, and other high-profile disasters. These trauma workers also maintain that far too *little* attention is paid to the lasting effects of chronic interpersonal abuse of the kind that Claudia had witnessed as a child.

As therapist Babette Rothschild has observed, no statistics have been gathered on the number of people who are suffering from PTS (post-traumatic stress, or little-t) as compared with those suffering from the highly dramatic symptoms seen in full-blown PTSD (post-traumatic stress disorder, or big-T). "One can guess," writes Rothschild, "that there are a significant number of trauma survivors with PTS, those who fall between the cracks—not recovered from their traumas, but somehow without the debilitation of PTSD."

As Rothschild notes, situations of unremitting tension generated by "an environment, life style or chronic situation that is constantly and extremely emotionally stressful . . . [and/or] . . . certain kinds of strict or neglectful childhood environments, dysfunctional relationships," and the like can at times be so overwhelming that they will in fact produce psychological and physical conditions that resemble the more disabling PTSD. A child's early experience of severe early stress is very like an adult's experience of a cataclysmic event in that it can shatter the individual's sense of basic safety in the world, of her or his invulnerability to harm.

Certainly, in the view of trauma researcher Bessel van der Kolk, witnessing terrible things going on inside your family is in many ways far *worse* than experiencing huge natural or man-made catastrophes. "The real trauma, and the actual cause of most post-traumatic suffering, is 'attachment trauma.' It's seeing people whom you love hurt each other in physical, horrifying ways," van der Kolk told me in the course of one of our many discussions.

We humans are, after all, social creatures, who grow up in the protective environments provided by our caretaking families. Thus, when bad things happen at the hands of the very people who are supposed to love and nurture us, our basic conception of ourselves and of the world we inhabit is inevitably impacted in enormous ways. Physical or emotional battering—or cold indifference and neglect—*within* the family group is at some basic level the most traumatic occurrence of all.

For this early exposure to domestic cruelty—or to callous disregard—transforms some of the crucially important figures within the child's world into creatures who cannot be trusted and who are fundamentally undependable. And in van der Kolk's view, it is this homegrown form of emotional injury that is the root cause of the vast majority of post-traumatic stress disorders that he and other physicians encounter.

Chapter Eight

—

FAMILIAR FEELING-STATES: THE BODY REENACTS

WHEN NEXT WE MET, CLAUDIA WAS IN MUCH BETTER spirits than the last time I'd seen her. The marriage seemed to be on an uptick, and she said, "Right now, I'm feeling hopeful," as she shrugged out of her brown suede overcoat and hung it over the back of a chair. She had arrived at the end of her workday, bringing with her a rosy-cheeked sense of nippy early spring and a strong whiff of pleasant-smelling perfume. As her quasi hostess, I'd put cheese, crackers, and two glasses of white wine on the low table between us; and Claudia's good mood served to augment the festive feeling with which the interview began.

As always, we started out by spending some time on her family genogram. This time I found myself focusing on the crosshatched line denoting both the marriage and later divorce of Claudia and her first husband, Steven. Looking at the scribbled notation just above that line—"5 years"—I thought once again that five years is not an insignificant length of time. I asked her what her first husband had done for a living.

She responded with a dismissive hand gesture and said, "Basically, nothing. And that was probably the major reason why the marriage didn't work out." She explained that when they'd first gotten to know each other, Steven had talked a lot about the thriving baked goods–distributing business that he owned. At the time, he'd told her that he was plowing all his earnings back into the company; but he had assured her that eventually—

gruntled, male-abhorring wife who didn't need a man in her bed, then we two hadn't remained merged and "as one," in perfect synchrony, as we had been throughout my childhood. "You can't have anything that *I* don't have," Patti Levin murmured on hearing this part of the story.

She was parroting back to me what I'd said about "the family pennant" earlier. I stopped, gave her a blank look, then asked what that meant in this context.

She gave me a quizzical look, raised an eyebrow. "If I don't have a man in my bed, *you* can't have a man in your bed. And if you *do*, it will make me feel bitter and vengeful." Those weren't the exact words I'd spoken, but they did echo their spirit, and I was taken aback. I'd surely never connected the competitiveness and ill wishing of my sisters with anything that had transpired between my mother and myself; the idea was simply unthinkable. It had no place in the cherished narrative of the loving, grateful bond I'd always shared with this deeply loved parent.

And yet the memory of that moment did reawaken another long-forgotten memory—something else that had occurred during that same, difficult visit. It had to do with my career as a science journalist, which was then just getting under way. Throughout the decade that was to follow, the 1970s, I did in fact turn out one *New York Times Magazine* cover story after another (and eventually see them brought together in a book of essays called *Body, Mind, Behavior*). But at the time my mother came to stay with us, I had only a small sheaf of published articles to show her. I remember presenting them to her proudly and then leaving her on the back porch to read them.

It was a pleasantly hot day in June, and the back porch on which she sat is at the base of a hill that rises in back of our home. The land our house is built upon was once part of inventor Eli Whitney's sprawling farm, and part of our view is an old drystone wall dating from the time the Whitney family lived here. The shape of the terrain we face is rounded and rising, like one side of a great bowl; and it's thick with old trees—tall oaks, some pines, some beech trees, and an ash or two. At midday, when the sunlight comes streaming down through the leafy foliage, the setting takes on a hushed, holy quality.

I waited, time passed; but there was silence aside from the occasional cawing of a crow. I remember going about a few kitchen tasks, feeling at some point in the future—it was going to make them a very wealthy couple. "We'd often drive past a certain building in which his company was supposedly housed, and I'd say, 'Let's go in.' But he'd always say that we couldn't, because he and his partner had agreed that they weren't going to get the wives involved."

The whole thing had been an elaborate setup. Throughout most of the five years of that marriage, Claudia had been made to believe that her husband was working at "the business" in the mornings and showing real estate in the late afternoons and early evenings—"Not very successfully, either," she remarked dryly. And while he was supposedly putting all his profits back into the concern, it was *she* who was paying the mortgage, the maintenance charges, the upkeep of the cars, and the electric and telephone bills.

"Steven wouldn't ever give me the phone number of his company; he always had a beeper. I would keep *asking* him for his business number, but he'd get mad and he would get in my face. Next thing you know he'd turn it around, and so now I was wrong; I was the one who was pushing. We'd get into a fight, and then what do you know, *I'd* end up backing off."

I said nothing for a moment but took note of the fact that once again she'd been maneuvered into the position of the bad guy. At the same time, many reactions to this strange story—and questions about it—began popping into my mind. How could she *not* have suspected that something was seriously amiss here; she had, after all, been the one who was shouldering all of the bills! And what, for that matter, had her ex-spouse done with so much empty time on his hands and nothing productive to occupy him?

When I asked Claudia if she had any idea just *how* Steven had spent all that blank time, her expression turned bitter. "What did he *do* with his time?" she said. "Slept and lied. He was a compulsive liar. Maybe he did real estate from about three to eight P.M., but he slept throughout the morning."

This lying, hypocritical state of affairs had gone on for five years. Ultimately, it was the issue of the company telephone number that had given her husband's bogus undercover life away. "I'd kept hounding Steven until he finally did give me what was supposedly the number of his business. But it was a scam; and the way he'd arranged it was that he'd had an extra telephone jack installed," she said. This secret jack had, in turn, been connected to a telephone answering machine, and the entire apparatus was then hidden in back of some stacked-up shoeboxes on *her own side* of the clothes closet. "The way it worked was that when I called I'd reach a recording of this so-called wholesale baked goods concern that he owned."

I stared at her. "So he was a total impostor," I said flatly.

She nodded, then went on to say that a steady buildup of odd incidents had finally caused her to do some active investigating; and that it had been this effort that finally culminated in her discovery of the concealed telephone jack.

I wrote the word *impostor* above Steven's name on the genogram.

Then I looked up at Claudia, as if prompting her to continue, and she picked up the tale with her discovery of the elaborate setup in the back of her closet. "I knew then that I was going to be leaving him, and I told him so," she said. "*His* reaction was that he came right up close to my face with this big, broad smile. And he asked me, 'How did you ever figure it out?'"

I noticed that her hands, which had been resting lightly on her lap, had become fists as she spoke and that her normally rosy skin had turned a grayish color, as if the life had suddenly drained out of her. "What a story," I said quietly.

Five whole years, I was thinking. Five years of cohabiting with—and being in a supposedly intimate relationship with—someone who was living a completely fraudulent existence, just plain *lying* to you about everything in his life. I paused, struck by the fact Claudia Martinelli had gone directly from a dad whom she described as a "holy roller and a total hypocrite" to a husband whose *exterior* life and whose *real* life bore no connection whatsoever. There was, it seemed to me, a somewhat poignant, daughterly sense of generational loyalty and continuity here—for what is a false life if not the very embodiment of hypocrisy?

Narratives and Myths About the Self

An arresting thesis, put forth by psychiatrist Charles Ford, is that it's not just the impostor but *all of us* who to some extent devise a "personal myth" about who we really are. This ongoing, self-told tale is basically the story of the self—a narrative we not only believe in, but organize our lives around.

This personal mythmaking is aided and abetted by a selective memory process that helps us to "remember" most clearly whatever fits into our schema and buttresses our images of ourselves. "We also present ourselves to others duplicitously, playing certain roles and providing selective information about ourselves. Responses from others confirm and help mold the resultant myth," writes Ford in his book *Lies! Lies! Lies!*

It is in the course of creating and elaborating upon such personal myths—a process that gets under way early in life, in our families of origin —that a particularly core, salient theme tends to come to occupy front and center of our awareness. For example, we may see ourselves in the central role of "the victim" or "the hero"; the "outcast" or "the entitled one"; the "nice guy" who is miraculously free of aggression or "the angry, injured guy," the person with a perennial chip on his shoulder. In this sense, we are all impostors to some greater or lesser extent—enacting for ourselves and those around us a life role that we've come to believe in.

Of course, there will be times when we're confronted with information that *doesn't* quite fit into the dominant story line: when the always unflappable "good guy" is feeling consumed by rage or the "tough, unemotional guy" feels weak, needy, and vulnerable. When this happens, our impulse is to quickly "stuff" these forbidden emotions, banish them from sight. The nice guy deceives *himself* as well as those around him by completely denying his own taboo feelings of aggression, just as the tough guy suppresses his intolerable sense of powerlessness and fragility. They are the secrets we keep from everyone, including from ourselves.

Needless to say, there is a close connection between the development of a personal myth and a person's development of his or her own individual self—by which is meant that subjective sense of "This is me, this is who I am" and "This is the body I inhabit." It is in this precise area that the impostor clearly differs from the rest of us. His inner sense of "who I am" and what manner of "self" his body contains is rudimentary, while his skill at being who and what *someone else wishes him to be* is often wonderfully well developed.

He is perfectly able to present himself as successful and competent to those around him—Claudia's husband had passed himself off as the co-owner of an up-and-coming baked goods–distributing company—while inside he is all emptiness, a vacuum, doing nothing. He is someone who lacks a secure identity and place in the real world and has therefore invented a fictional one.

Why should the impostor, who tends to be a highly intelligent person, want to renounce his individual personhood and playact at being someone he is not? You might say it's in order to get a free ride in life, with someone else paying all the fare; but most psychiatric experts working in this area believe there are other, far deeper reasons for his behavior. The most favored working hypothesis is that the very act of imposturing represents a person's attempt to fill up the painful existential void that yawns inside him.

For the impostor's playacting gives him an organizing, energizing "role" to play, which in turn fills him up with a jerry-built sense of identity—and a false identity is probably better than no identity at all. And perhaps more important, the act of imposturing transforms that individual's sense of himself as a weak and insignificant nobody—someone who has nothing inside himself and nothing worthwhile to show for his life—into a secretly significant, powerful somebody who is obviously superior to everyone around him. After all, hasn't he succeeded in manipulating and deceiving them all?

The Impostor's Dilemma

A surprising yet oft noted finding is that when the impostor's "cover" is blown, it's often *not* completely due to bungling or error. For the paradox of this individual's entire existence is that his major skills and achievements are in the area of manipulating and deceiving other people. So if those around him never *do* find out how brilliantly they've been taken in, they never will learn about his cleverness and superiority! They'll never realize what hopeless dimwits they've been or how masterfully he's led them along. Claudia's husband's slow smile of amusement and his disdainful question to his wife—"How did you ever figure it out?"—bespoke a certain pleasure in her mortifying discovery of how obtuse and gullible she'd been.

Indeed, her prolonged inability to "get it" does raise a question: Is there anything special or different about the kind of person who *can* be duped so thoroughly by an impostor—someone whose entire presentation of self is one gigantic lie? Is she a person who's simply been unlucky, someone whose too trusting nature has led her to ignore the manifold warning signals of which wiser, more wary heads would have taken notice? The current thinking about impostors and their chosen victims suggests that no single, clear-cut explanation for the vulnerability of the "target" is sufficient.

At a surface level, she can be seen as someone with an agenda of her own—an agenda that renders her all too ready to believe what she wants to believe. For example, if a woman's agenda is to find a mate and get married, she's prone to see whatever fits into her schema and to fail to take into account any information that doesn't fit into her self-constructed, highly optimistic picture. She may therefore view her potential partner as generous, competent, straightforward, loving, affectionate, and trustworthy, owing to the fact that she *needs* to see him in that light. In her own eyes, that person has all the attributes that she *wants* him to have, and if he seems to lack some of them, she goes ahead and fills in the blanks.

The individual she believes she knows is, in truth, a figment of her own fantasies, and the relationship they share is the one that exists primarily in the world of her imagination. It is as if she is committed to "not know" anything negative about him—to banish from her conscious awareness any potential doubts, fears, or painfully discordant feelings.

Errors in Judgment

As mentioned earlier, it has been well established that people who've been exposed to early trauma have a tendency to make gross errors in judgment when it comes to getting into intimate relationships. And in Claudia Martinelli's case, it could be said that both her current and her previous marital choices indicated that her "partner selection mechanism" was clearly out of kilter. Certainly her track record through life (which included several other ego-busting love affairs not described here) did indicate a penchant for getting into passionate involvements without any real sense of the other person's basic qualities—including his faults, his human failings, and the kinds of problems that might arise between them.

It was true that Claudia did, at one level, want to move ahead in her life and do all the normal womanly things that everyone around her expected of her—to marry, remain married, and have a family of her own eventually. At another level, though, her *behavior*—in terms of the partners she chose and the degree of emotional distance that always resulted—bespoke an equally powerful urge to *avoid* becoming intimate with anyone. For while she appeared to want a warm, trusting, gratifying relationship, her feet always seemed to walk her in a direction that would make achieving that relationship impossible.

A problem she was struggling with repetitively revolved, it seemed to me, around the issue of intimacy—specifically, the basic truth that it's impossible to become truly intimate without opening up and making yourself vulnerable. For many people, this feels dangerous—you could lower all your defenses and then meet with hurt, rejection, or abandonment—but it's *sure* to feel dangerous if you've experienced emotional injuries earlier in your lifetime. So Claudia, like many others, was full of warring wishes and contradictory-seeming motivations.

"The Body, Like the Mind, Is Subject to the Repetition Compulsion"

As I saw it, there were still some missing puzzle pieces here, some *other* leads to the mystery of why this lovely, intelligent woman had come to believe that the only relationship she was entitled to was a painful and humiliating one. And as I sat opposite her, what sprang to my mind was an extraordinary observation made by the analyst and author Joyce McDougall: "The body, like the mind, is subject to the repetition compulsion."

It is surely true that emotional experiences—fear, pain, and humiliation among them—are experiences *of the body*. These experiences do not, as we know, exist solely in an airy, abstract mental sphere; in reality, they involve a host of neurobiological reactions and many *physical feelings and sensations*. And it might well be the case, as McDougall contends, that a person's internal feeling-state—that is, *what is happening inside the person's body*—may, in certain instances, provide the unseen, underlying motivation for reviving and reenacting charged aspects of the past. The suggestion is that by recapitulating not only "the way it was," but "the way it *felt inside,*" a person can reconnect with the inner state of being he knows best and the bodily feelings and sensations with which he is most familiar.

Seen from this novel vantage point, it could be said that Claudia had, all unknowingly, sought out those kinds of relationships that would lead her to reexperience certain ways of being in her body—those internal feeling-states associated with feeling like a victim and living in an atmosphere rife with fear, abuse, and humiliation. For these were the familiar feelings and sensations she had known since time immemorial. Moreover, it occurred to me that she probably hadn't the remotest idea of what it would be like to live inside a *different* kind of body—a body that felt relaxed, full of trust, and gratified.

"Zoned Out," Yet Hyperaroused

Perhaps most central of all to an understanding of Claudia's current-day situation was an appreciation of the impact of traumatic stress—in this case, the witnessing of intermittent, unpredictable violence in her family of origin. For, as noted earlier, "zoning out," or dissociating from one's own emotional responses, is a frequent response in those instances where the caretaking parent is at the source of a child's suffering and pain. Young children have a powerful, *biologically based* need to form and maintain strong emotional attachments to the adult nurturers upon whom they're so utterly dependent. The human imperative is to maintain faith and belief in the instinctively adored, utterly irreplaceable parent—no matter what the psychological cost to the growing youngster and no matter how badly that parent may be behaving.

Again, in those unhappy circumstances involving an abusive, chronically neglectful, or emotionally exploitative caretaker, the child's best defensive action is often that of shutting down, not feeling too many things too deeply. Closing off access to her own internal experiences makes it possible to retain an all-unmerited faith and belief in the irreplaceable parent. It is for this reason that children who've been severely stressed during their earliest years will so often grow up to become adults who are deaf to their own bodily cues and warning signals.

Experience has taught them to believe it's safer to stay disconnected from this part of their internal wiring. Nevertheless, while someone in this situation may have managed well enough by shutting down many of her body's emotional warning signs and signals, her body's overall emergency warning system is on high alert and liable to be sounding off continually. For in the aftermath of traumatic experiences that have never been dealt with, a person's body is girded to confront the menace that is felt to be everywhere.

Her inner state is one of high arousal, and she is highly likely to respond in exaggerated ways to all sorts of minor challenges. Thus, a passing criticism from a boss, friend, or lover can precipitate the classic bodily reactions to a situation of crisis: a speeded-up heartbeat; clenched chest muscles; shallow, rapid breathing; and an outpouring of crisis situation neurohormones. Although outwardly the person may appear to be responding calmly, her body is in a state of perennial readiness to meet with threat, and perfectly ordinary, neutral kinds of events can be experienced as catastrophic ordeals.

In brief, the long-term consequences of growing up in severely stressful circumstances are twofold: First, the developing child tends to become disconnected from her own physiologically based sources of information —those subtle, body-based warning cues and signals—and second, she inhabits a body that feels tremendously tense and uncomfortable, for her central nervous system is in a state of perpetual defense readiness. She is so highly reactive to small occurrences, so braced to meet the next expected danger, that she never quite experiences her interior world, never knows it to be safe and under her control.

And because a person in this situation doesn't have a sense of owning the body inside which she lives—and is deaf to so many of the signals coming from inside it—she experiences her unruly feelings, urges, and impulses as if they're somehow attacking from outside. As a result, and as part of an effort to self-soothe and calm herself down, she will often become involved in addictive behaviors of some sort: drinking, drugs, gambling, promiscuous sex, or disorders involving food—which, of course, is the universal symbol of nurturance.

Actually, all of these addictive disorders can be viewed as attempted distractions from the roiling world within—a world that feels barren and fraught with dangers simultaneously. For even though people in this situation may be feeling "spaced out," in the most fundamental sense, they are nevertheless acutely sensitized to the plethora of dangers, possible betrayals, losses, and rejections that threaten them on every side. They are therefore drawn to any form of relief from their inner pain, no matter how self-destructive that behavior may prove to be in the long run—and not surprisingly, their lives take on a tormented flavor.

Unheard Dispatches from Within

Claudia came to our next meeting, the last of these interviews, looking as rattled as I'd ever seen her. She told me at once that she and Paul had had a bad quarrel this past weekend, then added quickly, in a defensive tone of voice, that she wasn't giving up on this marriage anyway.

This was because they'd eventually settled their differences amicably, and she'd felt *heartened* by that. It seemed to bespeak her growing capacity for hanging on to herself when the gale winds of one of their stormy, irrational arguments were blowing. In this instance, instead of "losing it," she had been able simply to walk away—something she'd been unable to do before getting into her therapy, which had begun two weeks before she'd gotten married and had been continuing in tandem with our conversations.

The fight with Paul had erupted the previous Saturday night, Claudia told me, flopping down on the sofa as if exhausted. Then she stopped speaking, looked dejected and lost in thought. I waited to see if she would continue on her own, but when she didn't I asked her how this past weekend's argument had gotten started.

Instead of responding to the question, she leaned forward, then put a chunk of cheese on a cracker and lifted it to her mouth with a slightly trembling hand. As she did so, I noticed that her skin had begun to look patchy, mottled with red blotches, as if her remembered anger had brought on a sudden outbreak of chickenpox.

The sense of her profound misery was such that I looked away, as if intruding on a moment that felt too intense and personal. I found myself staring at the wall behind her, which was lined with mahogany bookshelves and fully stocked with beautifully bound first editions—the kinds of books that appear designated for looking at rather than for reading. This valuable collection had once belonged to the grandfather of the apartment's owner, who was my friend and landlord.

"It's *Paul*—he has absolutely no patience, no tolerance," Claudia said, breaking the silence. "He just flies off the *handle*. For instance, we started going at each other because he pushed me out of the bathroom—*he* wanted to brush his teeth first!" I couldn't help but smile at the slightly comic quality of the complaint, and Claudia answered with a rueful smile of her own.

"I know, it's *so* ridiculous," she said.

The dispute had actually gotten under way earlier, when the two of them came home late on Saturday evening and found her husband's fourteen-year-old son, Christopher, entertaining a bunch of his pals in the living room. Although this teenage party had been prearranged and agreed to, Paul was ill at ease when he arrived and found those kids sprawled all over their brand-new, still pristine furniture. In Claudia's opinion, her husband had seemed self-conscious, stilted, "not himself," and not at all certain how to behave with his son's friends.

But as she saw it, it wasn't her problem, so she'd simply said a brief hello, then made a beeline into the bedroom area. Then she'd gone into the bathroom in order to remove her makeup and the contacts she was wearing. "I didn't think it was my place to start socializing with these boys; *I'm* not the parent," she explained to me crisply. But Paul had come dashing in after her and begun urging her to go out into the living room and talk with Christopher and his guests for a while.

"He wanted me to check the kids out, to see if any of them had beer or 'anything weird' on their breath," Claudia said. "But I told him, '*I'm* not going. Why should *I* go? *You* go!'" Her voice was rising indignantly.

"That's when he told me—I mean *ordered* me—'Move over, I want to brush my teeth.' And I said, 'When I get out of the bathroom, you will!' So he just *shoved* me out of the way so he could brush *his* teeth!" she said, looking completely furious.

A moment later, though, she seemed to have a change of heart, for to my surprise she said pacifically, "I think that Paul was probably dealing with a couple of different, and pretty complicated, issues on that occasion. First of all, I think he felt inadequate about going out there in front of his son and his son's friends—he didn't know what to say or how to be with them."

She was sounding as if she'd stepped into the role of her husband's counsel and was pleading his case before me, the stern, disapproving judge. I said nothing but felt somewhat confused about where this conversation might be going. Claudia had a way of stating her legitimate complaints and then backing off in an eyeblink. It was as if she were taking herself out of the equation somehow and nullifying what seemed to be her own appropriate reactions.

"Secondly, he *did* have a serious drinking problem earlier in his life, and although he's not touched liquor for the past seven years, I think he's still a 'dry drunk' right now," she said. In other words, his behavior was still *like* that of an active alcoholic in terms of his being provocative, controlling, and short-tempered. She was sounding more concerned, empathetic, and understanding about her husband's state of being than she was about any of the mental or physical distress she might be experiencing herself.

Claudia fell silent then, sat there staring out at the Manhattan skyline, which had lit up while we'd been talking. In the ensuing space of quiet, the distant sounds of honking horns could be heard, and a far-off ambulance siren blared the news of a distant crisis. But we were high up on the twenty-sixth floor of the apartment building, so the babble from the busy street below was not at all invasive. It was more like a humming backdrop to our conversation, one that gave the room an enclosed, safe, cocoonlike quality.

I looked at her thoughtfully, bemused again by the fact that this handsome woman, who had so much going for her, had hooked up with a husband who sounded so irascible, punishing, and blaming. Why hadn't she been able to recognize and react to those small, internal warning signs and signals—the knotted gut, the tension headache, the feelings of anxiety—that we all experience within our body/selves when we sense that something in our lives is going awry? It seemed evident that none of these small somatic alarms—which must have been sounding from time to time *before* the marriage—had been recognized and reacted to by her at the level of conscious awareness. Yet it was these very dispatches from the body's interior—a crucially important aspect of our everyday decision making—

that could have signaled her fair warning about what living with this partner was going to be like.

Deciphering the Data

There are innumerable life situations in which our bodies are sending out somatic cues, signals, and announcements—"Something's feeling 'off' here" or "I'm not sure this person can be trusted"—but transmitting this information in the form of vague physical discomforts or minor symptoms rather than through the more precise medium of thoughts and language. These body-based data contain vital information and need to be attended to on a routine basis—translated from what are crude physiological signals ("My stomach is in knots") into important bulletins that can at times be crucial to the whole person's well-being.

Of course, these messages *do* need to be decoded on a case-by-case basis: For example, a stomach pain may be symptomatic of a problem in your life, but it can also have to do with a medical issue or, for that matter, be traced to something that you ate earlier in the day. But in those cases where there is an unprocessed, unresolved history of trauma, one of the most typical reactions is that of going away internally—tuning out, becoming spacey, not fully present in one's mental or bodily self. The upside of this "solution" is that feeling distanced and not quite registering the disturbing experiences internally helps to keep the pain at a greater remove. You won't feel the "pain in your life" so keenly.

The serious downside, however, is that losing touch with this body-based feedback is highly maladaptive in the long run. For in the process, those gut feelings and responses—which so often bring us important, up-to-the-millisecond data about our true emotional state of being—become deactivated, blocked off. And as a consequence, a person may go charging forward in circumstances that might give someone more in touch with herself clear grounds for proceeding with caution.

Chapter Nine

—

WHAT LESSON AM I NOT LEARNING?

SOME THREE MONTHS AFTER OUR INTERVIEWS HAD CONcluded, I phoned Claudia at her office. This was meant to be a brief, routine follow-up call, but she sounded distraught and said she was very glad to hear from me. Her office was busy at this moment, but she told me that she'd call back that evening shortly after eight o'clock.

When she phoned it was with news, and it was bad news. She and Paul had just come back from a luxurious resort in the Bahamas, where they'd gone to celebrate their one-year anniversary. The "celebration" had turned out to be a hellish experience, and the two of them were now living apart—at this point, it was a trial separation.

As we talked, I realized that Claudia's voice sounded muffled, lower, almost an octave lower than I remembered. It was as if her voice were weighted down by strain and embarrassment, and I kept having trouble hearing what she was saying. She was clearly so depressed, so shaken to the roots of her being, that I hated having to ask her to repeat herself; but at times, during our long conversation, I simply had to do so.

As she described it, that anniversary trip had gone sour almost immediately on their arrival. They'd been unable to check in at the hotel because their room wasn't ready, so they'd been offered the use of a hospitality suite in order to change their clothes. "We had to get our bathing suits and stuff out of our bags, and I guess I took ninety seconds more than Paul thought I should have taken, and he blew up at me. I couldn't *believe* he was acting that way over something so ridiculous, but I heard him mumble a name at me under his breath. . . ."

What kind of name? I asked her.

She hesitated, then said, "Fucking birdbrain." She found it humiliating even to talk about, she said, but that incident had set her off, and after that she'd found it hard to shake the agitated feelings. Her *own* part in all of this was that once Paul got her going, she just couldn't calm herself down and let go of the issue. This was *her* problem—letting go of things—and it was something she'd been continuing to work on with her therapist. As always, she was eager to step forward and take her share, or more than her share, of the blame.

I did remember her saying that when Paul was acting moody, tense, or short with her, she could get pretty nasty herself. "I'm not too pleasant to be around. I obsess on things and pick them apart," Claudia had said at that time. Still, my own reaction was that if *my* partner had called me something like that, for a reason like that, I'd have had some trouble letting go of the issue myself!

It had been a *hard* vacation, Claudia repeated in that same heavy, teary tone of voice. At one point, the pair of them had strolled around for a while, and then Paul had decided he was hungry. They'd sat down, and he'd ordered a ham and cheese sandwich and a soda, and the bill had come to around $20. Claudia had thought that sum was really off the wall.

"What I said was, 'Gee, this place is expensive; God forbid that you come here with a family because you could really go broke.'" That remark had caused another eruption, for her husband took the statement to mean that she wanted him to spend all of his money on *her* and none of it on his kids.

Just recently, I recalled, there had been some sudden financial demands coming from his children, which had both infuriated Paul and made him feel guilty toward them. The largest of these demands had been his seventeen-year-old daughter's request for a new car, which she "needed" to get to school and to her part-time job. "There was just a whole lot of stuff flying between the two of us, and it wasn't good," Claudia said, her voice taut. They had come home that Monday night and separated shortly afterward.

"So, where is this marriage now?" I asked her.

"I definitely have one foot out the door," she responded, and I heard her begin crying softly, a low, throbbing sound. "I've been having a tough time these past weeks. It's been very, very difficult. And you know, I'm totally *ashamed* at this second marriage failing. I just feel so humiliated, in every way. . . . But as I told Paul, I just don't know if I'm *strong* enough to handle this relationship."

"Strong enough?" I asked. This seemed to me an odd way to characterize the situation. She was putting herself down, describing herself in negative terms—her "weakness" in contrast with her partner's "strength" —when there were many other words that could have been used to portray what was happening between them. At one point during our interviews, I'd actually met with the couple together and found Claudia's husband engaging, good-looking, fastidiously dressed, and very, very tense. During the course of that conversation, he'd acknowledged that he had a lot of anger inside him and had been angry as long as he could remember—he didn't know why. Now I said to her, "You do realize that Paul is very tightly strung? He's really on a short fuse; you can feel it."

"Oh yes," said Claudia, sounding relieved by that remark. Then she said, "You know, I told his mother recently that God forbid the pair of us ever get caught in bad traffic; I just can't believe the way he acts! And then he turns around and says he acts that way because *I'm* bugging *him*! That *I'm* the one who doesn't know when to back off! But you know, the last time we were out driving together, he told me that if I didn't shut the 'f' up, he was going to punch me in the mouth, and all my teeth would fall out! Or better yet, he was going to throw me out of the car and run me over! And he will say, 'Claudia, I'm not saying that this kind of talk is right—it's *so wrong*—but it's *you*. You just push me to the limit!"

I was startled. This was a degree of verbal violence that she'd never reported earlier. "There is simply no excuse for that kind of abusive talk," I said flatly.

"Well, that's where I am," she said wearily, and then began to sob again. "Maggie, I'm not *good* with this kind of stuff. And the truth is, with the exception of my first husband, I've always had every man break up with me. This goes all the way back to high school—everyone's always broken up with me. I did leave my ex-husband after five years, but I think any normal woman would have left that scam artist four years before I did.

So to make this final decision and walk out on Paul is really *hard*—I almost wish he'd do it to me."

She wished that *he* would be the one to break up the marriage, so that she wouldn't have to bear the guilt and be the "bad guy"—she felt so profoundly *bad* about herself already.

Claudia then told me there had been an entire year when she'd simply stopped dating any men at all, gone to see a therapist several times a week, and really tried to get to know herself. She'd tried to *be* herself; to live alone and *like* herself; and she'd really believed she'd gotten her act together during this period. "Eventually I started seeing different people, and then I started dating Paul, who was so kind and caring then; and we were together from that time onward. So I'm just sitting here, completely flabbergasted, and I'm saying, 'Here I am again, in this same position.' And I'm wondering, What lesson am I not learning, that I keep getting knocked over the head with the same thing?"

"I don't know, Claudia," I responded honestly. Then she began to cry again, and I simply sat there, listening, saying a soothing word from time to time. At the same time, I was thinking of how many similar situations I'd seen—instances in which a person had worked *hard* in psychotherapy, gained a new understanding of her or his ongoing problems and their origin in the painful experiences of the past, but then been unable to resist the magnetic pull toward repeating some version of the same history again. It was as if there were a deep stratum of the person's being that all this newfound intellectual and emotional knowledge had been unable to penetrate.

It may well be, as Bessel van der Kolk and other trauma experts have suggested, that this less accessible stratum of the self corresponds to that mysterious, wordless region of the "old, emotional" brain where our body-based feelings, sensations, and memories are believed to reside. But in any case, while the "talking cure" has surely been effective in helping people to make sense of, and give meaning to, a troubled past, it frequently *hasn't* helped them to change their repetitive ways of behaving and improve upon their present lives.

For example, Claudia, by maintaining her family's pattern of silence about matters that were *not* to be discussed (for instance, "bad behavior"), and therefore lying to Paul from the very outset, had almost scripted him to play a role in the secretive, abusive drama that was the story of her life. She was operating as if a certain internal "blueprint for being"—as forceful as it was invisible—had been incorporated by her, body and mind.

As it happened, it was during this selfsame period that I was starting to look seriously at some of the more offbeat, nontraditional, body-oriented approaches to treatment—therapies such as EMDR (eye movement desensitization and reprocessing) and PBSP (Pesso Boyden System Psychomotor)—which I shall be discussing at greater length further along in this book. These forms of treatment do much more than offer insight on an intellectual and emotional level; as shall be seen, they also *engage the body* at a somatosensory level, which is to say at the level of body-based feelings, sensations, and remembrances. And I believe it was my own sense of helpless, frustrated sympathy during this conversation with Claudia that galvanized me into accelerated action at that time.

For in the wake of this exchange, I began to look, with a new urgency and focus, for answers to a question I now viewed as the crux of the matter: Were there effective forms of therapy that were targeted specifically upon releasing, from the body, those painful secrets that could lead to repetitive, self-destructive behaviors and "familiarly uncomfortable" bodily states? I was to find, in the course of my work, that the answer to this question is yes.

Part Two

REPROCESSING

Chapter Ten

DETOXIFYING THE BODY'S MEMORIES: REPROCESSING

"WHAT LESSON AM I *NOT* LEARNING?" MANY OF THE PEOPLE I was interviewing at this time had, like Claudia Martinelli, raised this bewildered question in one form or another. And as a result, I'd begun to look outside the boundaries of the more standard forms of psychotherapy and to explore a variety of newer, very different modes of treatment. It was in the course of this odyssey that I became an invited guest at a packed training workshop where a therapeutic treatment called reprocessing (short for eye movement desensitization and reprocessing, or EMDR) was being taught to an auditorium filled with clinicians.

As a guest, I was able to attend daily lectures on the reprocessing method and observe—but not take part in—the experiential, hands-on part of the training. But as the three-day workshop progressed, the obvious and unmistakable power of the process made me wish I could experience it from the inside rather than being fixed, as I was, in the position of onlooker and outsider. I had absorbed all that I could by sitting in on lectures and observing the hands-on part of the training. Now I wanted to acquaint myself with the experiential part of the therapy—to dive right in by putting myself in the role of "the client."

I did so more in the spirit of learning the procedure than of personal problem solving, but in fact the sessions turned out to be a serious eye-opener for me. For as it developed, there were secrets I'd been keeping from myself—matters that I'd been carefully avoiding "knowing" but which I *did* know—experiences long "forgotten" that I was holding in my body and mind and that were affecting me at the very core of my being.

Targeting a Memory

Like most other psychotherapeutic encounters, EMDR commences with an initial assessment phase that is a schematic overview of the client's lifetime. This synopsis consists of biographical information, such as where the person grew up, the major events of her or his life, and an account of the person's medical, psychological, relational, educational, and career history.

Such an assessment will often include information about previous therapies—their success or failure; what was helpful, what was not—and a rundown of the medications or nonprescription drugs that the patient has taken or is currently taking. In the usual kind of situation, the client has come in with an unresolvable problem or is in the midst of a life crisis. However, my own goal, when I went to see EMDR facilitator Dr. Patti Levin in her New Haven office, was a distinctively oddball one: I just wanted to see what reprocessing therapy *felt* like. What then happened was much more than I'd bargained for.

Reprocessing the Past

I'd heard a lot about EMDR before ever seeing it in action. I was aware that it relied far less heavily on the spoken word and the clinician's abilities and sophistication than it did upon a carefully designed eight-stage protocol—a therapeutic recipe of sorts. I'd also heard a lot about reprocessing therapy from a clinician friend who used it often in her office and had found it to be remarkably effective. But when she'd first described EMDR to me, it sounded like some sort of therapeutic hokum.

At that time (the early 1990s), I'd tried to listen to my friend Katherine Davis, whom I knew to have an impressive amount of experience under her belt. She'd been clinical director of the Hamden Mental Health Service in Connecticut for many years before opening a private office of her own. Still, I listened dubiously as she described therapeutic outcomes that smacked of hallelujah cures—sudden resolutions of patients' long-standing problems that had come about when she made use of this reprocessing technique (still relatively unknown at the time).

One such case had to do with a trauma patient in her late twenties, someone whom Katherine had treated with conventional, insight-oriented psychotherapy for over a year. This client had suffered a harrowing loss: She'd seen her three-year-old daughter run down and killed by a speeding teenager who'd suddenly lost control of his car and careened into the child while she was riding her tricycle up and down along the sidewalk.

The mother had been standing nearby, watching over her daughter, and thus she was the helpless witness as the whole incident unrolled before her eyes. In the aftermath, the child's parent was so distraught that she could barely function in her day-to-day life; she'd simply remained transfixed in that terrible moment of the accident's occurrence. In session after session, this tormented client had dwelled upon the visual image of that horrifying scene, which preoccupied her thoughts and continued to flood her with a grief that was seemingly unresolvable. She was also experiencing many of the classical symptoms that follow upon traumatic events: intrusive thoughts, bursts of irrational anger, feelings of ongoing agitation, and horrible nightmares that sent her hurtling into wakefulness.

According to Katherine, this state of affairs had persisted for weeks, months, and then a year of traditional insight-oriented therapy, bolstered by antidepressant medication; still, nothing seemed to change things. The treatment was clearly going nowhere, and in fact, as Katherine later described it to me, it was in the nature of a frustrated, last-ditch effort to get the treatment moving that she'd first tried using reprocessing therapy. She herself was a novice, having just received training in the use of EMDR, and she hadn't actually tried putting her new knowledge to the test. What happened then amazed both therapist and client.

For in the wake of that single ninety-minute reprocessing session, the deadlock in the treatment came to a sudden, dramatic ending. Something remarkable had taken place—it was hard to understand just *how* or *why* it had taken place, but at the close of this meeting, the patient focused her gaze upon the therapist and said, "Okay, that's *it.* It's *over.* It happened, and there's nothing anyone in the world can do to make it *un*happen. It was and *is* horrible, but it's in the past. I have to get on with my life, but I feel that I can deal with it now."

"And that," Katherine told me, "was that." The therapy was essentially over, and in a few subsequent sessions, the young mother moved through a process of normal mourning.

Her tragic loss was no longer being experienced in the here and now—undigested and indigestible, stuck in her throat. Somehow, that single reprocessing session had enabled her to integrate a welter of thoughts, feelings, and images that had kept her locked in the moment of the trauma—the process had enabled her to swallow down and assimilate what her mind and body had been rejecting ever since her little daughter's death. The loss had been transformed into an awful memory, but it was now a part of the past—no longer something that was continually happening in an eternal, breathless, terrifying present tense.

Therapeutic Turnarounds

In the course of my work, I soon began encountering other clinicians who had the same kinds of amazing turnarounds to report. One New York analyst told me about a patient of his, a young college student whom he'd treated in psychotherapy over an extended period of time.

This young client had come in twice a week, every week, always complaining about the same problem—a painful relationship with an older, married professor. It was an affair she hated being involved in and wanted to break off, but somehow she couldn't bring herself to do it. She felt that the relationship was not only bad morally, but bad *for her* as a person; there were many ways in which her lover was being cruel to her, even sadistic, and she was well aware that this was so. Nevertheless, after months of psychotherapy, she'd been unable to bring this degrading attachment to a halt.

As had been true in my friend Katherine's case, this clinician had turned to the reprocessing method as a last resort, for he himself was in a state of "therapeutic despair." He was playing EMDR as a last clinical card, but in this instance, the patient hadn't appeared to respond—at least not in any way that was apparent.

During the rapid eye movement sets, she'd merely placed her hand upon her own body in different, innocuous-seeming places—at one point, her shoulder; at another, her arm; and then her forehead. But she'd had very little to *say* during the reprocessing procedure, and it didn't seem to her therapist that EMDR was going to have any effect. However, between that clinical session and the client's next appointment, her life took a startling 180-degree turnaround. Upon her arrival at his office, she informed her therapist that she'd finally ended the demeaning affair that had been causing her so much pain for so long.

She wasn't sure *why* she'd suddenly felt so capable of bringing that ugly situation to a close, but she *had*—and she felt really good about having done so. That was it. This young woman's presenting problem had been resolved with mysterious ease—and with few words having been said—in the aftermath of that single reprocessing session.

In this case, and in the many other clinical anecdotes I was hearing, reprocessing therapy had made a real difference in terms of bringing about clear and palpable change—not always with the same remarkable rapidity seen in the cases just described, to be sure. (Of course, in both these instances, the EMDR sessions had been preceded by extensive verbal psychotherapy.) Still, I will confess that such glowing reports had left me feeling skeptical, uneasy. For from a scientific point of view, how could miraculous resolutions of this sort possibly be explained? They sounded too sudden and dramatic, too good to be completely true.

Detoxifying Painful Memories

It was by serendipitous accident that Francine Shapiro, Ph.D., the originator and pioneer of EMDR, first stumbled across the peculiar notion that rapid eye movements might affect mental functioning in some unaccountable but distress-relieving fashion. She had been walking in a California park, thinking unhappily about some matter that was troubling her—she can no longer remember exactly what it was. Perhaps her mind was on the cancer, discovered and treated successfully a decade earlier (in the late 1970s). She was certainly in good health at the moment, but her physician had told her at the time of discharge that her disease might reappear, without warning, at some later point in time. This did happen to some cancer survivors, for reasons that were not at all predictable.

On that afternoon, Shapiro happened to be following a footpath lined by trees whose branches were swaying in the soft breezes. Strolling along, she eventually noticed something that was peculiar. As she walked, she'd begun feeling better. Much better. And by the time she reached the end of that pathway, the disturbing thoughts that had been preoccupying her seemed to have vanished from her mind. When and how had this happened?

She was puzzled, but grateful for this lifting of her spirits. At the same time, since she was a graduate student in clinical psychology, Shapiro's professional curiosity had been aroused. Not only her professional but her very personal curiosity, for she believed that mood-state, and its relation to the body, had some still undiscovered connection to the growth or regression of illnesses such as her own. What had brought about this sense of psychic relief? She called up other negative thoughts, in a purposeful fashion, and as they also vanished, discovered that her eyes had been moving diagonally, from side to side, very quickly, with the steady regularity of a metronome.

The year was 1987, and that trek through the park has since attained legendary status. Indeed, it has evolved over the subsequent years into the creation myth of a new form of therapy, one that has affected the lives of thousands and thousands of people. For having taken note of what had just occurred, and her own changed state of mind, Shapiro wondered whether emotional distress might be affected by the kind of rapid back-and-forth eye movements she had been making as she'd been walking down the pathway. Was it possible that rhythmical eye-tracking in this fashion had some effect upon the nervous system which no-one had noticed before?

In order to test out this strange notion, she summoned up another mildly anxiety-provoking concern that had been preoccupying her at that time. And as she did so, Shapiro moved her eyes back and forth at the same rapid pace and in the same arclike motion as before—following the motion of the branches from left to right and back again, in a continuously moving fashion. Once again, the anxious thoughts seemed to lose their emotional intensity. This was bizarre!

Had thinking those disturbing thoughts, in tandem with the rapid back-and-forth eye movements, tapped into some obscure neurophysiological mechanism that brought about the relief of psychological pain? It was an odd-sounding but nevertheless fascinating idea; and Shapiro, intrigued, began testing out the hypothesis informally with friends, acquaintances, and students—some seventy "volunteers" all told.

However, it didn't take her long to realize that a lot of people had difficulty making the desired swift left-to-right-and-back eye movements spontaneously. So she devised a method that involved asking the subject to bring up a distressing incident and then keep it in mind while eye tracking the movement of her index fingers, which she held up and waved back and forth rhythmically at a comfortable distance from the person's face. This simple procedure—bringing a source of distress to mind while visually tracking the rapid back-and-forth motion of a moving stimulus—appeared to have the curious effect of detoxifying painful, worrying thoughts and putting hurtful memories at a distance and in the past, where they rightfully belonged.

Next, Shapiro began to study this phenomenon within the framework of a formal research project, which was eventually to become the core of her doctoral thesis. The twenty-two subjects taking part in her study were all suffering from clear-cut cases of post-traumatic stress disorder that had developed in the wake of big-T events—such as rape, battlefield experiences, and childhood sexual abuse—and on average, their symptoms had persisted for some twenty-three years. All of them held low opinions of themselves (self-blame is commonplace in these situations), and all had significant problems in relating to others despite having undergone years of therapy.

After one sixty-minute session of EMD (eye movement desensitization, as Francine Shapiro first called her new technique), targeted upon a particular memory *that was troubling the person at the present time,* every one of the participants in this research reported feeling significantly better. The painful memory that had been focused upon had mysteriously lost its biting quality; moreover, all of the subjects felt more positive about themselves and more hopeful about the future. And at a three-month follow-up, many of the concrete gains made by Shapiro's research subjects seemed to have persisted with a surprising robustness.

A control group for this study consisted of PTSD subjects who'd been instructed to call up a troubling memory, which was then discussed at length. However, there was no periodic use of rapid eye movements during these individuals' sessions. It was talking therapy only, and these trauma survivors showed no improvement whatsoever. Shapiro, as astonished by her results as anyone, felt like an explorer who has suddenly emerged upon a wondrous terrain where no one has ever set foot before. True, there was solid earth beneath her feet, in terms of real research results, but where could they possibly lead her?

Desensitizing the Pain

At first it was Shapiro's belief that her new rapid eye movement technique belonged under the umbrella of behavioral therapy, for it involved the slow, systematic desensitization of unbearably hurtful memories—a treatment approach that had long been in use. This behavioral method entails carefully exposing the patient to the original traumatizing situation (often by asking the person to summon up the event or scene in his or her imagination), but at the same time managing to keep the level of emotional intensity lower, under control. The purpose is to enable the patient to feel comfortable enough to begin to *think* about, integrate, and process what did happen, while feeling anchored by the sense of safety provided by the therapeutic situation.

Then, if the treatment moves along according to expectation, the trauma survivor will become increasingly capable of tolerating feelings, thoughts, memories, and images—which come into ever sharpening, more vivid focus—*without* becoming overwhelmed by his or her own fear and terror. The basic theory here is that over time, repeated exposure to the alarming event or events makes what happened feel less horrifying (one becomes habituated to it, "desensitized") and that ultimately this proves far more curative than efforts to deny or avoid what actually occurred. Clinically speaking, denial and avoidance are strategies that may be helpful in the short run but don't work well over time. Painful though it may be, systematically confronting *what really happened* and slowly processing it is far more effective than trying to run away inside—which typically proves impossible anyway.

For when the traumatized person's truth takes the alternative low and secret road, it tends to erupt in the form of symptoms—memories that are split off from consciousness, obsessional ruminations, exaggerated startle responses (an unexpected touch on the shoulder may spark real terror), hyperagitation, and behavioral reenactments of the harmful things that happened earlier. But there is a problem inherent in the use of exposure therapy, which is that many traumatized people find it thoroughly intolerable. Returning to the scene of the trauma, even in imagination, is so agonizing that many patients freak out early in the process; they retreat from the process rapidly and then live out lives that are controlled by their post-traumatic symptoms.

Thus it was that Francine Shapiro—at least initially—viewed her new eye movement desensitization technique as a simple but wonderful tool to be used for making the process of desensitization more bearable. The rapid eye movement procedure appeared to make it possible for the client to bring up a racking, horrible memory and then use the swiftly alternating stimulation (left to right and back again) to draw the poisons from it rapidly and without the same degree of mental pain.

A Psychic Splinter

With the passage of time, however, and the appearance of a raft of psychological studies of the rapid eye movement phenomenon (many pro, a few con), Shapiro eventually decided to add the "R"—which stands for "Reprocessing"—to EMD, her strange-sounding but remarkably effective new approach. For by now she had come to believe that the rapid eye movements were actually initiating some kind of accelerated information processing within the central nervous system itself—one whose mechanism of action was very probably similar to what happens during REM (rapid eye movement) sleep.

This is the phase of sleep during which the raw data of the day's events are reawakened in the form of dreams—and the dreamer's eyes shift back and forth very swiftly, although she or he remains deep in slumber. A way of thinking about what happens during REM sleep is that these reactivated events are like pieces of a jigsaw puzzle that are being quickly scanned, assessed, then fitted together in some way that provides an integrated whole—a "portrait" or summation of the experiences that is meaningful and makes sense. When, like a picture puzzle that has been finished, it feels complete, it can be left behind: The events have been integrated into the person's wider understanding and become part of her or his history.

In Shapiro's view, and the view of other researchers as well, it had come to seem highly likely that there was some neurological analogue between REM sleep and EMDR. For in some mysterious fashion, EMDR seemed to enhance the brain's capacity to deal with those unassimilated bits of experience that had never been properly integrated and processed—which had, metaphorically speaking, become stuck in the patient's throat.

Simply by following the alternating, visual stimulus of the therapist's moving fingers—while keeping the mind focused directly upon those thoughts and memories that gave rise to distress—it often became possible for the person to process painful information that had hitherto existed within the brain as disassembled pieces of coarse, disorganized data. In some ill-understood fashion, the rapid eye movements helped the person to gather together the scrambled chunks and bits of stored material pertaining to the trauma so that it could be confronted and processed. Shapiro herself, along with a number of her colleagues, had come to believe that the rapid eye movements (rhythmic, alternating hand taps and ear tones have proven effective, too) were accessing some unknown, natural healing and integrating process in the brain.

At the present time, almost two decades since that famous walk in the park, many clinicians and researchers will attest that rapid eye movements *do* affect the brain in some mysterious fashion, but nobody is clear about *how* or *why* this happens (of course, still relatively unexplained are the bases of many drug actions, including the actions of most antidepressants). And in the meantime, psychologist Shapiro's reprocessing therapy has changed and evolved into a methodically ordered, full-fledged method of treatment that occupies its own clinical ground. However, as is always the case when a new kind of therapy makes its debut upon the clinical stage, a chorus of objections and criticisms has accompanied its emergence. One of the major critiques has been that EMDR works far too rapidly, a grievance that Francine Shapiro views as humorous.

She likes to compare her way of dealing with the aftermath of trauma to what happens when you remove a splinter from the flesh. A splinter can develop into a horrible infection if it's left to fester, but healing happens quickly once it is removed. So it is, she says, with toxic thoughts and memories. While nobody has been able to state definitively why reprocessing therapy works so frequently and with such rapidity—and while it is only grudgingly being accepted within mainstream clinical psychology despite a good deal of positive outcome research—it can be seen as taking out an emotional splinter. Once the splinter has been removed, healing can take place with surprising swiftness.

Similarly, maintains Francine Shapiro, once the raw, fragmented information—fractured thoughts, torn memories, partially obscured visual images, weird, inexplicable body sensations—has been integrated into the person's autobiographical history, it loses its dangerous intensity. The bad memory or memories don't go away, but they are now incorporated into the body and self in a different manner, and they hold different meanings. Thus, a sexually molested child who has grown up feeling that she's polluted in her very being can be helped to the realization that "I did the best I could, under the circumstances in which it happened." She can put the disturbing past *into the past* where it belongs and stop viewing herself as the soiled creature whom events that were in reality uncontrollable have caused her to believe that she is. Such views and beliefs are no longer part of an ingrained, negatively charged, often paralyzing sense of the self and the self in the world—which makes room for new learning and for the therapy client's interrupted life and development to move in a far healthier, more forward direction.

The Onlooker and the Outsider

I had been introduced to Dr. Patti Levin at one of the EMDR workshops and been impressed by her sensitivity; her tall, ramrod-straight dark-haired beauty; her quick intelligence and readiness to become engaged. When I went to see her in her office, we began with the initial assessment interview, which is the first stage of reprocessing therapy.

This information-gathering session is, it seems to me, in the nature of a fishing trip. The clinician is casting out a wide net in which she hopes to bring to the surface those toxic memories that existed within the client's brain and body—to bring them up and then "neutralize" them one by one. For the basic assumption here, as in so many other forms of therapy, is that the experiences of the past are often a hidden, driving force when it comes to what's happening in the present.

This happened to be true in my own case, for during the assessment process an unresolved concern I was struggling with did come tumbling out. It had to do with a recent bout of back pain that had kept me immobilized for several months. During this period, many friends and acquaintances had checked in with me frequently and been solicitous in numerous ways. But the two women whom I'd most depended upon to *be there* for me—one of whom I'd cared for daily after a bad accident—simply vanished from my life completely. They'd neither e-mailed nor telephoned—a radical behavior change in both instances—nor had they come to visit, although I'd asked them both to "please come and make a sick call." What had followed was nothing, silence.

Later on, when I was well and fully on my feet again, there were many proffered apologies, but the message that had come through was clear. These close, trusted confidantes were able to receive, but giving out was not on their agenda: If you were creating claims on their time or emotional resources, they'd move off until the demand was gone. I was shaken by such callous indifference and yet in some way not startled at all, for this was a familiar theme in my life—being ignored. After all, the first sentence of my autobiography, the one that always popped into my mind, was "I was born, and nobody noticed."

To be sure, I'd long known, at least at a certain level, that my most intense relationships were with female friends who hooked on to me when in situations of emotional need. It was as if I were giving off some sonar signal: "I will help you." They found me, and at a gut level, I found myself drawn in. As the daughter of my mother, I was the perfect partner of someone who needed nurturing; but in that situation I'd needed it myself.

"That must have been *hard* for you," Patti Levin said sympathetically, "when these women, on whom you were depending, didn't validate your own needs and act like friends. When they didn't even phone and say, 'How are you doing?'"

I smiled wryly, said that this lack of reciprocity was an old story, a pattern of unbalanced friendship I'd fallen into before. Patti nodded and asked me if I could pinpoint a time in my life when this prototypical relationship had first come into being.

I shook my head; I really couldn't. But my thoughts hurtled backward in time to long-ago memories of my two older sisters, who'd been locked in a poisonous, bitter rivalry as long as I could remember. They'd shared a bedroom, but like many children of a cruel parent, they'd turned on each other and begrudged each other any morsel of affection or attention, any good thing in life. I was out of the loop until much later on, when each of them wanted only one thing from me: to join in an angry coalition against the other.

My sisters scared me. The intensity of their mutual rage, which persisted long into adulthood, had the power to suck me into the vortex of a surging wave that could tumble me over and over and eventually deposit me back in a place to which I didn't want to return. In time, moreover, certain hurtful interactions began occurring—some around my budding writing career—and I came to realize that they bore ill will not only to each other, but to me. I had the notion that if a pennant bearing our family coat of arms had been fluttering over what remained of that household, the motto it bore would have been "You can't have anything that *I* don't have. . . . And if you do, it will make me want to kill you."

I met Patti Levin's gaze directly and said that in terms of internal supports, my mother's love for me was the sole bulwark I'd always clung to. She gazed at me briefly, then murmured quietly that nevertheless she believed that my older sisters' competitiveness and their wish to *use* me were issues that were being played out constantly in my current-day life.

I nodded; she was right. But at that moment, the recollection of a profoundly shocking incident—one that had nothing to do with my sisters—ballooned up from the subsurface of my being. It made me feel a little dizzy, and my heart began to pound; I found myself half rising from the chair. The vivid recollection of my mother's last visit to my home in Connecticut had suddenly assailed me, and it was a narrative that ran directly counter to all of the loving things I'd just been saying—something like a secret I'd been keeping from myself. As I sank back into my seat and began describing what had happened, Patti and I decided to target and "detoxify" this memory during the EMDR session that followed.

Chapter Eleven

—

FOLLOWING THE LIGHTS

MY MOTHER LOOKED SURPRISINGLY SHORTER—HER spinal disks had compressed with the passage of time—and she'd been like a taut bundle of rage from the moment she'd arrived. It was the early seventies, and she had been living in Israel, where she'd remarried. She was now convinced that her second husband was trying to defraud her of her small savings and income. Was it true? We couldn't ever confirm or deny it, not with certainty. When we'd met her new husband, he had seemed like such a sweet, scholarly man, and there was an overwrought, frantic air about my mother's anger and her accusations.

At the very outset of the visit, she'd marched upstairs to inspect the second floor (she hadn't seen this house before) and come right down with her chin jutting out triumphantly. "I notice that the two of you don't sleep in the same bed," she told me, her face alight with approval, "and I don't blame you. *I* don't need a man in *my* bed, either!" I was startled by this off-the-wall comment and stood there looking at her, speechless. Then I realized that she had mistaken one of our daughters' rooms, which had twin beds in it, for the bedroom my husband and I occupied ourselves.

"No, Mom, we do sleep together—in that big front bedroom, where there's a big double bed. Didn't you happen to look in *that* room?" I asked. Judging from her facial expression, the news was anything but welcome. She turned away from me coldly and went prowling through other parts of the house as if on a search for clues to a truth I was withholding.

I'd felt strangely at fault, as if I were letting her down. If I wasn't a discharged up, excited. My thoughts were filled with imaginings of my mother's pleasure and my own reactions to her pleasure—does anything ever equal the magical joy of a parent's admiration? But a half hour and then almost forty-five minutes passed by, and I'd reached that outer limit where anticipation begins to merge into worry. All this time I'd been expecting her to come inside and say something, but she hadn't. So at last I went out to the porch and asked, "What do you think of them, Mom?"

She was sitting there, motionless. The articles were beside her on our wicker sofa, and her horn-rimmed glasses had been placed on top of them. Her hands were folded calmly in her lap, and she said, "I have better things to read."

A Safe Place and Two Metaphors

Patti Levin now asked me, "When your mother said, 'I have better things to read,' how did that make you feel?"

I reflected briefly, could summon up nothing more than a hazy, out-of-focus recollection of having picked up the stack of articles and gone back into the house once again. "Stunned. *Not* angry, strangely enough. Confused . . . disoriented." I was experiencing an upsurge of the same feelings now, for the recollection of that incident was swamping me with the sense I'd had then—a desolate sense of being orphaned. This part of my life's story didn't really fit in with so many other loving, soothing, earlier memories of my relationship with my mother. In fact, it was a kind of counter-narrative, one in which all the affection and gratitude that existed at the surface threatened to give way to an underlying sense of disappointment and betrayal.

But this way of thinking felt aberrant. As far as I was concerned, the basic plot line of my childhood featured a brutally repressive father and a victimized, exploited mother who had nevertheless protected and saved me. And if certain events (such as the scene just described) had no place in the historical chronicle, I'd tended to discount and ignore them. I can't say I'd forgotten such discordances completely—only that they resided within my internal world as isolated, unintegrated islands of information, disconnected from the mainland of conscious awareness.

At this point in the preparation process, the EMDR protocol called for the establishment of what is called a "safe place." So Patti Levin asked me if I could summon up a kind of sanctuary inside my head—a spot I could go to (real or imaginary) that felt perfectly calm, secure, and comfortable. It might be a beach, a park, or some other mellow, relaxing spot that I recalled or could envision. "Do you have something of the sort that comes to your mind?" she asked.

I nodded; I had several. The beach at Cape Cod was certainly one, I mused aloud, as was the quiet dock in front of a lake cottage that we rent in the summers. But come to think of it, the safest place was probably a small upstairs sitting room in our house. My husband and I like to spend time there, reading, watching the evening news, listening to music on the stereo. "That little den," I said. "I can picture being there, with my husband, and we're both reading and I'm feeling peaceful and dozy. . . ."

"Okay, then," said Patti, "I'd like you to bring up the memory of feeling safe and protected in that room, with your husband nearby, and really feel it all through your body. And let's give it a word . . . a single cue word. . . ."

"I guess it would be 'home,'" I said, then amended quickly, "No, it would be 'the den.'"

She nodded and said, "'The den.' So I want you to bring up 'the den' and just follow the lights." Then she flicked the control switch on a device (it's called the Neuro*Tek* light scan) that she uses instead of recurring hand waves to guide the client's rapid eye movements. This ruler-shaped apparatus consists of a flashing row of minilights that keep shifting swiftly from left to right and back again. I tracked the rhythmically alternating visual stimulus, hearing Patti's soothing voice in the background: "I want you to *feel* that safe place inside you. How it feels in your skin. The sounds, the smells, the serenity, whatever makes you feel safe and makes you *know* that it's yours."

As my gaze followed the rapidly oscillating left-right-left lights on the bar, I could bring to mind the two of us sitting there, reading, and almost hear soft music playing—a Mozart quartet? I could smell the wool of my favorite rose-and-magenta shawl, which was tucked around my knees; I felt comfortable, relaxed. "Have you got it?" Patti asked me.

I said I thought so. "I'm getting sleepy," I murmured with a smile.

I felt a sense of relief throughout my body. I hadn't realized I was nervous about what would happen next, but at the training conferences I'd certainly seen some dramatic responses to the rapid eye movement sets. This brief, calming preliminary step served to give me the sense of a safe port to which I could quickly retreat if a storm of unexpected feelings blew up. Patti then offered me a set of headphones that come with the Neuro*Tek* light bar and can be used to augment the eye tracking. I tried them on and liked the *tick-tock* of the continually shifting sounds—a brief tone in the left ear, then a brief tone in the right, and then back to the left ear—that seemed to be in synchrony with movements of the lights. The sounds were bringing into play another of the body's sensory modes, making it possible for me to *hear* as well as observe visually the cyclic, continuous alternation from one side of the brain to the other.

The next order of business (familiar to me in my role as observer, but completely strange as a participant) was that of fixing upon the distance from the light bar that felt most comfortable to me. After this matter had been settled, Patti described the two major metaphors that EMDR clinicians often present to their clients before the actual reprocessing begins.

One is to imagine that you are getting on a train at point A and that your eventual destination is point B. At point A you are carrying with you all the troublesome junk that you want to unload, so that on arrival at point B, you won't be burdened with it any longer. "Along the way, you'll be looking out the window and seeing some of the stuff you're leaving behind—it's just scenery, and you're passing beyond it. At times you may want to avert your eyes, bring your gaze back on the train. That's okay; if it gets too uncomfortable, you don't have to watch it. At every stop along the way, when we pause and I ask, 'What are you noticing?' you can think of that as a station where dysfunctional information is being discarded and more functional information may be being taken on," she said, then paused and looked at me questioningly, as if to ask whether or not I understood her fully.

I nodded. Then she reviewed the other favored EMDR metaphor, which was to imagine that I held in my hand the remote control to a video that was playing on the screen of a large TV. The dysfunctional material I was processing was unfolding on that screen, and I was watching it as if I were watching a film. If the scenes I was seeing (such as that scene on the porch) were getting me upset, I could use the remote control to slow the film down. Or I could use it to mute the sound; I could speed up the film if I wanted to, or pause it, or just turn it off completely. What happened was entirely in my hands.

"Does one or the other metaphor appeal to you?" asked Patti.

"The train," I replied without hesitating. I realized that the image of embarking on a sea voyage into the past had been floating through my mind, but now my thought was that a train journey would do very nicely instead.

That Mother Was Not a Crazy Lady

During the preparation phase of the process, Patti had been typing occasional brief notes into the slender, envelope-shaped computer that she held upon her lap. Throughout this phase (not one but two prior sessions), I'd been trying to convey to her a sense of the deep fear that had pervaded my early family household. We children were like prisoners taken in a war we couldn't begin to understand. My father, the silent, steely-eyed commandant of the compound, was the source of a perennially threatened, unpredictable eruption about some issue that made no rational sense. My mother was the sane, reachable parent, but she was as much at my father's mercy as we siblings were. Nevertheless, I always saw her as doing her brave best to stand between his craziness and our vulnerability.

By the time she visited us in the early seventies, though, she was changed—a classic example of what Freud called "identification with the lost object" or, more simply, *becoming just like the person who is gone.* This process had begun shortly after my parents' divorce, when my mother had begun her strange transformation into someone remarkably similar to the husband she'd defied, resisted for years, then ultimately left—that is, fanatically religious, frowning angrily much of the time, praying constantly, unreachable.

One Friday evening during my mother's visit, my husband and I went out to dinner with one of his colleagues, a visitor from California. When we returned I went up to our third-floor guest quarters to kiss my mother good night, calling out, "Mom, Mom, I'm coming up for a moment!" as I'd run up the stairway. Perhaps she hadn't heard me—I'm not certain—

but in any case her false teeth were out, and my sudden arrival caught her by surprise.

I remember her leaning over the bed, about to slip in under the covers, then straightening up like a steely ramrod, looking at me with an expression of the purest, utmost rage and hatred. I stopped short. What had I done? Had I humiliated her because her teeth were out, which made her mouth look strange and sunken? Was she infuriated because we'd been out on a Friday night instead of welcoming the Sabbath with her? We didn't observe this ritual customarily, and she knew it, but the expression on her face was terrifying. I don't think anyone had ever looked at me with such murder in her eyes before; this had no place in my self-told narrative of our deeply loving, caring relationship.

Yet parts of that caring narrative *were true*. I thought of my mother as having saved me, in so many figurative and literal ways. She'd even given me the tuition for my third year of college—practically her last cent, as I understood it, and she hadn't been young at the time. So there were different parts of the story, parts of a larger puzzle whose pieces didn't fit. "Her own fate was so *hard*," I told Patti Levin, as if trying to explain how unentitled I felt to any feelings of indignation.

But then the full-blown memory of that expression on my mother's face burst back into my mind with a sudden force that felt assaultive. "I guess it's pretty obvious that she did *not* want me to live happily with a man, or sleep in the same bed with a man. And she did not want me to shine in the world," I said, thinking of her acid reaction to the articles I'd shown her.

Patti nodded. "You can't have anything that I don't have," she said, and her reiteration of that theme felt like the small but painful dislodging of an ax that had settled deep within me much earlier in my life. "Which is basically what was going on between your sisters. Nobody could have one tiny scrap of something that someone else didn't have, or the jealousy and rage would go wild . . . ?"

Her statement had ended as a question, and I could only nod and say that, yes, it had been a kind of primeval warfare. Then a feeling of colossal desolation descended upon me. I felt lost, obscured in a sandstorm of prickling, hurtful little thoughts about my mother, my sisters, and the two friends who had been "like sisters" to me and who'd vanished at a time when I'd most needed them—that is, during the months I'd been incapacitated by a painfully injured back.

Patti leaned forward, looked at my face intently, and asked me if I would like, now, to review the narrative of my mother—perhaps one that contained those seeming "inconsistencies" I'd been systematically deleting from my own idealizing account. I agreed with a silent nod of my head, for I could perceive the existence of a pattern here—some underlying game plan I was following whose end point, disappointment, a part of me was always expecting to emerge.

"I think that for a long, long time I've been telling myself just *half* the story," I said, hearing the incredulity in my own voice. "And what's been left out is the stuff about the kid whose hair wasn't combed when she went to school. The kid who never had clean clothes ready, who was not protected in any way, who wasn't even called in when it was time for dinner, as the other children were—the kid who was fending for herself from pretty early on, in many, many ways. Okay, my mom's life was hard, but she *could* have kept the house clean; it was always dirty, disorganized. She could have made sure her child had clean school clothes—a lot of people in tough circumstances *do*."

"Right," said Patti, and that single word made me feel validated, *heard*.

"Being a parent myself, I really don't understand it," I said unhappily. Patti shook her head from side to side, very slowly, as if to say she didn't understand it, either.

Then she returned to the target scene that we'd agreed we were going to focus upon today, saying, "Do you remember how you felt, *in your body*, when you showed her your articles and she said, 'I have better things to read'?"

Remember? I smiled wryly, for those feelings were coursing through me right now. "Stunned. Confused," I said. "As if I'm watching that scene at this moment and yet still can't decipher its meaning. Was it something to do with her ever growing religiosity—that she saw my writing as a bad, unwomanly thing to do? Did she mean that the Bible was better reading—or *what*?" I hesitated, then added with a shrug that I'd thought she might just be getting kooky.

Patti looked at me thoughtfully, then said, "Thinking back to your relationship with your mother, and keeping in mind the themes of competitiveness, jealousy, no protection, no validation—all of the suppressed parts of the narrative—can you bring to mind a memory or experience, a point in time, when you first realized that your mother wasn't perfect?"

I nodded; yes, I could. Our relationship had begun to deteriorate soon after my parents' separation, for it was then that my mom had started to take on religion with a thoroughly unexpected force and fanaticism. "She started behaving in ways that she'd always pooh-poohed in my father. And I remember her going wild and slapping me around because I'd brushed my teeth on one of the High Holidays; she was having all kinds of irrational outbursts at the time. I felt lost. We'd moved away from the neighborhood we'd lived in, and I'd had to change the high school I went to. But worst of all, I'd lost the mother I knew. *That* mother was not a crazy lady."

"So you realized then that your mother had become a crazy lady, and you'd never realized that before?"

I paused, looked at her in puzzlement, unsure what she meant. "No. . . . Why?"

"Wasn't it a little crazy to send a kid to school without her hair combed, and not to have her school clothes ready, and to keep a chaotically disorganized, disheveled house?"

I said nothing; I simply stared at Patti in amazement. I'd worshipped my mother so, and felt such sorrow on her behalf that I'd never entertained so perfidious a notion before.

The Worst Moment

The next order of EMDR business was to focus down sharply, as if with a high-powered microscope, upon the remembered point of maximal distress that I would target in this session. So Patti asked, "When your mother visited, and you showed her your articles, and she said, 'I have better things to read,' what was the *worst* moment of that experience? What is the image that springs to your mind?"

It didn't seem to me that I had one particular moment; it was more like a short reel of memory that began playing through my head immediately. It started with her sitting on the back porch, then moved to my coming out from the kitchen and asking, "What do you think of them, Mom?" Then, her saying coldly, "I have better things to read."

This was good enough for Patti, who said, "Okay, so when you think of that memory of your mother sitting on the back porch—and she's looking at your articles, and you come out and say, 'What do you think of them, Mom?' and she says, 'I have better things to read'—what is your current negative or irrational belief about yourself?"

"About myself?" I stared at her blankly, familiar though I was with the reprocessing protocol.

"About yourself," said Patti firmly, with a nod.

I couldn't imagine. I began casting about inside for some sort of answer but managed to come up with only a deep sigh, almost a groan. Finally I said, "I guess it would be . . . 'I'll never get what I need,'" though I myself wasn't sure just what that statement meant.

"And going back to that scene once again, your mother sitting on the back porch, looking at the articles, and you come out and say, 'What do you think of them, Mom?' and she says, 'I have better things to read.' Rather than believing 'I'll never get what I need,' what would you *rather believe now* as you think back to that moment?"

I laughed, embarrassed; it was not an easy question to answer. But Patti's expression remained serious, so I tried to think of a possible answer to the question. I couldn't. All that I was able to come up with was an answer in the subjunctive: "I'd rather believe that I *could* know how to get what I need," I said uncertainly.

She then asked me to bring to mind once again that memory of my mother saying, "I have better things to read," accompanied by the words "I *could* know how to get what I need." On a gut level, how true did that latter phrase *feel* to me?

I considered it momentarily. "Not very true, I'd say." I could hear the discouragement in my voice. Patti then asked me to represent my answer by a number on a scale that ranged from one to seven; the high figure, seven, stood for "completely true," and the low figure, one, stood for "not true at all." I assessed my degree of belief at about a one or a two; and she paused briefly to inscribe that figure on her laptop.

She looked up. "And when you go back to seeing your mother on the back porch, and she's looking at your articles, and you come out and say, 'What do you think of them, Mom?' and she says, 'I have better things to read,' and your thought or belief is, 'I'll never get what I need,' what emotions come up for you right now?"

"Stunned. *Not* angry," I repeated. There were no angry feelings connected with that scene, just an awful feeling of being lost, of being the daughter of a crazy mother. "It was over, hopeless . . . the relationship was gone." I shrugged, as if to say that the past was the past and I'd packed it all away years earlier.

But Patti looked at me searchingly and asked, "How upsetting does that scene feel to you at this moment—say, if you think of it on another, different scale, one where ten is the worst you can imagine and zero is no disturbance at all?"

I realized that the degree of distress I was feeling was pretty high and rated it at about an eight or a nine. She then asked me where, in my body, I noticed the disturbance. I pointed to my jaw, saying, "I feel it here. Actually, I never get headaches or stomachaches—any stress symptoms of that sort. But when I feel upset, my jaw clenches; and I feel it clenching *hard* right now." In fact, my jaw felt so tight that it was actually hurting. Patti typed a comment in her file, then nodded. The rapid eye tracking was about to get under way.

I'll Never Get What I Need

Patti said, "I want you to go back to that memory of your mother sitting on the back porch, looking at your articles. And you come out and say, 'What did you think of them, Mom?' and she says, 'I have better things to read.' *Hold that together with the words* 'I'll never get what I need.' Notice the feelings of being stunned, lost; of feeling hopeless, like the daughter of a crazy mother; notice, too, where you feel it in your body. And then let whatever happens happen." These brief instructions were followed by her switching on the bar of rapidly moving, fluctuating, left-to-right-to-left lights.

At first I couldn't focus upon anything but the light bar itself. The lights were flashing back and forth so swiftly that I couldn't quite keep up with them. Was I doing this correctly, or should I call a halt and ask Patti to slow down the scanning device—she'd already explained that the Neuro*Tek* could do that. But I said nothing and before long found myself keeping up more easily. I noticed a strange tingling in my jaw, but not much else.

Then the words "I'll never get what I need" began floating through my head in the bannerlike shape of some skywriting following in the wake of a plane. I thought of bits and pieces of my history as a daughter and as a mother, and of the good and not so good reenactments of the past that had occurred. I recalled occasional outbursts I'd had with my own kids—so reminiscent of my mother's flare-ups—and those unwelcome recollections filled me with self-reproach. But I'd never been involved in anything remotely like her hair-pulling fights with my oldest sister, and it occurred to me that my track record through life was actually far stronger on the plus side than it was on debits and failings. Then, like the sudden sprouting of a spring crocus, a new thought popped up in my mind: "Maybe it's not so hopeless after all."

It remained only briefly, and then the phrase "I'll never get what I need" appeared in my mental sky again. It was succeeded by a vivid image of Sisyphus pushing the same heavy rock up the same familiar hill. At that point, Patti stopped the flashing lights, told me to take a deep inhale and exhale, and then asked me what I had been noticing. I mentioned the tingling in my jaw, my guilt about not being the perfectly unflappable parent, and the sudden realization that nevertheless there were many good things in my life. Almost as an afterthought, I told her about the image of Sisyphus pushing a rock up a hill—the same rock that cascaded down eternally.

Patti made no interpretations of these remarks; she simply said, "Go with that," and started the reprocessing again.

I found myself keeping pace with the moving lights more easily, and I was pleasantly aware of the alternating ear tones; but no particular thoughts or images came to mind. Instead, I found myself diverted by the loud voice-overs of outside traffic, the screeching truck gears and howling of some passing sirens, for Patti's office is near a busy feeder to the freeway. Then my thoughts turned to my older sisters, and how, when I was a little girl, they'd seemed like such goddesses to me. They'd seemed so lovely, but out of reach, as if they existed in a rarefied realm that was utterly different from the one I inhabited.

For one thing, they'd had a room of their own, one the two of them shared. I was in a large front bedroom, where not only I but my parents and my baby brother slept. My brother was six years younger than I; and for reasons that were forever unclear to me, he hadn't remained in our household very long but instead had been sent off to a religious boarding school in another city. In his adult years, he'd moved to California and cut off all contact with the family.

Patti halted the movement of the lights, then, and told me to take a deep breath.

I inhaled, and when I exhaled I said, "My family dismantled itself. There's no 'there' there, in terms of a family. My younger brother speaks to no one, and I've had to pull away, too. . . ."

"Mmm," was all she said, a contentless, sympathetic noise.

"A friend of mine was telling me how close she was to her sister, and I thought of something one of my kids once said to me. She said, 'Your sister wants to harm you,' and I do have this scary feeling that it's true, it's really *true*. My daughter made that remark after our family had had a big celebration and my sister had been acting like Hedda Gabler, sowing ill will and conflicts everywhere she went." I paused, for not surprisingly, the statement "You can't have anything that I don't have" had popped into my head.

"Maybe she felt that I had some things that she didn't have—a flourishing career, whatever . . . ?" This was, of course, a rhetorical question, and Patti shook her head as if to say she could not possibly have the answer. Or had it been my intact marriage and family? I wondered. My sister had been divorced for years and living abroad. Her relationships with the children she'd left behind, in the care of her ex-husband and their stepmother, were understandably dicey. Another fact of her history, a tragic one, was that her second-born son had vanished under mysterious circumstances at the age of nineteen.

My nephew Richie had simply disappeared from the world and never been heard from again. There were differing accounts of the circumstances surrounding this event that we'd heard from my sister at various points in time. Still other versions had been told to us by her children, and we'd heard yet another story from one of her European friends, a psychoanalyst. Finally, we'd settled upon the only answer possible, which was that there was *no* definitive answer, at least none that we would ever learn.

Still, my sister's choices had been none of my making, and the notion that she could wish me actual harm was awful, a cause of harm in itself. Even at this moment, the idea filled me with an atavistic kind of fear, and my brain seemed to go blank; it was as if my thoughts had come to an inner barrier, someplace beyond which thinking was no longer possible. I felt as if there were nothing but empty space inside my skull, and I wanted to stop now; there was nothing further to be said. "I don't know what I'm— I'm not sure where all of this is leading," I said, feeling as if my internal compass had gone hopelessly askew and I'd lost all sense of direction.

"It's fine," Patti said calmly. "Go with it. . . . Keep going." She flicked the moving lights into motion once again.

Past and Present

The image of the moving train that periodically slows to a halt, unloads dysfunctional information, and then takes on other, more wholesome kinds of material proved consistent with my own unfolding experience. For once I'd resumed the rapid eye tracking, I felt as if I'd moved forward in the journey and entered a surprisingly different bodily and mental state. My breathing was deep and even, and I found myself yawning widely. As I followed the swiftly moving lights from one end of the bar to the other, I felt calmer, forgiving, even philosophical and ready to look at the wider context in which such things had occurred.

I held up my right hand, which is the EMDR signal that it's time to call the reprocessing to a halt. (The word *stop* in itself is not sufficient, for the client may be saying "Stop!" to an imaginary someone who's part of a disturbing event that's being reexperienced inside his or her head.) Then I said, "Part of this has to do with the immigrant experience, with being lost between two cultures. My mom once told me that when he was a baby she'd put my brother down in the basement at night so he could 'cry it out' and not wake the family up at night—something that I, as an American mother, would have considered unimaginable. So God knows what else she did with her babies—things that, given her own upbringing, she felt were perfectly acceptable." I sighed.

Then I said that no matter what, in my eyes my mom had been a magical being. I could remember a time when she'd taken me and my kid brother downtown on New Year's Eve. "There was so much confetti, and there were horns and so much excitement. And coming home at midnight on the trolley car—it was *thrilling*!" I smiled and said that whatever was good in my life had come from my mother, but that her own life had been a tough one.

In retrospect, I realize that my thoughts had migrated back to square one, my emotional default position: I was the all-forgiving, totally empathetic daughter of a loving mom who was a victim. But Patti let this pass without comment and merely said, "Go back to that memory that we started with. What do you notice about it?"

I hesitated. For some reason, I couldn't seem to call up the memory very clearly. I retrieved some hazy scraps—the porch, my mom, her comment—but it all seemed blurred and out of focus. What I *did* become aware of was an increased tightness, a rigid feeling in my jaw.

"All right, go with that," said Patti. "Notice your jaw." And she set the light bar in motion once again.

A Kind of "Sophie's Choice"

I followed Patti's instructions, but focusing upon my jaw seemed to make the rigidity and strange tingling sensations intensify. It felt as if tiny electric currents were coursing through those chin muscles, and instinctively, I brought both hands up to my jaw and held them there. Then I tried to divert myself by the fantasy that I was looking out the window of the imaginary train upon which I was traveling.

There, the scene that greeted me was one of being with my mother, the last time I'd seen her alive. That had been in Israel, just after she'd had a serious stroke; one side of her body was paralyzed. Alas, by then our relationship was so attenuated that it existed only at the most superficial level. My mother's rage at her second husband was the dominant theme of her existence; she made no pretense at being interested in me, my spouse, my children, anything about my life. Throughout our stay, her main concern had been making sure that any assets she left behind would go *not* to her husband and his grasping (according to her) family, but to a cultlike, Orthodox religious charity that had become dear to her heart. We were enlisted to arrange a secret transfer of her funds; and if we did have any importance in her eyes, rendering this important service was the source of it.

Two watershed events in my own life were in the offing at that time. My middle daughter, Betsy, was to be married in the early summer; she and her new husband would be moving to Dallas in the following September. That same fall, my book on women and depression, *Unfinished Business*, was slated for publication; but due to its then relatively taboo theme, few people expected it to garner much attention. To everyone's surprise, however, the moment was ripe for a frank discussion of depression, and the book was greeted by a blitz of newspaper, television, radio, and magazine publicity. I became caught up, rolled over and over, tossed hither and yon in my own personal tsunami.

As a result, my typically flexible personal schedule was being trumped almost as soon as any arrangements were put in place. My plan had been to visit my daughter's new home in Texas in October, but that intention was subverted by a highly pressured book tour that was whisking me all over the country; I was moving from city to city on a daily basis. What had begun as an exciting, novel experience soon evolved into a sense of constant strain and loss of control—a sense of trying to stay the course on a wild ride that was sapping my energy and keeping me balanced precariously between health and exhaustion.

My plans to visit Dallas kept changing, for I was flying off in other directions, coming home, recovering, and working out fresh plans for a Texas visit that then had to be altered. "I think Betsy's getting upset," I told my husband, worried.

"No, she understands," he assured me.

But he couldn't have been more mistaken. By the time the blizzard of demands upon me had begun to lessen, Betsy was feeling hurt and absolutely furious. No matter *what* might happen next, I decided, the conflict between "mom time" and "me time" would be decided in Betsy's favor.

But on the eve of my departure for Dallas, my mother suffered a second stroke, one that left her in a deep coma. So I was presented with a kind of "Sophie's Choice" between a parent who I'd been warned would not be alive by the time I got to her bedside—she couldn't even know I was with her—and a daughter who was feeling aggrieved, ignored, and abandoned.

"I went to Dallas," I said to Patti Levin bleakly. "And so when my mother died I wasn't there. Neither were my sisters or my brother; she'd been so far distant from every one of her kids for so many years, in every sense of the word. And realistically, trying to make it there in time would have been a pointless maneuver. . . . But I never got to say good-bye."

Then a surge of loneliness and grief swept over me, as did the realization that all my efforts to evade or bypass such feelings had not been notably successful. My mother's death had not been truly mourned, and in some way I hadn't really parted from her. "I never got to say good-bye externally *or* internally"—the words emerged slowly—"and it's probably time to connect with all the sadness." I sighed, almost a groan, for a weary feeling had swept over me, as had the thought that I'd run and run throughout a lifetime without achieving much real distance from home base.

"Go with that, Maggie," instructed Patti, directing my attention to the light bar once again.

Nurturer/Nurturee

When I recommenced the rapid eye tracking, the imaginary "train" that was carrying me began to wind its way through a different, though neighboring, kind of terrain. The metaphor of the railway journey was proving marvelously apt, for it was congruent with the experience I was having. As I moved along from one reprocessing episode or "set" to the next one (each consisted of some twenty-four back-and-forth eye movements), with brief halts along the way, I found myself gazing out at a landscape thick with images and memories of various relationships I'd had with women friends over the years.

Most of these girl relationships had been structured in strikingly similar ways; they'd tended to be or become asymmetric and short on mutuality. Routinely, they'd been pervaded by a soothing, comforting parent–needful child flavor, for which my bond with my mother had surely been the prototype. Not surprisingly, the role I'd typically assumed was the role I had been playing since the dawn of memory: I was forever struggling to help and comfort a female friend who needed caretaking, and feeling profoundly, very personally involved in and responsible for her fate.

This was, of course, an all-too-familiar scenario, a replication of my earliest bond with my mom: "I'm going to fix things for you; I'm going to make you happy; I feel so guilty about the troubles and misery in your life." Always the wise giver, without needs of her own, I existed as the dedicated helper of a dependent, appreciative receiver; and the friendship always felt cozily familiar and completely appropriate. The underground "deal" here was that I never had to expose my suppressed dependencies or even face any sense of my own vulnerability, for the spotlight of the friendship's attention was always on the beleaguered other person.

I needed to focus more on finding *peers*, I thought, though without any sense of self-condemnation or alarm. On the contrary, I heard the sound of my own regular breathing in my ears, and each breath was deep, long, as peaceful as if I were meditating. Then the memory of a friendship in which the basic structure had been similar but the roles reversed—I myself had been the nurtured one—sprang into my mind's view. I was revisiting some vivid images of being with my friend Valerie (a pseudonym), now deceased, with whom I'd initially had a long, wonderful "friendship honeymoon."

Val, warm, funny, smart, and eleven years older than me, had taken me and our young family under her capaciously nurturing wing when we'd first arrived in New Haven. Given her seniority in terms of age, the fact that she knew her way around the new community, and her generous but imperious nature, she and I slipped right into the roles of all-knowing mentor and compliant disciple. I had never had so unstintingly nourishing a friend before, and not only our own lives, but the lives of our families became intertwined.

This gratifying state of affairs lasted until my aspirations as a writer began to be realized; then, however, I found that I was violating boundaries I hadn't even known existed. The difficulties had probably begun surfacing even earlier, when I'd spoken to Val about an article I was contemplating writing. The subject was to be a new method of inpatient psychiatric care called milieu therapy, which was then being pioneered at Yale–New Haven Hospital. Val was appalled by the idea.

On behalf of our friendship, she told me firmly, I shouldn't think of involving myself in such a project. Since she herself was a practicing clinician (a psychiatric social worker), there was a real danger that if I, her closest friend, were to get it all wrong and write something foolish, she would find it hugely embarrassing. What a pliant, perfectly obliging creature I had been! I'd actually pulled back and not begun researching the article until Val and her family left New Haven for a European sabbatical.

I found myself smiling at the recollection, bemused by the memory of that request. "What's coming up for you?" Patti questioned me after bringing the reprocessing to another temporary halt.

I answered by telling her the story of this friendship and about the way it had started foundering badly when my first *New York Times Magazine* piece was published. That article had marked both the beginning of my career as a science journalist and the initiation of what became a hurtful, confusing, unresolvable struggle between Val and myself. As I told Patti, with a brief, helpless little shrug of my shoulders, "It was the very article about the mental ward that she'd asked me—no, commanded me—*not* to write."

"Because she had better things to read," said Patti dryly—a remark that struck me as a blow of revelation. I'd always believed that I had oriented toward Val as a benign older sister, but perhaps the relationship had actually been more in line with my mother's dicta and her behavior.

The message in both instances was that I could be loved and cherished if I operated within the prescribed limits that existed in the other person's mind. But all affection and nurturance were up for grabs if I set my own goals (which weren't, as it happened, approved goals) and pursued them. In short, loving meant always following the stated and unstated orders about who I should be and become, while moves toward independence and autonomy were accompanied by threats—not idle ones—of rejection, loss, and abandonment.

I Can Get What I Need

As we recommenced the rapid eye movements, an unbidden, novel, hitherto unthinkable thought appeared front and center in my mind. It was, "Mom, you just don't care about me, not *for me*. You just care about me in terms of *you*." When I reported this to Patti at our subsequent rest stop, she nodded in silent, sympathetic agreement.

Then I said, "My feeling is—and I don't mean to sound trite—that I have to get hold of a self that's really *me*. In so many of my relationships, I tend to come on at one end of a tilted seesaw—either 'Take care of me' or, far more commonly, 'I'll take care of *you*.'"

Patti nodded, said that, yes, many of those old caretaking issues were being recycled in my present-day relationships—namely, the two sister surrogates I had supported through some hard times but who'd vanished when *I* was the person in need. I had to learn an important lesson, one I'd never fully internalized, which was how to find equality in my close attachments when it came to giving out and getting.

We fell silent for several moments. I was thinking about how often I'd been amazed by the ways in which so many people I was interviewing were engaged in reenacting the unresolved issues of the past. I'd wondered how this came to be without anyone's realization that what was happening now bore an uncanny resemblance to what had happened earlier—but here I was, heavily involved in much the same thing and at best dimly aware of what was occurring. I had some major reassessments to make.

"Now," said Patti, "when you go back to that original memory, what do you notice?"

The question seemed to me to come out of nowhere, and I found myself staring at her blankly—I found myself unable to recollect what that memory had been! But I did recall that Patti had recorded it in her computer, so I asked her if she would read it back to me now.

She shook her head in the negative, saying that she wanted to see what was left of it, or if there *was* anything left of it, and to hear about it in my own words.

I searched inside my head, located some wispy scraps of that scenario with my mom on the back porch of our house. "It's there, but it's more distant, less vivid," I said in a confused tone of voice. "But I do have some feeling in my jaw."

"How disturbing is that feeling on a zero-to-ten scale?" Patti asked.

I thought for a moment. "Not very disturbing."

"Give it a number," she said.

"I'd give it a one or a two."

"Okay, let's focus on that," she said, and we began the eye tracking again.

This time, however, something strange happened as soon as I began following the lights. I had the impression or vision that my mother was sitting out there on the patio and my body was feeling light, weightless. I was feeling so light that I was floating up the hill that overlooked the porch, and I was calling out, "Good-bye, Mom, good-bye, Mom, good-bye! . . . I wish I could feel real anger at you, because you were a neglectful parent, but I guess I just don't feel it. I appreciate the good things you did!" Then I seemed to see myself drifting up and away into the nimbus of sunlight at the top of the hill, and a vast sense of peace and resolution descended upon me. I did feel tears springing to my eyes, but at the same time I felt absolutely wonderful. "I can get what I need," I decided.

Part Three

BEVERLY, KAREN, JOANNA

THE BODY'S MEMORY "NUMBING OUT"

EXTRAMARITAL AFFAIRS

Chapter Twelve

—

SECRETS FROM THE SELF: BEVERLY CHANGES THE LOCKS

AS I MYSELF HAD COME TO REALIZE, A PERSON WHO HAS grown up in severely stressful, often secretive or semisecretive situations can be seriously compromised when it comes to recalling just what *did* take place on certain highly charged occasions. Nevertheless, there are times when "what the body knows" pops into awareness without warning and presents a person with unwelcome but unavoidable information. In Beverly Scanlon's case, a shocking, long-suppressed memory had suddenly risen to the surface of consciousness, owing to the particular context in which the remembering was taking place.

Beverly was in her mid-thirties at the time of our interviews, but almost a decade earlier, when she'd been in her twenties, she'd held a very responsible position as assistant to the dean of the Department of Human Genetics at a major teaching hospital in Boston. Although she'd subsequently left this job to go on to graduate school, where she'd earned a master's degree in computer science, Bev had taken that administrative position very seriously and felt proud of the harmonious way she'd managed to keep the department running.

But there came a time when she was given a routine project that involved changing every lock on every door in the entire human genetics unit—and this simple task soon developed into a uniquely personal calamity. Her mandate had been to secure, and if necessary rekey, all the offices and laboratories, which involved much lock checking, jiggling of doorknobs, and opening and shutting of the doors to see if they closed securely.

"I would start out each morning to work on this project," Bev told me, a scared frown settling upon her face. "But it always happened that after about fifteen minutes or so, I'd start feeling really uncomfortable—*physically* uncomfortable. Short of breath, heart pounding, completely unable to *focus*—and I'd end up running back to my office. I know this is going to sound crazy, but I was completely panicked. I couldn't figure out why this was happening, and I kept thinking, This is nuts! I felt guilty, too; it was so *unlike* me not to act responsibly, to do the best job I could."

As the days and weeks passed, this strange dilemma didn't seem to resolve itself; on the contrary, matters worsened, and Beverly found herself feeling ever more shaken, driven by impulses that were utterly out of her control. She decided to consult a therapist, but even that got her nowhere, for after weeks of treatment she'd made no headway with the precipitating concern. "The only conclusion I could come to was that, for whatever reasons, I *could not go on with this project.*" It had simply been impossible—*physically* impossible—for her to carry out the seemingly mundane duty assigned to her.

Bev broke off this narrative momentarily to hold up her hand and show me how much it was trembling merely by virtue of remembering that time. "See what I mean?" she asked me, or perhaps the better word is "demanded." Then, in a more subdued tone of voice, she said, "What was the worst, the absolute *worst,* for me was the actual sound of the door opening—you know, the clicking sound that the latch makes when the door opens and closes? That would really *get* to me, and after a while I'd run back to my office and slam the door behind me. I just couldn't go on with it!"

She and her psychotherapist had reached an impasse; the treatment wasn't going anywhere. Then, said Bev, in the midst of one of the sessions, a vivid image suddenly popped into her head. "This happened—literally—in the middle of a sentence, when I was going on and on, feeling very *agitated* about the problem with the locks!" Even as she described this incident her body stiffened; she sat up rigidly in her chair as if an iron spike had hit her between the shoulder blades.

I gave her a quizzical look, but she shook her head as if asking me not to disturb her train of thought. "This image—it was like a photo that you look at. . . . But I wasn't just observing it, I could *feel* it, too. And I felt terrified! The picture was of a little girl in a white nightgown sitting on a bed, with her legs tucked underneath her, waiting for the sound of a door opening." Beverly looked and sounded young and frightened at this moment.

I said nothing, and she sat there staring at my face without seeming to recognize my presence. So I asked her if, when that picture came into her mind, she'd felt as if she *were* the little girl or she were *watching* the little girl. She didn't reply; she merely held up her shaking hand once again to show me how this memory was affecting her. I nodded, murmuring, "Yes, I see that."

Then she repeated her statement to the effect that while she was looking *at* the little girl, she was feeling the terror simultaneously. "Do you know where *you* are in the room?" I asked her. Was she on the ceiling, in a half-opened closet, in a corner? Or where else in the room might she have been?

Bev squinted thoughtfully, as if to summon up all the details of the scene that were available. She was watching, she said slowly, but she wasn't sure where she was watching *from.* "And it's not a dispassionate kind of looking," she repeated. "I'm looking, but I'm also *feeling*. I'm feeling *afraid.* There's also a tremendous tightness in my back, and the tightness is in my legs—*both* my legs—too."

A natural suspicion sprang into my mind, one that was intrinsic to the scenario she was describing. Had the frightened little girl in this picture been trying hard to hold her legs together? I asked Bev if, when she reflected back about that scene—the scared child and the door that was about to open—the door ever *had* opened, eventually?

Oh yes, the door did open, she answered dryly. Then she shrugged her shoulders briefly, as if to indicate her utter helplessness in the face of the events she visualized unfolding. "The door opens," she said. "I don't see a face, but a male figure comes in. Then I get this very smothered feeling, this sense that I can't breathe, and I'm fixed there, absolutely paralyzed. . . . I can feel that paralysis right *now*, but I've never been able to put a face on that person." Her own face was a dark storm cloud of distress at this moment.

We were both silent for a period of time. Then Bev said, "To this day, I'm not exactly sure what did go on. The best way that my therapist and I could put it together . . . because I still do have these huge memory gaps . . . is that whatever happened probably didn't involve intercourse, just some sort of fondling or rubbing."

What impulse was it that led me, then, to ask what *time* of day or night she thought it had been when that bedroom door began to open? "I don't know," she said quickly. Did she think it might have been around bedtime or sometime during the middle of the night? I asked her. Bev then said, "It's ten o'clock; I know that," now with no uncertainty in her voice.

I noticed that she'd switched into the present tense, and this was no surprise. For Bev, like so many people who've been through traumatic experiences, wasn't so much remembering a painful past as she was *reliving* in this moment what had happened. "You're sure of the time?" I asked her, and she nodded.

"It's ten o'clock," she said flatly. I asked her how she knew that. "I *do*, I just *do*," she replied, speaking in a clipped, tight-lipped tone of voice, like a reporter announcing news of a catastrophe. On the spot I decided to bring this interview to a gentle ending as soon as possible, so I told her that I had one last, general kind of question—one that she could respond to or not as it suited her. "When you think back to that time, does anything else spring to mind, in terms of *other* things that were happening then?"

"What I remember most is wanting my *mom* to come home," Bev said resentfully. The expression on her face was that of a sullen, angry child. I waited for her to say more.

"My mom had taken a job around that time—I can't remember what it was, exactly—but she was away from seven P.M. to eleven. So the way it worked, she was there to give us dinner, and then my dad would pick her up later on; but *he* was the one who was in charge of putting us kids to bed. And so I suppose, thinking back—and thinking about the bizarre nature of my relationship with my father, who always treated me like his little wife—there's very little doubt about what did happen." Still, said Bev, she had no conscious memories of any seductive goings-on and had never been able to put her father's face—or *any* face—on the male figure who came through the door.

Disconnected, Disjointed Images

This was, it seemed to me, a classic demonstration of the effects of that "upside-down U curve of remembering"—which is that rising levels of fight-or-flight-related brain biochemicals act to enhance memory retention, *but only until the summit of that upside-down U has been attained.* Then the *opposite* effect begins to emerge, and as the surge of fight-or-flight substances continues, the quality of remembering declines. Eventually, the individual's overwhelmed central nervous system reaches a critical juncture (the top of the upside-down U), beyond which memories become splintered and disorganized or vanish from consciousness completely.

Then, instead of being able to bring to mind the sequence of events in the order in which they happened, the individual may recall only fragments of what occurred—or summon them up in disconnected images—or simply forget that they ever took place. In other words, he or she may suffer either partial or total amnesia for aspects of his or her own life's history. Even so, while the memories seem completely gone, the branching, forking, interconnected neurons of the brain and body cells *do* remember. In their own mysterious fashion, they retain the encoded documentation of long-ago events that have seemingly vanished from the narrative—or at best lingered on as isolated thoughts, random remnants of a lost puzzle, or disjointed, disconnected mental images that seem to make no sense.

Amnesias

"It's true that my dad had a thing for me," Beverly now said. "He liked to take me everywhere he went and surely never made a secret of his preference for me; but I have no recollection of there being any *sexual* component to that. And I have to say that even *after* that picture flipped into my mind, I spent weeks of backtracking in the therapy—weeks and weeks of trying to convince the shrink that I'd probably made the whole thing up."

Her clinician had not bought into this revised, more benign version of events. The very way in which the picture had suddenly materialized in

Bev's mind—like an undeveloped negative that's been plunged into a chemical solution—seemed to argue otherwise. "That image actually came to me in the midst of a session when I was going on and on, just *obsessing* about that rekeying project. I remember telling the therapist that I just couldn't do it—and then *bam*, that picture flashed into my head. It was so *vivid*—I *saw* it and I *felt* it; and in some way I *became* that little kid, sitting there, waiting for the door to open!"

She stopped, scrutinized my face, as if wondering whether I doubted her or believed what she was saying. Then a confused look crossed her features, as if she weren't sure she believed in this remembered image herself. I said nothing, merely nodded, as if to say "I'm with you." I did believe her, for regardless of what anyone might have to say about the fundamental untrustworthiness of "recovered memories," Bev's story didn't have the ring of anything that had surfaced from the sludge of a favored daughter's long-ago erotic fantasies.

Besides, as experts in the field of trauma will attest, amnesias are common in the wake of cataclysmic experiences. As Jonathan Shay, M.D., has observed, a traumatized person's memories cannot be summoned up at will as ordinary memories can be. "Traumatic memory is not narrative," Shay writes. "Rather, it is experience that *reoccurs* [my italics], either as full sensory replay of traumatic events in dreams or flashbacks, with all things seen, heard, smelled, and felt intact, or as disconnected fragments." This is a particularly apt paraphrase of what happens at the "overwhelming challenge" side of that upside-down U-shaped curve of remembering. On one side of that inverted U-shaped curve, the individual isn't concerned enough to remember—the events aren't sufficiently significant—and on the opposite side, remembering is intolerable.

Pathways to Remembrance

What rouses dormant memories and stirs them into wakefulness? When Marcel Proust, our foremost poet of memory, dipped his famous madeleine into a cup of tea, the purely physical sensations—the taste of the little cake, the smell of the brew—opened wide a gateway that propelled him into the magical, almost forgotten world of his childhood.

One of the two overarching themes of Proust's masterpiece, translated as *Remembrance of Things Past,* is the way in which some random sensory event—a bite of a familiar pastry, a sip of steamy tea—can trigger a semi-automatic summoning up of the memories archived within our densely interconnected neural circuitry. The other central theme has to do with the way in which significant memories, *once accessed via physical sensations* (such as taste and smell), can be reexperienced with as much immediacy and emotional intensity as they had when the original experiences occurred.

Truly, this exquisite ability to retain within and revisit the past is one of the great glories of our humanity; but in terms of trauma it can be the cause of great suffering as well. This is especially true in those undramatic and yet chronically damaging situations where an individual's coping capacities are under chronic assault and eventually become overwhelmed. In those situations where neither fighting back nor escaping is a realistic, viable choice, the person's only option is to freeze in place, zone out, and surrender to the inevitable. In the process, his or her basic assumptions about personal safety are shattered.

Many examples of this kind spring readily to mind—an obvious one would be Claudia Martinelli's witnessing of her brother's savage beatings. Another would be that of a young child hearing his alcoholic mother shouting insults at his father, knowing that ultimately the pair would get into a loud physical brawl. The petrified youngster can neither stop his parents' hysterical battling nor escape the situation—where would he go, and who would take care of him?

Still another instance of this kind of unremitting, frightened helplessness would be that of a soldier, hunched in a foxhole night after endless night, with deadly mortar shells flying overhead—any one of those shells could land upon him and kill him. In all of these cases, there's obviously nothing that a person can possibly *do* in terms of taking clear-cut, self-protective action. The individual is immobilized, a rabbit frozen in the headlights, waiting for whatever-will-occur to overtake him.

Internally, though, he is experiencing the huge burst of energy that's been summoned up to sharpen and focus his physical and mental resources upon effectively fighting or fleeing the situation. Concurrently, however—since he can do neither—he's consumed by a terrible sense of his own vulnerability and powerlessness. He is paralyzed in place, and the physiological forces that have come into play *remain* in play, for there's no effective way to utilize and ultimately discharge them.

This state of perpetual mobilization-to-meet-the-danger can affect the human organism profoundly. Traumatic experiences can and often do provoke changes in brain and body functioning that can take years to dissipate and sometimes never fully disappear. Then, much as any of us might want to move forward in our lives and put behind us painful aspects of our personal histories—those times when we felt helpless, inadequate, unworthy, unable to take action—our vast dossiers of encoded memories are what accompany us in the effort. We carry them along with us not only in the evanescent "mental" sense, but in a patently material, bodily sense.

The reality is that memory itself is, ultimately, a series of bodily—neurophysiological—occurrences.

Selective Highlighting

For one person, it can be the powerful aroma of pine needles as she walks through a forest that suddenly floods her with feeling. She may not quite recall the incident itself—one summer at camp, when a boy she was in love with took her in his arms and kissed her—but the pungent smell, the way the sunlight is filtering through the tree branches, and the sweet languor of the afternoon air fill her with a sense of gladness, the goodness of just being alive upon this earth.

For someone else, however, that same smell—the pungent smell of pine needles warming in the sun—may evoke feelings of a radically different kind. She feels herself tensing up and looks around to see if any strangers are hovering nearby. While she may, or may not, bring to mind the leering tramp who suddenly exposed himself one peaceful afternoon when she was reading in the park, the sensory data that she's receiving—plus the woodsy context in which she's receiving it—light up her internal warning board, connecting instantaneously with the part of her cerebral wiring that was laid down in relation to that "forgotten" incident that occurred so many years earlier.

As we all know, there are many such situations, ones in which certain sensory cues evoke a host of seemingly inexplicable, even downright irrational feelings. There are actually times when it can take nothing more than a change in weather to trigger a significant emotional reaction. For example, a period of humid, rainy drizzle—weather reminiscent of long, frightening days in the danger-filled jungles of Vietnam—can make a veteran of that war feel edgy, hypervigilant, tense, unable to sleep and to concentrate at work. "This situation can repeat itself for years—literally—without that individual ever associating his unease and fearfulness to those long-ago wartime experiences," as trauma expert Steven Southwick told me.

The link between the terrifying past and a present-day trigger of memory—in the case just mentioned, the "feel" of the persistent light rain—creates a sense of imminent danger that, at a superficial level, feels completely out of whack. The returned vet is at one level perfectly aware that he's now safely home in America and that the war in Vietnam ended many years earlier. Still, the self-preservation lessons that he learned at that time (You must be ever vigilant! Watch out! Be ready to fight for your life!) linger on within him; and an environmental cue such as a soft, steady rainfall can raise them to the murky surface of awareness. Well though that person may realize that there *is* no realistic threat, his body and brain cells are reacting to sensory cues that connote danger and responding with messages of emergency.

What can explain the persistence of such strong emotional responses, which can occur so far in time from the long-ago lover's first embrace (that kiss in the woods) or the long "forgotten" original fear situation? Once again, the explanation is that these powerfully encoded responses *do* make good biological sense from the point of view of species survival. For we humans are well served by selectively bookmarking those situations that excited and attracted us, in the interests of courting and mating. But *above all else*, we need to keep vividly in mind those situations that have threatened our safety and integrity, for the evolutionary bottom line is always that of staying alive long enough to reproduce and create a new generation.

Nature has, in short, equipped us to learn, and learn well, those lessons that have been invested with survival significance.

The Loss of Mittens the Cat

I have written elsewhere (*Intimate Partners*) about a story originating in my own early life, but I will retell it here, for it is so apt an example of the way in which vital lessons are highlighted within our nervous circuitry: In the 1960s, when our three daughters were very young and my husband, an economist, was teaching at Stanford, we lived on the university campus and had a tiger-striped kitten with pure white paws that looked liked mittens. "Mittens," in fact, was the name we had given him.

Our closest friends, during this era of our lives, were the Ds. They were roughly the same age as we, just moving past the twenties and into their early thirties. I customarily spent a good deal of time with the wife, Anne, and had opened myself up to the relationship completely. She was a part-time social worker, who taught at a school for autistic children. On Wednesday afternoons, I took care of her seven-year-old daughter. So aside from other visits, there was always that predictable time together, when Anne came either to pick up her child or to drop her off.

Our two husbands, who were colleagues on the Stanford faculty, were as close to each other as Anne and I were. The friendship had, in fact, originated with the two men. Although the two of them related to each other differently than we—they enjoyed getting into long, heated, abstract discussions—they were also, especially for males, unusually disclosing and personal with each other.

In short, the relationship between our two families seemed to work at every level and in every permutation—between the varying adult twosomes, between the four girls of the junior generation, and between each child and any of the respective parents. We had misunderstandings and tensions from time to time, to be sure, but we functioned as a quasi–extended family; problems could and did arise, but our attachment to the Ds was never in question. Going out in the evening meant going out somewhere with Anne and Larry, and we did so as often as we could manage it. We went to small restaurants in San Francisco, to the movies, to occasional nightclubs, and to afternoon baseball games. As families, we went on hikes, picnics, excursions to the beach at Santa Cruz, and sometimes camping in the Sierra Nevada mountains.

It was on our return home from one such trip, to Yosemite National Park, that we discovered that in our absence Mittens had wandered away.

I had actually begun to get anxious about the cat on our way home—I wasn't sure why. We had, before leaving for five days in the mountains, made the usual arrangements for his care. Our neighbor's daughter, a reliable twelve-year-old, was to come in daily and feed him; she was also to change his litter box. Mittens was, as always, allowed to stay outside in our large enclosed garden; this arrangement had never led to any problems in the past. But as we wended our way homeward, I began to worry about his having strayed off and met with some sort of accident.

This was ridiculous, I told myself, for he never wandered far from the back patio—not even when the gate of the stockade fence was left open. I felt, nevertheless, extraordinarily uneasy.

Perhaps it had to do with a crazy feeling I'd had, while up in the mountains, that something was different about the Ds. On the journey back, too, we'd taken a long detour through the old towns of the California Gold Rush country; I'd been a passenger in Anne and Larry's Jeep for a while. I'd felt somewhat confused while riding with them, felt that something I couldn't understand was taking place.

Something was wrong—or was I imagining it, this difference in the air? I sensed something strained and unnatural about Anne—her wide blue eyes were glassy and blank—or was it Larry who was behaving strangely? Was a fight going on between them? I had seen them when they were overtly angry at each other; neither one seemed angry at the moment. But the atmosphere was subtly toxic . . . or was it my imagination?

"Something is *wrong*," I said to Herb when our family had reunited in our own station wagon again. The Ds' Jeep was moving around and past us at that moment, and I nodded my head in their direction. "*What's* wrong, Mommy?" a voice piped up from the backseat.

"Nothing," I said, signaling to my husband that we would discuss it later on, when the children's attention had turned elsewhere. But when we were able to talk privately, Herb assured me that he had noticed nothing odd or amiss about the Ds. He believed that I was imagining problems where no problems necessarily existed.

I let myself accept this explanation, even though there had been something *different* about them—about Anne in particular, who'd been there in body but utterly absent. It was, however, in the wake of this brief discussion (conducted sotto voce) that I began to get so alarmed about the cat.

As we approached Palo Alto, I remember, my sense of foreboding—about something having happened to Mittens—was experienced as an almost physical, intensely anxious discomfort. I couldn't wait to get out of the car and into the house to prove to myself that I'd been mistaken! But my fears, on this occasion, had been prophetic: Our pet was not there to greet us, and we could not find him anywhere. He was nowhere in the house or in the garden; his food, uneaten, was drying in his blue-and white dish.

Our young neighbor, contrite, told us the cat had vanished from the garden a day earlier and had not returned at feeding time. She'd searched the entire area but had been unable to find him. No one, she reported, had seen him—or at least noticed him—and she had no clue as to his whereabouts. She was clearly very upset, and we had to set about reassuring her.

It was not her fault, we told her. Mittens had merely wandered away and was very likely to wander back to us eventually. In the meantime, we ourselves would take over the search. Reasonable words, reasonably spoken; yet even as we stood on the front lawn talking to her, I felt a sense of queasiness, a sense of awful grief. I could not understand where that feeling emanated from—a missing pet is, after all, low on the list of life's potential tragedies! Nevertheless, I was deeply—seemingly irrationally—upset.

Later on, when the children were in bed, I talked about this with my husband, who was able to offer me an explanation that I'd been unable to offer myself. He reminded me of a story I'd once told *him*, in the early days of our relationship, but then had apparently forgotten. It had to do with an incident that had occurred on the day of my own parents' separation, a separation that led to their eventual divorce.

I was twelve years old at the time, and the furniture was being moved out of the house. But for me the most terrible part of what was happening was that our cat had gotten his neck caught in the outdoor coal grate. He had hurt himself so badly that the two men from the animal shelter, called to his rescue, had had to carry him off with them.

"Oh yes," I said to Herb, recognizing that for me that cat had been the symbol of the intact family. The loss of the cat was connected, in my own mind, with the family life that was being taken away.

At the age of twelve, one is in part an adult but also to some large degree a child—still able to give credence to magical ideas and notions. I suppose, looking back, that I probably maintained the belief that if our pet were to return, so would my world's stability. Or perhaps my preoccupation with the loss of the cat—so intense that the breakup of my parents' relationship seemed almost incidental—was due to my finding it easier to confront and mourn the loss of the family pet than to mourn the *intolerable* loss, which was the ending of my parents' marriage.

In the case of the Ds, history proceeded to repeat itself. For a few days after our return from that camping trip on which I'd experienced the Ds as "different," my husband appeared at home—unexpectedly, in the middle of the afternoon—with the warning that he had some bad news to tell me. The children were, at that moment, listening to records on their toy phonograph. He and I went outside, to the far end of the garden, and sat across from each other at a picnic table under a blooming wisteria vine. Anne had, he said without preamble, told Larry that she wanted a divorce.

She had, it appeared, been having an affair for most of this past year; now she was leaving her husband for her lover. He—the other man—wanted to marry her and had already left his spouse. I sat there, open-mouthed. I was doing my utmost to assimilate this barrage of new information but found it enormously hard to concentrate.

Other matters commanded my attention, such as the perfumed smell of wisteria blossom and the sight of a lazily droning bee scouting for a likely source of nectar. Also, there were the distant voices coming from the record player; the children were listening to a fairy tale. The only thought that crossed my mind, which felt emptied of ideas, was of the cat who was still missing. Will he ever come back again? I wondered . . . and then realized, at once, that it was not the cat that really concerned me.

There is actually a horrible addendum to that Mittens story—one of those incidents in life that are hard to recall without flinching. It concerned the original memory of my parents' separation—and most particularly, the memory of the *way* in which the SPCA workers had carried the cat away that day. Our family pet's neck had been secured in a halter so that the rest of his body hung down stiffly. He was dead, but why did they take him out in that cruelly indifferent way—not cradled gently in their arms, but with his head lolling and his limbs dangling down disrespectfully? "Now I know that life is terrible," was the anguished thought I so clearly remember.

And it was that image that surfaced in my mind, these many years later, when the unthinkable thing, the impossible thing, proceeded to happen. For even as I listened to my husband describing the details of the Ds' separation, and Anne's long-standing affair—and realized that *I* had been the lovers' babysitter on the Wednesday afternoons when they met!—I looked upward and caught sight of Mittens's body, high in the trellis above the picnic table on which we sat. He looked as if he were suspended in midflight, his body caught in the thickly tangling vines but elongated tautly—for a mad instant, I thought he was alive and we'd found him. But what had happened became clear at once: The cat had been leaping upward at a bird and had hit a live electric wire. Mittens was dead; in rigor mortis; arrested in the performance of that final act.

I stared at this scene in disbelief, and although I was, at this point in my life, miles away in time, place, and circumstance from the world of my original family, the grief and fear I'd experienced on the day of my parents' breakup assailed me with all the intensity of the original experience. This sorrow and terror-driven memory—the shattering of a marriage and the brutal fate of a beloved pet—had been forgotten, stashed away for years in my mental out-of-circulation files. At that moment, however, my body "remembered" everything that had occurred and presented it to me in a cascade of vivid feelings, sensations, and imagery—evoking an anxiety that hit me like a punch in the stomach. It felt as though it were all happening *right now*, for experiences of this kind seem to have a timeless quality, a way of remaining alive and fresh in an unending present.

Triggers of Memory

As world-renowned researchers Larry R. Squire and Eric R. Kandel (a recent Nobel laureate) have observed, there are three major avenues or cues to memory's awakening. These are 1) *sensory experiences*, such as Proust's tasting of the special cookie and my visual image of the elongated body of the cat; 2) *context*, being in a place or a situation that is very *like* the one in which the original memory was laid down; and 3) the *internal, bodily state* of the individual doing the remembering.

I have already talked about the first important spur to retrieval on Squire and Kandel's list—sensory experience, the way in which certain sights, sounds, smells, and so forth can jostle slumbering memories into the spotlight of conscious awareness—so now let me address the other major triggers of memory they cite. In regard to the second one—context—there is now a large scientific literature supporting the view that being in a setting that is *very like the setting in which the original experience took place* makes remembering that experience much easier and more efficient. There are a number of demonstrations of this phenomenon in the scientific literature, but one I found particularly intriguing was an experiment in which the subjects who took part were all deep-sea divers.

In this study, every one of the participants was asked just to listen to forty unrelated words. However, some of the divers were standing on the beach when doing the listening, while others were standing under some ten feet of water. "Subsequently, they were tested in one or the other of the two contexts, and were asked to recall as many words as possible," report Squire and Kandel in their book *Memory: From Mind to Molecules.* The results of this research showed that *the words learned underwater were best recalled underwater* and *the words learned on the beach were best recalled on the beach.* Simply being in the same situation served to render memory more accurate. Context matters.

So does the third trigger of memory, the individual's *internal state of being.* The impact of a person's neurophysiological status upon his or her capacity to remember was vividly demonstrated by Dr. Steven Southwick and his colleagues at the West Haven Veterans Administration in Connecticut. Their remarkable research showed how effectively and rapidly an altered interior state can summon up a legion of emotional memories and reactions.

The design of the Southwick et al. experiment was wonderfully simple: The researchers asked a group of twenty Vietnam War veterans, all of them identified as suffering from post-traumatic stress disorder, if they would volunteer to receive intravenous injections of a drug called yohimbine. Yohimbine, which is often used as a research tool, is a psychoactive substance derived from the bark of a South American tree; it has the effect of stimulating a rise in levels of the activating fight-or-flight brain hormone norepinephrine.

Yohimbine (which was often used to treat male impotence before Viagra appeared upon the scene) acts to rev up the nervous system by causing a brief increase in the body's norepinephrine. For most people, yohimbine has insignificant or no side effects, but in *this* situation—which involved men who were already experiencing the symptoms of PTSD in their daily lives—the drug elicited immediate and striking reactions. As the investigators reported, nine of the research participants had panic attacks, and six of them experienced frightening flashbacks. That is, they felt transported backward in time, as if they were in the midst of the terrifying battle experiences they'd undergone in the jungles of Vietnam many, many years earlier. These reactions occurred in the absence of any external *sensory* cues or of a *context* that was reminiscent of the traumatic situation. In other words, a *changed internal, bodily state* had propelled these harrowing memories directly to the center of the veterans' conscious attention.

Flashbacks

A word about flashbacks is in order here. A flashback is like a trip through a psychological time machine, inasmuch as what occurred "then and there" is suddenly being experienced as if it's occurring in present time, right here and right now. To cite just one example of this eerie phenomenon, one of the volunteers in the Southwick research was a forty-seven-year-old helicopter gunner who'd flown dozens of missions in Vietnam and witnessed many scenes of death; he'd suffered from PTSD for many years afterward. In the course of the study, this man reacted to the active yohimbine treatment by experiencing a panic attack and a flashback.

"During the flashback," wrote the researchers, "the patient was highly agitated and described a helicopter crashing into flames. He could see the flames, hear the crash, and smell the smoke. He appeared to be in a dissociated state, responding as if the traumatic episode was occurring in the present." This man wasn't merely *remembering*; rather, he was *living through* a full-blown, fully elaborated scenario in the moment—and it had been evoked by nothing other than the rising levels of norepinephrine in his nervous circuitry.

Because his brain and body cells were being exposed to a heightened state of arousal, generated by the drug yohimbine, he'd begun to feel the same way he felt *at the time of the original trauma*; in consequence, his memories of that event erupted onto wide-screen consciousness again. This well-recognized kind of reaction goes by the technical name of "state-dependent remembering"—a term that is basically a synonym for *internal state*, the third of the three important cues to memory retrieval cited by Squire and Kandel.

Basically, the message here is that when a person's internal bodily climate feels *just the way it did* when a traumatic memory was laid down, a vivid reexperiencing of the overwhelming episode becomes far likelier to occur. But actually, when I think back upon that Mittens story, I recognize that *all three* prompts to memory retrieval were present. First of all, there was the powerful visual stimulus of the cat's body, stretched out so unnaturally in the wisteria vines above me. Second, there was the situational context, which is to say the Ds—a couple who felt so much like "family" —were breaking apart and, in the process, revealing themselves as people whose real lives had been shared with us far less than we'd ever imagined. Third, there was the factor of "state-dependent remembering": my internal state of rapidly fermenting agitation and fear about what would happen next. Then, an added fillip to all of the above was the fact that Anne, my trusted "replacement sister," had betrayed me; she'd been lying to me for a long period of time. This too had its precedent in my history with a real sister, so it's no wonder that this incident hit me as hard as it did.

Implicit and Explicit Memories

It must be acknowledged that this discussion of memory research has been excerpted from a vastly more extensive, extremely complex scientific library now dedicated to the subject—a library, I should say, that has sprung up recently in stunning "Jack and the Beanstalk" style and shows no signs of having reached its full growth as yet. The entire field can't be reported upon here—no chance of it!—but I do think it important to make one more point before moving on, which is that modern scientists make a clear distinction between the two ways in which long-term memories are stored.

One of these storage systems is called “declarative memory” (also known by other names, such as “explicit memory” and “semantic memory”). It’s this kind of memory that we’re generally referring to when we use the word *memory* itself; it refers to our conscious knowledge of facts, ideas, and events that have occurred.

Declarative or explicit memory consists of information that can be summoned up verbally—“London is the capital of England”; “My vacation was great, but too short”—or in the form of mental imagery, such as the annoyed look on the boss’s face yesterday or the memory of how much smelly garbage was floating in the Venetian canals the last time you visited that city. It is basically the vast storehouse of information that *you know that you know*.

The other major system of memory storage is called “nondeclarative memory” (also known as “implicit memory” and “procedural memory”). This form of remembering exists at a nonverbal, semiautomatic, partially or completely unconscious level. Nondeclarative or implicit remembering is, for one thing, about the “how to” aspect of memory; it includes skills and habits such as riding a bike, driving an auto, and brushing your teeth on a daily basis. We don’t have to summon up an entire set of memorized instructions each time we hop into the driver’s seat of the car; we simply put in the key and perform a series of actions without thinking or reflecting. Also, very important, implicit memory encompasses emotional responding, reflex actions, and classically conditioned behaviors—to wit, that Vietnam War veteran’s experience of feeling agitated and out of control during a period of humid, drizzly weather, even though the war had been over for more than twenty-some years. Another example, of course, would be my feelings of anxiety about our family cat (even though I’d lost track of the original memory until my husband reminded me about it) and the subliminal connection made somewhere deep in my nervous system between “lost pet” and “something deeply amiss in a relationship that had great meaning to me.”

As we all know, psychoanalysts have long maintained that our lives are always being strongly affected by powerful implicit memories with which we have no conscious contact—and the recent hard evidence emerging from a good deal of highly sophisticated memory research appears to bear this suggestion out. We do indeed retain many implicit, nonverbal memories within our cerebral circuitry, where they are thought to exist in patterns of neural associations—you might think of them as a person's "basic wiring,"a kind of wiring that is admittedly difficult but by no means impossible to access and to change. For there are now fruitful strategies for bringing such changes about—reprocessing is an important one of them—and these will be further examined and illustrated in the stories of Karen, Joanna, and Deirdre that follow.

Chapter Thirteen

—

THE WORLD TURNED UPSIDE DOWN: EXTRAMARITAL AFFAIRS

AS KAREN BARRY-FREED RECALLED IT, THAT SUMMER had been a smoldering one, and she herself had been feeling perplexed and disoriented. It was as if she'd been aware of certain subsurface tremors that were still too negligible to suggest the scope of the impending earthquake. True, her husband, Jon, had been strangely unavailable to her and the children during the long, stifling August afternoons: He'd had a series of minor illnesses and had spent much of his time sleeping in the garden hammock. Eventually, though, she'd felt her patience giving way. "When you're not here you're not here; and when you're *here* you're not here," she'd complained, but the conversation hadn't led anywhere.

"I was clueless, totally clueless," Karen recounted. "I had no idea; never discovered lipstick on his shirt; none of *that* sort of stuff. I never found out until he *told* me." Her brown-fringed hazel eyes were staring and enlarged, and her open, friendly face seemed drained of life and color. It was as though the memory of that domestic catastrophe weren't five years in the past, but as current as the headlines in this morning's newspaper.

Throughout that summer's end and the beginning of fall, the Barry-Freeds' lives went on as usual. "In many respects, the marriage we had was like a business," said Karen. "We had a partnership; we ran a home;

we were raising children; and that was it. Sex was not great, and to the extent that I thought about that, I thought, Maybe I'm just not a sexy person."

Sex was to her something on the order of an obligation—you had to do it once a week, but it wasn't particularly interesting. She'd never given much thought to how this might be affecting Jon, never wondered about how *he* might be reacting. Having grown up in a family where flawless conduct and keeping up appearances were of paramount importance, Karen was relatively oblivious when it came to the world of feelings. Therefore, she was thoroughly unsuspecting and unprepared—"hurt, insulted, *devastated*"—when her husband's feelings erupted with cataclysmic suddenness and he let her know how barren the marriage felt to him.

That upheaval happened in October, somewhere around the time of his fortieth birthday. Karen's gift to Jon had been a three-day vacation for the pair of them at Canyon Ranch in the Berkshires; but when he'd opened the gift envelope, he was clearly taken aback.

"I was surprised—hurt—by his reaction. I thought, How can you *not* be happy? We're always overwhelmed by these children, and won't this be a great chance for the two of us to get away? But he started making all kinds of excuses, saying he wasn't sure he could spare the time—business reasons, something like that." Jon had seemed downright shaken by her present, as if no prospect could be more threatening than an intimate getaway for the pair of them.

"I pointed out that it was an open reservation; we could go whenever we pleased," Karen said evenly, "but of course it was the last thing he wanted to do with *me*."

The following week had been characterized by appreciable silence and a sense of polite constraint until she'd felt the need to probe again, "I don't know where you *are* anymore, Jon. Where *are* you?" He hadn't offered up any explanations or answers, for he *did* know where he was, and it wasn't with her and with their family. Another week went by, and eventually she made some puzzled comment about the fact that they hadn't made love on his birthday, and they hadn't made love on their anniversary, two significant events that were just a few days apart.

"Not that I was an overly sexual kind of person at that point in time; I really wasn't," Karen hastened to add. "But again, these were *occasions*. . . ." Her voice trailed off momentarily, and then she said, "It just seemed odd. So I brought it up, and he said, 'I have to talk to you. I'm just not—I'm not real happy.' And I said, 'Oh, okay.' But we didn't talk about it that night. I did find myself wondering what was going on with Jon, but strange as it sounds, the thought of another person in the picture didn't even occur to me."

That evening, the Barry-Freeds finally sat down together to talk. "The children were in bed, the house was quiet, and the two of us went into the living room to have this conversation. I can't remember everything he said, exactly, but there's a kind of image of that scene that's just burned into my brain," said Karen, touching both temples with the tips of her fingers. Jon had been sitting in the rocker (she pointed to it at this moment), and she had sat on the sofa, facing him. Then, without any preamble, he'd told her that what he wanted to talk about was the fact that he wanted a divorce.

"It was just like that—that direct—and I couldn't *believe* what I was hearing. I felt as if—as if I'd taken this massive punch to the stomach, and all the wind had been knocked out of me! . . . I mean, this couldn't be happening. . . . This was so surreal. How did I not see this? I just sat there, looking at him, and what he said was, basically, 'You're a wonderful woman; you're the most wonderful mother, the most moral, ethical person I've ever met. I feel just terrible, but I'm very unhappy and I want a divorce. I think you should get an attorney.' It came out just like that, pretty much all in one sentence.

"I was in shock. I really was in *shock*. But I think when there's been as much creeping distance in a marriage as there was in ours, you have no clue whatsoever . . . and I really wasn't clued in." In the course of this short, astounding conversation, her whole world had lurched crazily, rocked back and forth for a few breathless moments, and then came crashing down around her. "At some point, I looked at him, and finally the light is dawning," Karen continued. "It's dawning slowly, and I said, 'Is there another woman?' He couldn't answer me; he just nodded his head up and down—there was. Even so, it didn't seem possible. I mean, I did know this conversation was happening, but at the same time I couldn't take it in, couldn't *believe* it."

In retrospect, the most wounding words she'd heard that evening were not actually about herself; they were what Jon had to say about his responsibilities toward the children. He had always been the most caring and devoted of fathers, but when she asked him, "What about the kids?" he'd bristled and said coldly, "I've got only one life to live, and they'll be fine."

Nevertheless, Karen hadn't responded angrily or even *felt* angry; she'd felt dazed—numbed. Despite everything, her first thoughts had been focused solely upon saving what could be salvaged from the wreckage. Her proposal had been that the two of them go into marital counseling—work on repairing the relationship and forgiving whatever needed to be forgiven—but above all, try to keep the family intact.

Jon was willing, and agreed to participate in twice-weekly therapy with Karen; but at the same time, he had an underlying agenda. He was unhappy in the marriage, in love with someone else, and he wanted out. "He kept talking a lot about 'adventure,' about his craving for more excitement in his life. About his wanting to go white-water rafting, stuff like that. Let's face it, he was just turning forty, and the message was that he didn't want to be living in this house in Lincoln, Massachusetts, with this wife and these three children."

Betrayal Trauma

According to psychologist Ronnie Janoff-Bulman, the essence of trauma is the abrupt disintegration of the victim's inner world. Unbearable, unthinkable experiences have a way of demolishing the basic structure of the self, shattering those fundamental assumptions that have served to make life feel livable and safe. In Janoff-Bulman's view, such assumptions or core beliefs can be subsumed under the following propositions: 1) that the world is benevolent; 2) that the world is meaningful; and 3) that the self is worthy.

Most of us take these reassuring assumptions as facts of our existence —givens—and they usually exist outside our conscious awareness. But when overwhelming, inconceivable events—in the case just cited, the treachery of a trusted partner—demolish and scramble these bedrock beliefs, the injured person's inner world becomes an alien landscape, littered with the debris of destroyed convictions.

"Victims of trauma have come face-to-face with a highly unstable, dangerous universe, which has been made all the more frightening by their total lack of psychological preparation," writes Janoff-Bulman. It is as if a harsh, glaring light has suddenly illuminated the full panorama of the individual's existence, and the terrible fragility of the self has become painfully apparent. Not only is the self vulnerable in ways not hitherto realized, but the person experiences him- or herself as besieged by lies, malice, and meaninglessness in a world that offers no real stability or protection.

At the same time, a loud internal emergency alarm has been set off—one that can't readily be modulated or extinguished. The revelation of the betrayal has put the shocked partner's body into a state of high alert—one that can precipitate a wide range of the familiar physical and mental symptoms that follow upon traumatic experience, such as chronic anxiety, confusion, "flashbulb" memories of certain painful scenes, mood swings, irritability, sleep disturbances, depression, feelings of estrangement, shortness of temper, deep-rooted, ceaseless anger, digestive problems, substance abuse, chronic fatigue, and a host of other greater and lesser difficulties.

However, when it comes to making a formal diagnosis of post-traumatic stress disorder—in the big-T sense—the revelation of a partner's infidelity doesn't qualify. Although such an event is clearly shattering to a person's view of the self and of the world, it doesn't meet the current criteria of the *Diagnostic and Statistical Manual of Mental Disorders,* which stipulates that a PTSD finding must be reserved for traumatic occurrences that involve actual or threatened death or serious harm to the self or nearby others—in other words, horrifying occurrences that put at risk the victim's physical survival.

This is obviously not the case in extramarital situations, for most people don't die as a result of learning about a trusted partner's lies and deceptions. Nevertheless, a number of researchers and clinicians working in the field of EMS (extramarital sex) *have* come to recognize that betrayed partners often respond in ways that are characteristically present in other traumatic situations.

Interpersonal Trauma

Prominent among these EMS experts is the late Dr. Shirley Glass, who has posited the existence of a phenomenon that she has termed "interpersonal trauma." As Glass told me in the course of a series of conversations, she believes the word *trauma* to be apt because it captures the true extent of the stupefying emotional wound inflicted by a disloyal mate upon his or her trusting and believing partner. For the betraying spouse's behavior has in fact been an assault on her fundamental sense of who she is and on many of her most cherished assumptions.

Until the time of the affair's exposure, she's seen herself as someone unique and special in the eyes of another special person—the intimate partner who has bonded with her and promised to prize her above all others. Thus, when faced with the indisputable evidence of his horrifying dishonesty, her self-respect suffers a monumental reversal. In the wake of the revelation, she experiences herself as anything *but* special; she feels inconsequential and discardable, as if she'd been relegated to a kind of human waste dump.

Many of her most basic beliefs about her own personal qualities—her looks, her lovability, even her good judgment—disintegrate precipitously. She may have viewed herself as sophisticated and mature when it came to *other* people's dalliances, but nothing in her experience has actually prepared her for the jolt of coming face-to-face with her own trusted partner's incredible duplicity.

It is so dizzying, so destructive an experience that everything she thought she knew comes suddenly into question. Her world has been shaken from its assumptive foundations—hit by malevolently powerful forces—turned completely upside down. And while the exposure of the partner's sexual betrayal is not *mortally* threatening, it often is experienced as a death—the death of faith in a critically important attachment and the loss of a secure base in a world that makes sense and is meaningful.

A Self-Willed Obliviousness

Later, Karen was to wonder why she had remained so hopelessly ignorant of what was happening during the months leading up to the revelation of her husband's affair. Perhaps it had been what she called the "creeping distance" in her sixteen-year marriage that explained her total lack of awareness, but in retrospect she did recognize that there had been *numerous* indications that something out of the ordinary was taking place.

Among them had been Jon's nervous primping before the mirror on certain mornings just before going into work. He would keep changing his shirt and his ties, keep asking her advice about which tie looked best with the suit he was wearing. Recollections such as these were particularly galling once she realized that this had occurred on the days when his lover—a woman who worked for an affiliate of Jon's family-owned shoe-manufacturing business—was flying into Boston "on business." Although he'd always arrived home in the wee hours on these occasions, her suspicions had never been awakened.

In hindsight, she found her naiveté stupefying; indeed, she felt moronic about the whole thing and looked upon the blindness of that time as her own very personal failing. But in fact this reluctance to register the knowledge of a trusted partner's betrayal is much more the commonality than the exception. So is the sense of perplexity and disorientation that Karen remembered experiencing throughout the period leading up to the extramarital affair's revelation. For even though the sense that something wasn't quite right had been palpable—in the conjugal air, somehow—she'd managed to keep the unthinkable information from her conscious awareness. Karen Barry-Freed, like so many other bright, intelligent people, was ready and eager to deny what was happening before her very eyes, and to do so right down to the wire.

What motivates this kind of self-willed obliviousness? You might explain it on the basis of the old "love is blind" cliché; but many deceived partners are in long-lasting, committed relationships rather than the early throes of romantic passion. What makes them cling so steadfastly to the irrational belief that nothing's amiss, even in the face of accumulating signs and signals to the contrary? Or if they should raise bewildered questions, what makes them so strangely prepared to accept the betraying mate's lies and misrepresentations? The superficial answers to such questions may vary widely, and they do; but they all boil down to the ordinary truth that the thought of a beloved, trusted partner's defection is often too intolerable to penetrate the mind's defenses against experiencing pain.

"Refusing to Know"

Another example of a person "refusing to know" was that of Anne Bailey, who was in her late twenties at the time of our interviews. Anne told me that she had been strangely aware and yet unaware of her husband Mark's extramarital affair for a period of many months but had refused to acknowledge on an overt, conscious level what she *did* know. As she put it, "I just couldn't let my thoughts go down that track." It was as though she'd had the intuition that certain associative tracks could lead directly to a marital train wreck.

In Anne's case, as in that of Karen (and those of so many other deceived spouses), the affair had become known only when knowledge of it became completely unavoidable. This happened to Anne Bailey when she, her husband, Mark, and their six-month-old son, Timmy, were vacationing on Nantucket island. The whole matter came to light by the merest chance—when Anne picked up the downstairs phone to make a call and overheard a scrap of whispered, excited-sounding conversation. It was Mark, talking to a woman, someone whose voice was faintly familiar.

Startled and confused, Anne had replaced the receiver immediately. Then she stood where she was for a heart-pounding few moments. She knew she recognized that person's voice, and yet she couldn't quite place it. After a short interval she tiptoed halfway up the stairs to see if that strangely overheated conversation had ended.

It was quiet on the second floor, so she hurried downstairs again. Come to think of it, she *had* heard the phone ring sometime earlier, so she quickly dialed *69 and found herself connected to the sender of the last call that had come in. "Hi," said the woman at the other end of the line in a bright, friendly tone of voice.

Anne did recognize the voice this time. She knew the person to be one of the young postdocs who'd been working in Mark's laboratory since the previous winter; she replaced the phone on its cradle without speaking. But in that moment, she *knew* with complete certainty everything she'd fought so hard against knowing before.

"It was like having a rug pulled out from under me—not the rug of a room, but the rug of the whole world—and I felt as if I were spinning. It was like whirling through space, breaking apart into pieces—I was *demolished*. And the thought that came into my head was, My life is just *over*."

At the same time, said Anne, those terrible feelings had been accompanied by a strange sense of relief. For so many crazy, confusing things had been going on for such a long period of time, and now she understood why those things made sense. "All of a sudden, things clicked into place, and I could *understand* why I'd been feeling so strange—so unlike myself, so weepy, so mad at the world, rejectable, and quick to take offense."

Scanning backward in time, she realized how long and how elaborately Mark had been lying to her. What a stupid idiot she had been! There had been so *many* clues that he was involved elsewhere—blatant symptoms of an underlying malady for which she now had the firm diagnosis. How *had* she managed to dismiss a whole series of seemingly insignificant incidents from her awareness? The telephone calls he'd been getting at odd hours—from an annoying, klutzy new colleague, he'd said. The unusually long hours he'd been spending at the lab—leaving so early in the morning and coming home so late almost every night. He'd had to work harder than ever on his government grant, he'd told her, for the money was getting much tighter.

It had all been an ingenious stew, a mixture of half-truths and blatant deceptions. She did recall questioning him about one incident along the way and remembered being puzzled by the guilty expression on his face. "I wasn't clear on what *that* could be about. But let's face it, a part of me didn't *want* to push matters. Maybe it was because Mark was so miserable at the time, worried about his laboratory's funding. Maybe it was because my own job was so demanding, and we had a young baby, and I was so involved *there*."

She had done her best *not to know*, but on the morning of that overheard phone call she *had* known with a sense of furious certainty. So she'd marched directly upstairs to confront her husband, said directly, "Look, I have to talk to you. . . . I know you're having an affair."

Mark was working at a small computer in their bedroom, but he'd stiffened, then jumped up, almost knocking over his chair. The two of them had just stood there, staring. Anne remembered the scene vividly: the ragged sound of her own breathing, the way she'd crossed her arms over her chest as if to shield herself from him. Mark, looking hangdog, had let out a long sigh, then admitted that it was the truth.

The effect upon his wife was volcanic. It was as if a stockpile of rage that had been silently building up inside her had erupted on the instant. "I felt like I was exploding, literally blowing apart—as if I wanted to *kill* him—him or *myself*, I wasn't sure!" The worst part was having to keep it under wraps for a while, because at that moment the baby woke up from his morning nap and started crying for someone to get him from the crib. It was already close to eleven A.M., and the Baileys had houseguests who were due to arrive somewhere around lunchtime.

"Even now, that whole weekend is a big blur in my mind," Anne recounted. "But what *is* vivid is the memory of being alone with Mark at bedtime. . . . How *embarrassed* I felt getting undressed in his presence, because now he was someone *strange* to me. I didn't want to be seen by him. I felt so soiled, so humiliated, so utterly *betrayed*."

The Body Reacts

It will come as no surprise that in the aftermath of an affair's exposure, the betrayed and bereaved partner is likely to develop post-traumatic stress symptoms and reactions. Acute hyperarousal was surely one of Anne's most evident reactions, for the exposure of Mark's infidelity had quickly shunted her into an amphetamine-like "high"; she'd felt pressured, supercharged with seething energy, chronically agitated, and unable to calm herself down. Plagued with intrusive thoughts and disturbing images of the lovers' embraces, she'd been preoccupied by fantasies of murdering her deceiving mate or of committing suicide. It was impossible to get to sleep, and when she did manage to do so, she was often wakened by violent nightmares. She simply couldn't soothe herself, calm herself down.

From the point of view of outward behavior, Anne's reactions were completely different from those of Karen Barry-Freed, whose responses looked completely opposite. Instead of speeding up, Karen had slowed down, almost to the point of complete immobilization. Hers had been the second kind of bodily reaction—"freezing" or numbing out.

Karen didn't rage or feel vengeful; she felt "as if I couldn't move, as if I were weighted down with stones." It was as though she were some confused survivor staggering around in the wake of a devastating catastrophe, seeking foggily for some points of orientation in a bizarre world that was no longer safe or familiar.

"In one sense, I knew everything that was happening, but in another sense it all seemed like it was happening to someone else—I was so *out* of it," Karen said. "When I drove my kids to school I didn't even *hear* them when they spoke to me. They kept saying, 'Earth to Mom! Earth to Mom!' because my thoughts were just elsewhere—no, not elsewhere, but *nowhere*. It was like the inside of my head was . . . blank. And I was so disoriented, I could get lost just driving to the grocery store."

At times, for no specific reason, tears would start running down her cheeks; yet those tears felt strangely unconnected to any emotions such as sadness or grief. By and large, she felt *numb*—a leaden feeling that would be pierced now and then by sudden visitations of horror. It was usually an impromptu visualization of that scene in the living room when Jon had sprung the news that the marriage was over and she should get herself an attorney.

That image, when it popped into her mind, had the power to make Karen double over, her entire body gripped by anguish and fear. Sometimes she even imagined she was *hearing* the words that had been spoken—hearing them aloud, in the moment. This made her fear she might be going crazy, for wasn't "hearing voices" a sign that something deadly might be happening?

Fight, Flee, or Freeze

Clearly, here were two women who had reacted to the same traumatic revelation in polar opposite ways. Karen had closed down and become almost paralyzed, while Anne (like Claudia Martinelli) had become visibly "hyper." Anne had been filled with bubbling anger that continually threatened to boil over in some rage-driven destructive act. Despite all outward appearances, however, *inside* Anne's and Karen's bodies a similar physiological situation prevailed.

For the biological bottom line is that when we humans are faced with threats of a potentially overwhelming nature, an inner siren is triggered and we switch into an altered state of high readiness to meet the challenge at hand. Even as we make an instinctive, instantaneous assessment of the danger, an upsurge of neurohormones and neurotransmitters is activated. These substances inundate our brains and bodies: Our hearts start pumping faster; our muscles contract; and our blood vessels constrict in order to reroute blood flow away from those organs most vulnerable to serious damage. On the instant, we are primed, psychologically and biologically, to face up to the threat, to attempt to escape it, or to freeze and "play dead."

This swift bodily reaction to stressful circumstances is, as we know, highly adaptive; it promotes survival. But again, what is generally a vital asset can become a burdensome debit in those life circumstances where neither fight nor flight is a remotely plausible option. We are then simply faced with our terrible inability to do anything about the threatening situation, which therefore remains unresolved; and this in turn leaves our bodies in a state of unremitting preparedness—that is, chronic hypervigilance and readiness to meet with danger. From a physiological point of view, traumatic stress leaves the body's engine running in overdrive.

Thus, despite the fact that Karen looked immobilized and Anne looked intensely souped-up, the two women were in very similar internal, bodily states. This is also true of the many individuals who respond to a faithless partner's deception by ricocheting back and forth from "lows" of frozen, dissociated numbness to "high" bouts of explosive, uncontainable fury. In other words, however disparate various individuals' outward responses to the insult of infidelity may appear to be, the same sorts of reactions to this intense stressor exist within the body itself.

Chapter Fourteen

PARADOXES OF INFIDELITY

BEGINNING WORK ON A FAMILY GENOGRAM IS ALWAYS A slightly odd experience. When you start out, you're sitting opposite someone who is a relative stranger; yet you're aware, from a vast amount of former experiences, that you will soon know that person much better than many of the people numbered among his or her closest friends and acquaintances.

Since Karen Barry-Freed had already told me that her first marriage—the marriage to Jon—had ended in divorce, I drew a horizontal line on the sketch pad. This is the "matrimonial" line, connecting the symbols that read "female" (a circle) and "male" (a square). Then I drew the double-slashed, vertical line through it, which symbolizes "divorce," and asked quietly how long that union had lasted.

They had been married for sixteen years, she said in the hushed voice of someone making a confession; and at the time of their separation, Jon had moved to an apartment house nearby. Afterward, despite that chilling remark he'd made about the children on the night of the revelation—"they'll be fine"—he'd remained a highly involved and caring father. Karen, who'd enjoyed her role as a mother from the outset, continued parenting their three daughters as devotedly as she could. But at the same time, she realized she would have to figure out how to create a professional and social life of her own, one that was different from her former self-definition as "contented suburban housewife."

And she *had* been contented beforehand, she told me quickly—

perhaps subliminally aware, but never really threatened by the "creeping distance" that existed between herself and Jon. "The relationship was really spiraling down, but I didn't know it. At that time I probably didn't know what a good relationship *was.*" I tilted my head to one side, raised a questioning eyebrow.

She paused, then said thoughtfully that her parents, both still alive, were basically good, kindhearted people, but there had been "no vocabulary for the emotions" in her own original family. "So I was *dumbfounded* on that October evening when he told me he wanted out. Because, to be truthful, I was actually pretty satisfied, myself. I had my kids, I had my house, I had wonderful friends, and my life seemed good. Also, I was pretty much used to the fact that Jon's business necessitated his traveling abroad for long periods—to Europe, South America, often for two to three weeks at a time. So we'd sort of grown apart, and I think, in retrospect, that he must have been feeling that loneliness acutely—particularly so after his father died."

Shortly after that shattering conversation during which Karen had learned that the marriage was over and she should get herself an attorney, the Barry-Freeds had begun to see a therapist together. But while Karen was struggling to keep the marriage together, Jon was far more invested in his relationship with his mistress. He was in that state of rapturous enchantment where two are as one, perfect company; and as a consequence, he was busily rewriting the history of his marriage so as to view it in its most negative light. This is something that tends to happen in these particular circumstances, when the deceiver is trying to assuage his own guilty feelings and justify his behavior.

Currently, from the vantage point of hindsight, Karen saw that entire affair—which hadn't lasted even a year—as a "fantasy relationship," a midlife re-creation of an exciting, far-off time when Jon had been young, single, and unencumbered. The lovers had been eating out at fine restaurants and staying at first-class hotels, and Jon's mistress had been giving him all of the full-beam, wonderful attention he'd been craving. "There were no screaming kids, no 'Who's taking out the garbage tonight?' kinds of situations," said Karen dryly.

By the following spring, however, the other woman had given Jon his walking papers. For he'd moved out of the family home, which from his lover's point of view made the romance increasingly untenable. She herself was a divorced parent; and while she'd been enthused about those dreamy, periodic trysts, she wasn't interested in taking on the added burdens of domesticity that a serious commitment to Jon would have involved.

So he was on his own. And although by then he and Karen were living apart, they were consulting a marital therapist together—a slow and painful process that didn't seem to be going anywhere. For even though, technically speaking, it was she who was the wronged party, Karen was the only one putting in any real effort. Jon was licking his own emotional wounds and remaining distant, disengaged, and coolly critical.

He was insisting that *Karen* was the one who needed to do some serious changing—she needed to lose ten pounds; to make some improvements on the cooking front; to give him a big hello when he came home in the evenings—he'd even complained that one of the major problems in the marriage was that he was no longer "the apple of her eye." And while Karen had recognized the childishness of this statement, her self-esteem was taking a beating.

"There's no way I can describe the *pain* of hearing 'You're just not sexual, you're not desirable; this other person was so different, so exciting' . . . and buying into all of that when I heard it, which I did. I felt—it's hard to even describe it—so totally *invalidated* as a woman," she said. Any hope of reviving the relationship soon faded, and Karen continued to experience waves of nausea, migraines, intense stomach pain, and insomnia. Moreover, having been out of the workplace for many years, she was feeling directionless and more frightened than she could ever remember.

A Trite and Ordinary Story

Karen and Jon had arrived at the bleak consummation of what she knew to be a trite and ordinary story—but one that *felt* like the dead-ending of her entire lifetime. However, as time passed, matters moved in a more positive direction. Realizing that she would have to go to work in the near future, Karen enrolled in a nearby college and earned the credits necessary for teaching physical education on a part-time basis. She also began to join some singles groups and form strong new friendships, some with women who were in positions similar to her own. And although she didn't begin dating until after her divorce, she eventually became involved in two important relationships.

The first was with a divorced man, someone she had known for many years, whom she described as a caring and wonderful person. But early on, the pair of them had recognized that the relationship wouldn't go anywhere in terms of marriage, because they were very different people with divergent points of view on every topic—religion, politics—imaginable. Eventually they had parted, on the best of terms, Karen said. Then she paused, gave me an assessing look, and took a deep breath before continuing.

"The other big experience that I had was with a young teacher, a colleague, who was twenty-something years old and so *handsome* that he could have been a male model. I couldn't *believe* it when he let me know he was attracted to me, but he was, very much so . . . and that was good." He had made her feel like the sexiest dish alive, she said, and that had done a lot for her still-damaged ego.

"My divorce was actually the beginning of my birth as a person, in many ways." Karen's eyes widened and her expression brightened as she spoke. It was certainly, she said, the time when she'd given up on being an intimidated little girl and begun getting to know herself as a grown-up, sexual, desirable woman. So in that respect, the traumatic crisis hadn't been the end; it had been a beginning.

A Matter of Timing: Trigger Points of Infidelity

As Hamlet reflects in Shakespeare's famous play, "There's a certain providence in the fall of a sparrow. If it be now, it will not be later; if it be later, it will not be now. . . ." When a sparrow *does* fall, however, we humans usually hunger for some understanding of the meaning and context of the event. *Why* did it happen? What caused it to happen *now*?

In cases of marital infidelity, the reasons given vary widely, but the most commonplace explanations tend to cluster under the headings of "falling in love," "desperate emotional neediness," "irresistible lust," "tantalizing opportunity," or some heady combination of all four. Typically, the explanations given are ones that anyone can understand, and as such, they seem to be complete in themselves.

There are, however, often other, more subtle questions to be probed—questions that fall into the "why *at this time*?" domain. These often have to do with a fateful but unnoticed confluence of forces, involving not only the pressures of the present moment, but far more distant issues rooted in the partners' families of origin. These issues and concerns, which may have lain dormant for many years, tend to waken at certain trigger points in the life cycle, such as the birth of a first baby (the trigger in Anne Bailey's case), the graduation or wedding of a grown child, a break with a valued career mentor, or the looming retirement or death of a parent. Clearly, these times of transition involve additions to, or losses from, the family system as an emotional entity.

The Loss of a Dad

In the course of my conversations with Karen Barry-Freed, which ranged over various periods of her life, I became aware that her husband's affair seemed strongly linked in her own mind to Jon's father's final—fatal—heart attack. It had been only a matter of months after Jon's dad's massive coronary—which had been the culmination of many attacks over the preceding years—that Jon had embarked upon the affair.

Karen knew that her husband had been feeling profoundly lost and abandoned at that time, for father and son had been extremely close—*so* close that she'd been somewhat jealous of their relationship. The two had always talked on the telephone almost daily, and she'd sometimes had the sense that after her father-in-law's death, there was nobody else in the entire world—"and I include myself," admitted Karen—who could make Jon feel adequately validated and self-sufficient. Her father-in-law had heaped approval on Jon all the time, told his son how special and wonderful a person he was—so much so that Karen sometimes wondered if the upshot was that Jon never felt good enough all on his own.

I paused, then asked her directly if she saw some connection between his dad's death and her husband's affair. I'd begun to wonder if Jon was one of those seeming adults who've managed to leave home, in the geographic sense, without having fully individuated—grown up, achieved a sense of being a fully autonomous person who's no longer dependent on a parent (or both parents) for ongoing support and guidance.

She paused to draw in a breath, then said on the outbreath, "To answer your question—*yes*. The loss of the person Jon loved most in the world—the only person who, he felt, really understood him and loved him unconditionally—was very *much* connected, in ways I still don't fully understand, to everything that followed."

Isn't Everybody Doing It?

Pragmatically speaking, doesn't marital infidelity involve the breaking of a promise that nobody's really expected to keep? Isn't extracurricular sex a commonplace—no calamity, but simply part of normal everyday life? *The Random House Dictionary of the English Language* describes normalcy as "conforming to the standard or common type . . . usual; not abnormal; regular; approximately average in any psychological trait. . . ." In other words, what is common to most people, that which occurs in most cases, is what is "normal."

In the late 1940s and early 1950s, pioneer sex researcher Alfred Kinsey and coworkers surveyed sexual behavior in the United States and came up with findings that astonished many Americans. His results indicated that a full *half* of all married males had been unfaithful before the age of forty, and so had more than a quarter (26 percent) of their wives. In other words, *one in every four married women* had been unfaithful before the middle of her life.

Were Kinsey's statistics reliable? They were certainly greeted with disbelief and controversy, but later surveys seemed to bear them out. A study conducted in the early 1980s by psychologist Anthony P. Thompson indicated that the rates of infidelity among committed couples were not only high but rising in the female population. Thompson's best estimate was that "at least 50% of married men" engaged in extramarital sex and that the rates of infidelity among married women were swiftly ascending toward the same level. And in 1981, sex researchers G. D. Nass, R. W. Libby, and M. P. Fisher published their "educated guess" to the effect that 50 to 65 percent of husbands and 45 to 55 percent of wives had been unfaithful before reaching that magic forty-year-old age mark.

These studies appeared to confirm the now widespread impression that infidelity rates were not only high but continually rising. However, more recent sex surveys tell a mixed and somewhat ambiguous story. In their 1992 study of extramarital sexual activity, researchers Shirley Glass and Thomas Wright found that less than half of the husbands and one-quarter of the wives in their sample had had at least one sexual experience with someone other than the mate. These figures were slightly lower than—but generally in line with—the Kinsey data, but they were very *different* from the findings of the National Opinion Research Center (NORC) at the University of Chicago.

The NORC figures are derived from random annual surveys of the population carried out in the decade of the 1990s, and these surveys involved more respondents than had ever before been polled about their sexual behavior. When presented with the question "Have you ever had sexual intercourse with someone other than your spouse when you were married?" only 21.5 percent of ever married men and 12 percent of ever-married women acknowledged having strayed from the connubial fold. These surprising figures suggested that the rates of extramarital sex might in reality be *lower* than anyone has thought since the Kinsey findings erupted upon the cultural scene. Had the incidence of infidelity changed owing to the fear of AIDS and other sexually transmitted diseases? Or had Kinsey's figures been erroneous in the first place?

After the publication of the NORC results, some critics suggested that the manner in which the surveys were conducted—which involved interviewing people in their homes and therefore in the bosoms of their families—affected the accuracy of the answers that the researchers received. However, the NORC interviewees weren't actually asked to talk about their sexual behavior *during* the face-to-face part of the interchange; they were simply asked to fill out a self-completion form in private, then place it, unsigned, in a sealed envelope and mail it off later on.

Nevertheless, it's difficult to be absolutely confident that the NORC's much lower figures *do* reflect the actual rates of infidelity in America; it's just as likely that many individuals decided that answering a sexual questionnaire truthfully was *not* the better part of discretion. So the question itself is still out there: *Is* infidelity the norm, and *is* everybody doing it? The definitive, incontrovertible answers aren't in, and they probably never will be, for we'll never know how many people are willing to talk frankly about their sexual behavior.

What's more, many other issues are worth bearing in mind when it comes to assessing rates of infidelity—for example, what constitutes an act of partner betrayal? When we're talking about extramarital sex, is oral sex or only genital sex to be counted? Is a highly sexualized relationship that takes place only on the Internet to be considered merely a game, or is it a form of real marital deception? Are we distinguishing among a one-night stand, a brief fling, an affair involving sex but no real emotional relationship, and an affair involving an intensely sexual *and* emotional connection? Many of the extant surveys lump together some or all of these behaviors in ways that reflect none of the serious differences among them.

Moreover, the current EMS data doesn't take into account the fact that many *unmarried* couples are in seemingly sexually exclusive, committed relationships. In these instances, despite the absence of a marriage license, learning of a partner's betrayal can be just as horrible an experience but never be reflected in the overall sexual treachery statistics.

The Trust Issue

During a preliminary telephone conversation, Karen had told me that she was in a second marriage. So in the course of this first interview, I drew a fresh marital line and asked her how long she and her current husband had been together. It seemed like a simple question, but she hesitated and looked at me strangely, then asked me which marriage I was referring to.

My pencil remained aloft in the air. "This marriage," I said, pointing to the line I'd just drawn on the sketch pad.

She looked at it, nodded, then warned me that in terms of time frames, the discussion might get confusing: Her first and second marriages were to the same man.

She smiled broadly, obviously amused by the startled look on my face. Then she told me that although she had gotten married to the same husband on two different occasions, her first and second marriages were very *different* in her own mind and in their day-to-day reality as well.

Karen explained that after a year of heavy-duty marital counseling, the marriage—their *first* marriage—had taken on a Humpty-Dumpty quality.

Despite Jon's breakup with his lover, and her own desperate efforts to save the relationship, they couldn't put it back together again. And at last, the Barry-Freeds had given up trying to do so; their long separation ended, and the divorce was finalized. This seemed to mark the definitive ending of their conjugal story, for both ex-partners were by now firmly set on their different and disparate life paths.

Then, one blustery winter afternoon a few years later, Jon called and asked his ex-wife if she would do him a favor. He had the flu and was running a temperature; there was a prescription waiting for him at the local pharmacy, but he was feeling too sick to go out and get it himself.

Karen agreed to drive down to the drugstore and pick up the prescription. But when she brought it up to his apartment, Jon met her at the door and said that there was something he wanted to talk to her about. She stepped just inside the doorway, and he asked her, in a muffled, humble tone of voice, if she would give some consideration to going out for a friendly dinner with him some evening, with absolutely no strings attached. Surprised, Karen hesitated, then agreed in principle that at some undetermined time in the future she would do so—right now it was impossible, for the Christmas holidays were almost upon them.

A couple of months later, the ex-partners *had* met for dinner, and this in turn had led to more meetings—all enjoyable, if permeated by an undertone of strain and wariness. On one such evening, a few months after these casual "dates" had begun, they sat in Jon's car for a while, discussing the plot of a film they'd seen—in an uncanny way, the plot resembled some of the things that had happened in their own lives. And suddenly Karen realized that Jon was weeping.

Then he began talking, in a choked and muffled voice, about what a damned fool he had been. He accused himself of having sabotaged everything in his life that had any real meaning and done so much damage to the people he loved in the process. He told Karen that there was no *way* he could apologize enough—he realized that it wasn't possible—but that he would, if given a chance, do anything, *anything*, to put their marriage back together again. He did understand that if this should ever come to pass, the relationship would have to exist on a different footing entirely.

Now, the balance of power between the members of the pair had shifted dramatically. It was Jon who was pressing to restore the marriage, while Karen remained dubious about getting reinvolved. "I'd arrived at a place in my life where things felt pretty stable, and I was skeptical about making myself vulnerable again," she said, two fingers flying to the base of her throat, as if a body sliver of pain had lodged itself there.

Still, she'd agreed to Jon's request to join him in a fresh round of couples' counseling, even if only with the modest goal of better understanding what had gone wrong between them. "We started back into therapy, and that's when it really got heavy—*that's* when we got into the difficult stuff. . . ."

"The difficult stuff?" I asked.

"Well, the *trust* issue," she said tensely. "I said to Jon, 'I've been lied to and I've been betrayed; and I don't know that I will *ever* trust you again!' I told him, 'You can apologize to me until forever'—and he *has* apologized to me, just endlessly—'but still, I can look at that scar, and it's *there*—and a part of it still hurts—and I think it always will. . . .'" Her hand had drifted downward, and she held it palm inward, fingers splayed wide, against the middle of her chest.

I said nothing; I simply met her gaze and nodded sympathetically to let her know that I'd heard what she was saying: The loss of a certain wholehearted, innocent faith in the safety and security of her partner's love was gone and wasn't ever going to be replaceable.

"Usually it doesn't hurt; it's pretty much healed by now," Karen said slowly, reflectively. "But you know, I don't know that I'll *ever* be free of that little nagging sense. . . ."

Nevertheless, said Karen, she'd be the first to acknowledge that all the suffering they'd been through had actually had a colossal upside. For during this second course of couples' therapy they'd *both* become deeply engaged in the process; and their relationship had opened up and deepened in ways they hadn't ever thought possible. They had come to know and accept each other as the very different individuals they really were, and this had helped them feel less threatened by their differences, much more willing to come closer. In the course of time, this second courtship had resulted in the partners' decision to marry each other again. And by the time our interviews got under way, Karen had been in her "second marriage" for a little over two years. She did seem to have a buoyant air about her, and she told me that this marriage was infinitely happier and more intimate than her "first marriage" ever had been.

The Paradoxical Aftermath

The marked improvement of the Barry-Freeds' relationship in the aftermath of the affair was actually a development that's not at all uncommon. At the outset, the impact of the revelation had shattered many of the couple's long-held assumptions, jarring violently and then demolishing the framework of the marriage that had existed earlier. The damage wreaked by this psychological tornado had left in its wake a sense of desolation and emptiness—a bleak nothingness where all of the comfortable beliefs and soothing predictabilities of their long relationship had once existed.

It was in this atmosphere of disillusionment that the couple had begun confronting the scary truth that making sense of the relationship would require a degree of honesty and disclosure that hadn't existed between them before. If they were to face up to the "creeping distance" that separated them, they would have to be dangerously forthcoming—speak to each other openly about all of the frustrations, disappointments, and polite evasions that had been there *before* the marriage's eruption.

It was a slow, agonizing enterprise, yet after the fact, Karen was very clear about one thing: In the wake of the affair, her marriage to Jon was much happier and stronger. This sort of outcome is not at all uncommon, for one great paradox of infidelity is that while it has all the high-octane potential to decimate a relationship, there are many situations in which the couple's life together improves dramatically in the wake of an intimate betrayal.

Indeed, the truly *atypical* aspect of the Barry-Freeds' story was not the radical turnaround and marked improvement of their relationship. The most unusual part of their tale was the fact that they'd gone through all the wrenching agony of a divorce, and the turmoil around a family breakup, then reversed course after all the hell they'd been through. It was as if these partners had had to completely obliterate the old marriage before rolling up their sleeves and undertaking the labor of restructuring their lives together anew.

A Garbled Plea for Change

After the initial havoc of an extramarital crisis has been weathered—if it *is* weathered, and that's always a big "if"—a significant number of couples will do what the Barry-Freeds eventually did. They will construct a marriage that's much closer, more honest and mutually satisfying than it ever was beforehand (but very rarely will they have divorced in between). It's not at all exceptional for an affair's exposure to serve as a catalyst for change in a relationship that feels lifeless, stunted, and shut down.

Why should this be so? One possible explanation is that adultery often serves as a compelling form of communication—a harshly strident, attention-grabbing announcement, delivered in the language of behavior, whose content boils down to one very essential statement: "For me, this marriage isn't working."

In this "communicative" sense, the affair can be viewed as a *challenge* to the marital relationship, a garbled plea for change that has not been otherwise articulated. The Barry-Freeds' narrative can serve as a fitting example, for prior to the extramarital crisis, their way of relating to each other had been structured along the lines of a "businesslike arrangement"—one that both of them experienced as emotionally disengaged and sexually dormant.

At the Level of the Body: Keeping Score

Since denial and avoidance were the couple's main ways of managing their differences and difficulties, their sense of profound disconnection was not being acknowledged at the level of conscious awareness.

At the *level of the body*, however, defensive strategies such as denial and avoidance are not available; the body's nervous circuitry is always keeping score in terms of what is actually occurring. This is why many people experience only *in their viscera* the unthinkable messages they can't bear to receive—messages that may come to them as feelings of inner emptiness, physical deflation, isolation, abandonment, or the like. But when an individual has lapsed into a state of emotional shutdown, body-based communiqués of this sort are *not* consciously linked to the hurtful thoughts to which they might give rise. For, like Sleeping Beauty in the well-known fairy tale, the person has fallen into a form of pseudo-death; and though "alive," she remains numbed and frozen, walled off in an emotional slumber that serves to shield her from painful knowledge in a menacing environment.

It was not a kiss, but Jon's abrupt confession that had shocked the Barry-Freeds into full wakefulness. It had presented them both with an in-your-face confrontation about what had been happening—and *failing to* happen—between them. His admission had exposed the underlying truth of their marriage, which was that their intimate connection had become so tenuous over time that they were living together in an atmosphere of insincerity and estrangement.

This underscores another paradox of infidelity, which is that there's a real sense in which many extramarital affairs can be understood as a discouraged, unhappy partner's way of being *truthful* about a relationship that has actually stopped functioning beforehand. As one marital therapist told me in the course of an interview, "I've always found it curious that a partner who doesn't want to hurt his partner's feelings by telling her how disappointed and miserable he's feeling will turn around and get into an affair instead. It's a peculiar form of politeness: In the effort to avoid wounding the mate by talking with her openly, the betrayer becomes involved in something that will, when the truth emerges, strike at the very heart of her being."

The huge upheaval created by an affair's revelation, and the chaos and despair attending its painful aftershocks (finding out the identity of the other person; the length of the affair; mutual friends who've been in on the secret all along; and so forth), does pose a mortal threat to the relationship's survival. And even if the marriage endures, its innocence is gone and will not return. According to a recent survey, most psychotherapists consider extramarital affairs to be second only to physical violence in terms of the emotional damage they inflict.

Still, you can't ignore the *other* reality, which is that an extramarital crisis can and frequently does have exactly the *opposite* effect. If the initial blowup doesn't spin so completely out of control that the marriage deteriorates beyond repair, that selfsame crisis may create the conditions for mutual soul-searching, enhanced openness, and the growth of a new, deeply satisfying mutual understanding. The admittedly ambiguous truth of the matter is that while infidelity can sometimes kill a relationship, it can sometimes bring a dying relationship back to life.

Chapter Fifteen

REENACTMENTS OF THE PAST: THE BARRYS AND THE FREEDS

WHEN IT COMES TO A DILEMMA IN THE PRESENT SUCH as an extramarital affair, why bother looking backward at the partners' earlier lives in their separate families of origin? If you were to ask each member of the couple what *caused* the affair, you'd be likely to get two diametrically different answers, yet *both* partners' explanations would be fixated on whatever was going on in the here and now of the current moment.

Typically the betrayed mate would, like Karen, view the partner's lying, sexual cheating, and the other person in the triangle as the main *reasons* for the turmoil in the marriage, while the deceiving partner, like Jon, would be more likely to see the affair as the *effect* of all the disappointments and deficits in the marital relationship. Overall, the focus of attention would be upon who bore the major responsibility and on whose shoulders the burdens of shame and guilt most rightfully belonged.

Did the misery in the relationship precipitate the affair, or was the affair a consequence of the slow-burning anger and alienation someone was experiencing beforehand? In general, the partners are so caught up in the chaotic emotionality of the moment that the importance of the baggage each of them has brought to the relationship often goes unnoticed. And although in fact the affair has often been motivated by unresolved struggles rooted in one or both mates' earlier family histories, the crucial, underlying connection between the "here and now" and the "then and there" is never really explored or addressed. As a result, the couple suffers without ever making sense of what happened; and even if they do manage to stay together, nothing is learned, and nothing changes. What this amounts to is an opportunity lost, for a crisis without real learning, and ensuing change and growth, is a crisis that has been wasted.

Karen's Family: Keeping Up Appearances

As I learned in the course of sketching out the couple's multigenerational genogram, Karen Barry had grown up in Minnetonka, Minnesota, a suburb of Minneapolis. Her family had lived on a quiet cul-de-sac where all of the neighbors were good friends. And as she described it, the communal life they'd lived there was in many ways idyllic.

There were skating parties when a nearby river froze; there were wonderful, progressive New Year's Eve parties, which involved all the parents and the kids moving from house to house for each course of a long night's dinner, then ending up sleepy and ecstatic as they all counted down to midnight. There were hunting parties for the men and boys—her dad usually took her older brother, Scott—and family camping trips and cookouts in the summer. "I really felt there was this magic bubble. . . . Bad things did *not* happen to the Barry family from Minnetonka, Minnesota," Karen said.

Growing up in that world had been harmonious and pleasant—it had been nothing *but* harmonious and pleasant—yet as she now recognized, it had also been emotionally flat and highly conformist. An unstated but strictly enforced rule of the household was that keeping up appearances was of paramount importance: It didn't matter how you actually felt as long as you *looked* as though you felt all right. Thus, while the family she'd grown up in had felt secure and very sheltered, it had also felt inhibited and devitalized. "There was a low-energy, 'flat tire' kind of a feeling. At the dinner table, people passed the plates around, but no one had very much to say."

As Karen saw it, what had been missing in her family was some way to connect at an emotional level; and if she complained about something—perhaps an incident at school that had hurt her feelings or made her angry—her mother's response was always "You shouldn't feel that way."

"I wasn't *supposed* to feel that way," she said emphatically, "but I *did*. So as a little kid there was always the sense that I shouldn't be feeling what I was feeling, but I *was*. And this kept me wondering, What's wrong with *me*?" I nodded in sympathy, for this sort of emotional invalidation can make a person feel that her normal emotions are really *bad*. Then she observed that the main unwritten rule of her family had been "Don't stick out; don't be different from anyone else." "It was never anything like 'You're great' or 'You're special.'"

It wasn't that she'd felt unloved as a child, Karen hastened to say, but there had been no interest whatsoever in what was going on *inside* her—in her feelings, her thoughts, on who she *was* as a growing human being. She had simply been expected to go along with the family program—follow the rules, do well, get good grades—but never behave in ways that would make her stand out too much or command an excess of attention. And she *had* done what was expected of her, always, as long as she could remember.

Jon's Family: A Novel, More Vivid World

Meeting Jon's family, shortly after they'd begun going out with each other, had come as a revelation to Karen; she'd found herself entranced by all of them. Like Dorothy leaving Kansas and finding herself in Oz, she'd had the sense of a black-and-white existence suddenly becoming radiant with color and emotionality. For life among the Freeds was so different from the family life she had known: Everyone was lively and challenging; people leapt into the ongoing conversations, bantered with one another, talked easily and openly about their feelings.

It was wonderful, but it made Karen edgy, too, for she'd felt disconnected from so many of her own feelings and emotions at the time. She told me this with a bemused smile, as if recalling what a prim, constrained, wide-eyed girl from the Midwest she had been.

Since Jon's background was Jewish and his parents were observant, I asked Karen whether there had been any objections to their interfaith romance from either hers, his, or from both sets of parents. She shook her head and said there had been none from her side and none from Jon's father, either. "His dad was—well—such a genuinely *loving* human being." Her father-in-law, now deceased, had been a man with a truly generous heart, someone who was always building everyone up in the most affectionate way, making people feel good about themselves.

"With Jon's mother, it was different—her love was more conditional." Karen's expression clouded over. She said she now knew—but hadn't suspected at the time—that her mother-in-law, Anita, had been vehemently opposed to her son's choice and had been doing everything she could to prevent the relationship from getting too serious. "I myself, with my innocent, fresh little Minnetonka Girl Scout persona, had no idea that these monumental tidal waves were being churned up. . . ." True to her own family's tradition, she had been "clueless" when it came to being aware of anything distressing or unpleasant going on beneath the surface.

The Freed Legend: "We're the Greatest"

In terms of family style, Karen Barry's family had been benign but bland and disengaged, while Jon Freed's family was warm, demonstrative, lots of fun to be with, and highly overinvolved. I had the notion that a significant part of the couple's initial attraction had stemmed from Jon's capacity to offer Karen a taste of intense emotionality and her capacity to offer him some degree of autonomy and space.

But Jon's doting, overinvested parents hadn't found it easy to see him marry and move off into a life of his own. Even after the pair were married and living in a place of their own, Jon's parents would arrive for dinner bringing his favorite meat from the kosher butcher. His energetic, overzealous mother would then make her son hamburgers in special little presses, carefully explaining to the young bride that this was the way her new husband liked them best.

"Jon was their golden child, their only son; he could do no wrong." His older sister, Sandy, now complained that as the older child in the family, she'd had all the rules and the "No, you can't!" responses, while her brother got away with everything. "Jon just charmed everyone around him," Karen said.

"So he was Prince Jon?" I asked with a smile.

She laughed. "He was Prince Jon, he was *definitely* Prince Jon! And if we came to his folks' house for dinner, and he didn't like what they were serving, his mother would make him a special meal of his own."

I laughed, too, then asked Karen, "If you were going to call your husband 'Prince Jon,' what would you call his sister, Sandy?"

"His sister was definitely not a princess, so I don't know. . . . I might call her 'Cinderella,'" Karen replied. I asked her how well Sandy and their dynamo of a mother had gotten along.

Karen hesitated for a moment, then explained that in the Freed family there was never any question of *not* getting along. There were rules or ways of being, and everyone was supposed to abide by them. The most important rule was that you weren't to go against Mommy and Daddy. "The basic idea was that 'This is how we raise kids, and this is how we're expecting you to behave.'"

Unlike her own original family, for whom a major concern had been appearances—what the neighbors might think of them—Jon's family had required only *internal* loyalty, and the youngsters could deal with the outside world as they chose. "I think Jon got a very different message from the one I got. His was 'Push the envelope'; 'Bend the rules'; 'You're a Freed'; 'the Freed legend'; 'You do what you want.'"

I raised an eyebrow, smiled, and asked, "And what exactly is the Freed legend?"

"It's 'We're the greatest'; 'We don't need anybody but us'; 'We're terrific people'; and 'If you're in my family, I want you, and if you're not in my family, I don't really want to deal with you. I may not even want to sit *next* to you, because I like my family as it is!'" She was smiling, too, but at the same time rolling her eyes and shaking her head ruefully.

"So I should think it's a hard family to get into?" I asked, thinking of a young midwestern Protestant trying to find her place in this tight-knit Jewish family who lived in the affluent Boston suburb of Newton, Massachusetts.

"No kidding!" said Karen, and we both started laughing. But I was thinking that while the Freed family was probably not only hard to get into, it sounded equally difficult to leave.

Karen, Jon, and Echoes of the Past:
The Good Girl and the Renegade

The curious reemergence of old family scripts in a new generation is a somewhat mystical, if thoroughly commonplace, occurrence. As my interviews with Karen Barry-Freed proceeded, I continued filling in more of the informational dots and connecting lines in an effort to look at the Barry-Freeds' marital crisis in its more extended, familial context.

Karen was, like Jon, the younger of the two children in her family. She was also the favored child, the one who made her parents feel good about themselves: She could be relied on to do everything that was expected of a nice, *nice* girl and not behave in ways that would make her stand out unduly or command an excess amount of attention. But if she was the family's good girl, her older brother, Scott, was the renegade, the outsider.

There had been a six-year difference between herself and Scott, so Karen felt that she'd never really known him well. He'd been married by the time she went away to college, and she'd gone *far* away—to a university on the East Coast. "Anyhow, Scott was always kind of a loner, a different kind of kid. A *very* different kind of kid. He really *did* push the envelope, in all sorts of ways," said Karen in a flat, unemotional voice, as if she were chatting about a stranger.

I had an odd sense that she was tiptoeing around a subject she didn't want to talk about. But eventually she said, as if in defense of Scott, that her brother hadn't been involved in anything that was outright *illegal*; he'd just loved cars and motorcycles. He could fix anything on wheels, and as a teenager, he'd always had some hot rods that he was upgrading. "He could transform old roadsters, and they were *beautiful*," said Karen. Her words were upbeat, but there was a growing edge in her voice, and her facial muscles had stiffened.

I wasn't sure what was happening, so I glanced down at the sketch pad on my lap, eyes seeking the square box in her family's genogram inside which I'd written the name "Scott." Then I looked up again and asked Karen where her brother was now. Was he married, and did he have children? What did he do for a living?

But she'd begun to shake her head in the negative as soon as I began asking these questions, and finally she raised her right arm, palm facing outward, in the universal gesture that signifies "Halt there." "My brother is dead," she said flatly.

"Dead?" I stared at her. "How old was he?"

He had died at thirty-four, she answered, eyes wide and unblinking. My gaze fixed upon her face, I asked her what he'd died of, expecting to hear the word *cancer* or to hear about some other illness. But Karen told me that he had been murdered. "*Murdered?*" I repeated disbelievingly.

She nodded, said, "Yes," in the same dispassionate, almost reportorial tone of voice. Then she went on to say that her brother had dropped out of college after one year because of a shotgun-type marriage; he had definitely *not* wanted to marry the girl he'd gotten pregnant, but intense pressure from both sets of parents had forced him to do so. This teenage marriage had produced one child, a son, but had ended in divorce five miserable years later. After that, Scott had drifted from one unsuccessful job to another and finally gotten into some sort of trouble—she wasn't sure *what* kind of trouble—in the drug scene. He'd begun using various drugs himself, mostly cocaine, she believed, but the whole story was still murky in her own mind.

She still didn't know whether Scott had actually been *selling* drugs or whether he'd had a lot of cocaine in his possession, Karen told me. All she knew for sure was that her brother had been arrested at one point, then agreed to cooperate with the police in lieu of serving jail time. Had he been killed because he was slated to testify in an upcoming drug trial, which was going to court a few weeks hence? Or had it happened because he'd owed a lot of money to someone?

Karen shook her head, said with a small, helpless shrug of her shoulders that all her speculations had remained just that—speculations. By that time, she herself had been long gone from Minnetonka. She was married, the mother of her first child, and living in the Greater Boston area; and everything in her brother's life had been happening at a great distance. The family *did* know that Scott had been beaten and tortured before being shot in the head three times, execution style, she added, her tone of voice remaining even and controlled. But her brother's killers hadn't ever been found, and the case remained unresolved.

I must have looked puzzled by the dispassionate way in which she was relating this awful story, for Karen leaned forward, as if to meet my gaze more fully. "Most of the pain I felt at the time was for my poor, mild, inoffensive, good-hearted parents," she said. "The police called my dad at three in the morning to come down and identify the body. . . . I can't even *imagine*, as a parent, having to do anything like that." She shuddered.

I couldn't imagine it, either. And what seemed especially incongruous was how little this startling tale of torture and murder seemed to tally with that "magic bubble" she'd described—life on the pleasant, family-oriented cul-de-sac in Minnetonka, Minnesota. What malevolent trajectory had carried her brother from his close-knit, suburban upbringing to a "loner and outsider" sense of self, and then to a shotgun marriage, an interrupted education, a divorce, and a series of failed efforts to find some sort of suitable occupation? How had a boy from this quintessentially "nice" midwestern family fallen into the life of a drifter, a druggie, and ultimately a victim of murder?

I asked Karen what she could remember about her own reactions on first hearing this catastrophic news, and she grew silent, stared at me without replying for a few moments. Then she said, in the hushed voice of someone telling a ghost story, that she'd felt "eerie," "surreal"—as if everything around her, and she herself, were both real and unreal simultaneously. She'd had the weird sense that the news she was hearing couldn't *possibly* be true—yet knowing that it *was* true—even though it felt as if it were happening to someone who was living on an alternative planet.

"Also, what I remember *vividly* was the feeling of time having slowed down. . . . Then, on my way to the airport, I had the strange feeling that the people passing me on the street were receding, floating, like figures seen in a film in slow motion," she said. She'd felt at a remove from everything that was happening around her, like an actress playing in a scene of daily life that she herself was watching.

This kind of reaction is associated with the "numbing" response to traumatic threat, which is one of those three instantaneous bodily reactions—fighting, fleeing, or freezing—to situations of immediate danger. Of course, we don't *choose* among these response options after weighing each of them carefully. Our brains and bodies simply assess the circumstances in an instantaneous, decision-making flash, and they react. Karen's response had been to freeze—to shut down, zone out, and feel emotionally distanced from what was happening. This was her means of protecting herself from experiencing the full shock and pain of the family's loss—its sense of shame as well, for "bad things did not happen to the Barry family of Minnetonka, Minnesota."

"You know, my parents weren't strict, but they did put great stock in *obeying the rules*. That was their mantra," Karen said. "The most horrible thing we kids could ever do was somehow bring embarrassment to the family, through some kind of bad behavior. And I really *heard* their message and I said, 'Okay'; but my brother heard it and he said, 'Forget it.'"

"So Scott's position was that if there was a rule around, he'd bend it or break it?" I asked, and she nodded.

"Exactly," she said disapprovingly, "and it's interesting, because my husband's exactly the same way. And Jon has a low trigger point for anger, as Scott did, too."

I hesitated, my attention caught by this comment. For when Karen mentioned those basic similarities between Scott and the man she'd chosen as her life partner, I couldn't help but notice that an old family theme—one involving the polarized roles of "the good, well-behaved female" and "the difficult, unruly male"—had suddenly materialized in her current-day existence. And it occurred to me that there might have been a bit of a replay going on here—a newly updated, modernized version of an old family scenario involving a conscientious, rule-abiding girl and a restless, rule-bending renegade.

At a surface level, Scott Barry and Jon Freed would seem to have had very little in common. And yet Karen spoke of them both (not only in this, but in subsequent interviews) in similar terms as individuals who had "certain issues with authority," a tendency to "bend the rules" and to "operate outside the box." Had it been a certain recognition that her husband, like Scott, would always live by his *own* rules, that had been a subliminal part of the attraction when she'd first met him?

Repetitive Patterns of Relationship: The Way It Felt Inside

As therapists and theorists Christopher and Lily Pincus have written in *Secrets in the Family*, "We all have a tendency to get into repetitive patterns of relationship that are motivated by wishes in unconscious fantasy form and derived from the way earlier needs were satisfied." In simpler terms, we are drawn toward certain kinds of interactions because they conform to the internal blueprint for being in relationships that each of us begins to develop early in our lives. These are the relationships that feel *right*, because they are the ones with which we are deeply familiar. They have about them a sense of deep recognition, of coming home; it's as if our minds and bodies *know* that we've arrived in a place where we belong and where we're clear about how we're supposed to behave. Just as a woman who's been raised in a violent household *knows* what life is like in a violence-prone relationship, Karen Barry *knew* some things about what life would be like in a relationship with a partner who operated "outside the box" and who had "certain issues with authority."

This brings me to a point well worth noting, which is that there are many instances in which an attachment will feel *right* to us—because it is so *familiar*—but it will not necessarily feel *comfortable*. In many instances, the attachment will feel anything *but* comfortable; but even so, it's a *familiar discomfort*, one that reconnects us not only to "the way it was" but to "the way it felt inside," in terms of our body's well-remembered feelings and sensations. For the old, familiar relationship patterns—the ones that hark back to our earliest experiences in the world—are accompanied by familiar internal states of being.

And in this way they serve to bring us "home," to link us to aspects of the past in subterranean ways of which we're often not consciously aware. Thus, while Karen might have had her issues and grievances about a relational scenario involving an even-tempered, rule-abiding Girl Scout and an overentitled, restless, quick-to-anger, rule-bending male, there was a certain sense in which she'd resurrected in her current life a female-male relationship that she already knew a great deal about, one with which she was deeply familiar.

Jon's Parents: A Royal Match

As Karen saw them, both her in-laws were fundamentally good, caring, affectionate people. However, it was true that in terms of guiding and disciplining their children, they'd divided their parental roles into that of the bad cop and the good cop. Jon's mother, Anita, was seen as the more difficult one; she could be demanding, controlling, at times impossible to please. His father, Stan, had always been the softy—the far more nonjudgmental, generous, gregarious member of the pair.

"My father-in-law was a man who was just *bigger than life,*" Karen said warmly, earnestly. "He was universally loved by everyone who knew him, and *his* love was unconditional. He would always know how to smooth out his wife's ruffled feathers—settle any difficulties between her and the kids. And as far as his one and only son was concerned—well, Jon could do no wrong." But then she frowned and, almost as an afterthought, said dryly that Jon's father could at times be "inappropriate," too.

"How so?" I asked.

She paused, then told me that even to this day—so many years after the event—the peculiar way in which she and Jon had become engaged was something she didn't understand. Why had Jon's father, rather than Jon himself, been the man who'd actually proposed to her?

That proposal had come simply out of the blue, one afternoon when she'd been asked to go out for a friendly lunch with her steady boyfriend's dad. It was during this repast that Stan Freed had suddenly put his silverware down upon the table with the air of someone who's made a decision. Then he'd looked directly into Karen's eyes and asked her if she really loved his son.

"Can you *imagine,* coming from Minnetonka, where we don't talk about feelings at *all*? To have this person ask you straight out, 'Do you really love my son?'" Karen's eyes widened, and she giggled uneasily, as if the memory made her squirm even now.

"I didn't know what to say, so I just blurted out, 'Well, yes, I think I do.' And then his dad said very enthusiastically that he thought Jon loved me, too, and that our feelings for each other were pretty strong, and *he* believed the two of us would be great for each other! 'So you have to join the family,' he told me. That's how he put it—'You have to join us.'"

"That's odd," I said, thinking that it sounded more like a proposed adoption than it did a proposal of marriage.

"It *is* odd." Karen nodded and, as if anticipating my next comment, responded by saying, "Yes, of *course* it was Jon's job to do the proposing, not his dad's."

Emotional Triangles

Most adult sons would have been *furious* in a similar sort of situation, I reflected. "Talk about being overinvolved," I said aloud. And it occurred to me that Jon and his father might have been in some sort of political collusion to override the heated objections of his "demanding, controlling" mother, who didn't want him marrying out of the faith. If this were so, then Stan's proposal, made "on behalf of the family," would have halted all dissent immediately. It would also serve as a prime example of what family therapists call a "perverse triangle"—that is, a hidden alliance between two members of different generations (in this case, father and son) against a third party (here, the mother, who'd had no prior knowledge of the plan).

Emotional triangles—that is, two-against-one coalitions—are an inherent aspect of family life. Generally speaking, these alliances emerge and then fade away as the problematic issues that spawned them are resolved. As new concerns arise, the involved players may then occupy radically differing positions—someone who was an insider in the last triangle may be temporarily out in the cold. Transient triangles are an aspect of many family and other close relationships—for example, two siblings who are gossiping unkindly about a third sibling are teaming up as the "insiders" in a triangle, while the object of their discussion occupies the triangle's outside leg.

Thus, triangles come, and triangles go, and they usually present no enduring family problems—*except* in those situations where they take on a fixed, enduring quality. Unchanging, rigid triangles have a way of keeping everyone in the group "stuck" on old dilemmas that are no longer relevant in the present, and the triangle involving a parent and child against the other parent is a truly classic one. In the Freed family, Anita was often in the bad cop, outsider position.

As for Stan, it seemed to me that there were many ways in which this loving, gregarious, benevolent father could be pretty controlling, too. Although his way of handling matters was much more genial and velvety than his wife's, Jon's dad was very much the social engineer: He'd put it to his son's prospective bride that in order to marry Jon, she had to "join the family." In his amiable, affectionate way, Stan had taken charge and was shaping the course of events.

Come to think of it, Karen had characterized her husband's role in his family as that of a golden prince—"Prince Jon." And who is a prince but the offspring of a king and a queen? Traditionally, in royal households, the matches were always made by the parents, not the children; it was they who would carefully select a mate deemed suitable for inclusion in the royal family. In this instance, Karen Barry was not the ideal consort Jon's mother had in mind. Yet—despite the evident differences between the lovers—her prospective father-in-law was informing her that he was championing this match and graciously permitting it to go forward. As reigning monarch of the family, Jon's father was also letting her know that she would have to join the ranks of the younger generation of this family—in some symbolic but very important sense become one of the Freed family offspring.

A Time of High Anxiety: The King's Mistress

A mere six weeks before what Karen always referred to as her "first marriage," a sudden catastrophe had sent her husband-to-be's entire family spinning. Jon's father, who'd seemed so healthy, vital, and fit, suffered a first but very serious heart attack—one so severe that it compelled Stan Freed's retirement at the impossibly young age of fifty-five. "Obviously it was traumatic for everyone," Karen said quietly. And naturally there had been much discussion about whether or not the wedding should be called off; and if so, for how long?

The ultimate decision had been that the ceremony itself would go forward, but that all the surrounding festivities, including the reception afterward, would be canceled. Stan's doctors thought that even a small party might create too much emotional strain for their patient. And then there were other, more sub-rosa reasons for the anxiety and apprehension coursing through the Freed family system. The story being circulated was that Jon's dad had been on the golf course at the time he was stricken, but in actuality he'd been with another woman when it happened.

Here, I think it worth mentioning that research has shown that men are more prone to suffer heart attacks during sex if they're having sex with someone *other* than the customary partner; they very *rarely* have heart attacks if they're having sex at home. This sort of statistic leaves you wondering if this has to do with much higher levels of sexual excitement or with the tremendous intensity fueled by secrecy and the thrill of the forbidden. It may just have to do with performance anxiety or with plain old-fashioned guilt—guilt that could be related either to the fear of discovery or to strong feelings about violating one's own strongly held code of ethics.

In Stan Freed's situation, any of these explanations could have been on target; but it did seem to me that the looming marriage of his beloved son was probably as relevant as any of them. For Jon and his parents—and most particularly his father—were extremely close, and it sounded as if this "princely" offspring was serving as the repository and container of his family's dearest hopes, dreams, and expectations. He, in turn, was receiving daily supplies of support and affirmation from the older generation—an image of himself as a superior being, heir to the family legend.

Key Family Transitions, and Affairs

As mentioned earlier, many extramarital involvements get under way around key family passages, even joyous ones such as a wedding or the birth of a child. These are times when the emotional system must undergo a profound, earth-moving shift, and certain individuals are likely to be experiencing not only happy feelings but painful feelings, of loss and abandonment. In Jon's father's case, that extramarital affair—seemingly disconnected from the young couple's imminent marriage—might have been the older man's way of seeking solace for the pending departure of his son.

For this was a defining moment in the life of the family: The Freeds' "golden" son and last unmarried offspring (their daughter, Sandy, was already married and living in upstate New York) was moving off into his own adult existence. The family baton was being handed along, and somehow I had the idea that this benignly controlling and directing father—who was such a *presence* in the life of everyone around him—might have been feeling as if part of his own inner self were being wrenched away in the process.

Wall-to-Wall Avoidance and Denial: A Bargain with the Devil

How had the facts of Stan's whereabouts at the time of his collapse become known? Karen herself wasn't sure. Her understanding was that the few facts that were known about Jon's dad's extramarital relationship had come through his sister, Sandy. "I'm not clear on many of the particulars, but somehow Sandy *knew*. . . . Also, when Jon's father came home from the hospital, the woman he'd been involved with—she was a legal consultant working with the company—kept calling the house frantically for news of his condition."

As his colleague, the woman *did* have a pretext to call, because they had a professional relationship. But she would often phone around dinnertime and ask frantically, "How is Stan? How is Stan?" "I think it freaked Jon's mother," Karen said. "She'd ask, 'Why is that woman *calling* here all the time?' And of course nobody answered. We'd all just look down at our plates and then the subject would get changed."

Had Anita Freed ever learned the truth, or hadn't she? According to Karen, this was a question that nobody in the family could answer to this day. All of the specific details surrounding the event—how had Stan gotten to the hospital? who had called his wife?—were hazy in everyone's mind, and the subject of the other woman had been whisked out of sight almost immediately. There had been an initial flurry of discussions between Jon and Sandy, but then this hot-potato topic was dropped, and their mother never, ever broached the subject with either one of her children.

In the wake of Stan's dangerous heart attack, it felt natural for the family to focus their attention upon his symptoms and state of health, while avoiding all allusions to the circumstances in which the emergency had occurred. And within a period of weeks, the phone calls from the other woman had ceased, so the family circle's cardinal mythology—"We're the greatest: We're the most loving, mutually cherishing couple with the brightest, most devoted offspring"—was never openly questioned or challenged. There were never any fierce quarrels, agonizingly candid discussions, expressions of remorse or conflict resolution endeavors of any kind—at least none that Karen knew about. On the surface, the Freeds' family relations seemed to be as unruffled and harmonious as ever.

The crisis had been "settled" by being met with wall-to-wall avoidance and denial. But alas, one of the side effects of a shutdown of this sort is that while it protects the people in the family from experiencing their bad, painful feelings, it also shuts off many of their good, spontaneously happy feelings. The Freeds had, in effect, made a bargain with the Devil, for the need to censor certain topics made it impossible for them to be fully *present*, in touch with what was happening inside themselves in terms of their true thoughts and emotional reactions.

And all the while, the unresolved dilemma remained, for when major issues of this sort are buried in this fashion, they inevitably begin to release pernicious toxins. The sharp disjunction between the family's newly revealed reality and the treasured Freed legend had in fact turned the system on its axis. And no matter how strenuously the truth of the situation was being disavowed, their central vision of themselves—"We're the best, we're the greatest"—had been seriously undermined.

Family "Solutions": Extramarital Affairs

As Bessel van der Kolk has written, severely stressful experiences "can alter people's psychological, biological and social equilibrium to such a degree that the memory of one particular event comes to taint all other experiences, spoiling appreciation of the present." In such instances, the awful memory remains front and center and doesn't permit normal life to continue. In other instances, though, old, heart-stopping experiences can *appear* to be completely forgotten, then be revived and acted out in "real time" without being recognized as thinly disguised repeat performances of actual past events.

Such resurrections of old scenarios, which are not knowingly linked to things that *did* happen, are like strange artifacts or fossil remains of familial history that have suddenly emerged at the surface. When this kind of reenactment takes place, the painful memory is not only being revived in terms of the traumatized person's *behavior*, it is also being reexperienced at an emotional, physiological, and neurohormonal level. All of the suppressed feelings and sensations associated with the original event spring into being, and they *feel* as potent and present tense as ever. For our bodies hold the archival history of everything that has happened to us, including experiences that may seem to be lost in the past and long forgotten.

In the period following Stan Freed's almost fatal heart attack, his health began to improve and his strength to return more rapidly than anyone had expected. And within a few short years, the family's life appeared to be as warm, close, and enjoyable as it had ever been. Jon and Karen had two children, and Jon's sister, Sandy, married to a pediatric surgeon, was the mother of two sons.

But all was not as benign as it appeared to be, for themes of the family's past were beginning to spill into the present. Sandy had become immensely attracted to a fellow member of the choral group with which she frequently rehearsed and sang. The man in question (Dennis) was divorced and was certainly *not* the sort of person who could be guaranteed to meet with her parents' approval: He was a high school sports coach, easygoing, Protestant, comfortable with himself, and unambitious. Over time, Sandy and Dennis had gotten into a deep, confiding friendship, and although they hadn't become involved in a sexual affair, she knew she was in love with him and that her feelings were returned.

Sandy felt blessed, for Dennis was attentive, friendly, warm, appreciative, loving—everything her husband was not, for her marriage (like her brother's) had grown increasingly distant over the years. Still, despite the fact that she was being loyal to her vows, in the technical sense, she felt guilty and conscience-stricken; she knew that she *was* being unfaithful emotionally.

At last, feeling suffocated in a situation that was filled with lies and evasions, she'd decided to bring the matter into the open. But she'd been astonished by her husband's reaction, for he'd greeted this confession with a chilling air of calmness. In his most composed, medical fashion, he heard her anguished story out and then, seemingly untouched, told her that given the circumstances, it was his belief that an amicable divorce would be their best option. (Much later, she discovered that he'd been involved in an affair of his own at the time.) So despite the outraged, scandalized protests of her parents—for divorce had no place in the Freed legend—Sandy's marriage to the archetypical successful, professional Jewish husband ended right there. Within months, the elder Freeds had a new son-in-law—Dennis—a son-in-law who had no place in the legend and would never meet with their unequivocal acceptance.

Do You Feel You Can Trust Him?

Thinking in terms of romantic triangles, past and present, this forbidden love of Sandy's did bear some resemblance to that love affair of her dad's that had ended with such abruptness some four years earlier. For as Sandy had once confided to Karen, she believed her father's extramarital relationship had been deeply significant to him—by no means a casual fling but, rather, a true affair of the heart. Thus, there was a sense in which she might have been acting as his unconscious delegate, on a mission to bring that interrupted, extramarital romance to its ultimate, satisfying conclusion.

In any event, Sandy's recapitulation of her adored father's "secret" narrative was already part of the family's never discussed story, one that had been assimilated into their basic script. For this event had not only stated a theme—specifically, the problem of how you deal with "creeping distance" and disillusionment in an intimate relationship—but provided a model for the way in which the problem could be resolved. If you're feeling discouraged and alienated from your disappointing partner, you don't confront the difficulties directly; you slip quietly off to a place where he or she can no longer affect you—that is, you become involved in an emotional triangle.

Stan could humor his wife when she was being a difficult, controlling bad cop, but he never did defy her directly. Instead, he kept the myth of the perfectly harmonious family intact and moved off to engage his true self elsewhere. Clearly, this was a pattern of managing the inevitable tensions and disaffections of married life that was to have an impact on the lives of *both* his adult children eventually. And who could say whether or not it had existed in previous generations? Perhaps the real origins of this "solution" stretched further back than anyone knew, and there had been secret or semisecret extramarital liaisons in the family in which Stan himself had grown up. As anyone who works with genograms will tell you, when a problematic issue—be it infidelity, depression, alcohol addiction, eating disorders, or illegitimacy—appears on one branch of the family tree, it is more than likely to pop up in other places as well.

Thus, I couldn't help but wonder whether Karen felt that this, her second marriage, was now truly betrayal-proof or whether she had some lingering concern that this pattern of dealing with marital tensions—emotional distancing that could at any moment metamorphose into sexual disloyalty—might recur at some later point in time. "Do you feel you can trust Jon?" I asked her directly as our last interview was drawing to a close.

"Oh yes," she said swiftly, automatically, "I *do*. I—" But she stopped herself in midsentence, began tracing two fingers along the hairs of her right eyebrow, as if to smooth out her own honest thinking on this topic. Then she shifted in her chair and leaned toward me with a mischievous expression, as if to share a particularly juicy bit of confidential information.

Premarital Negotiations

Karen smiled broadly and explained that when Jon had been pressing her to marry him again, she'd come up with the idea of a prenuptial agreement. He had been unhappy about this idea and said that it was painful to him, like having a separation agreement written in advance—a routine they'd been through already. Karen viewed the process differently, said that in her opinion it had been "very collaborative" and they'd been able to compromise.

Then she laughed. "Of course, if Jon were here, he'd say, 'Are you *kidding*? She got everything!' And it's true. Should we ever separate, I get practically everything we own." Karen said that she had made that happen—that every time her lawyer had come up with yet another proposal, Jon would groan and say, "I can't believe I have to look at this again! I can't *believe* I have to fork out all this money to these two attorneys to work out a separation agreement from a woman I love and want to marry in a few months!"

Ultimately, though, he'd agreed to everything; and later on his attorney had said to Karen, "He really wanted to marry you, because you got just everything; it's ironclad."

"What that entire process really did was to empower me, to let me know that I would always have a voice in this marriage," said Karen, sitting up erectly in her seat. She took in a deep breath, and as her chest expanded she seemed to grow in authority. But then she halted suddenly and looked at me questioningly. "I suppose this might sound very negative to you?"

"No, quite the contrary," I replied.

In this second marriage, an altered power situation had been established. At the time of the remarriage, Jon had been the one pressing to remarry and Karen had been the one resisting, so the reins were in her hand. This prenuptial agreement was her insurance against ever finding herself in the same one-down position she'd found herself in before. It was wise, and it was also clear that she herself had grown and changed greatly over the course of this long crisis. She was no longer living in the fictional "bubble" of her girlhood; she was a grown woman who was aware that life was complex and that bad, unexpected things could happen.

I did, however, notice that the question of whether she now trusted her husband—trusted him instinctively, *in her gut*—hadn't actually been answered. She sounded as if her reasons for trusting him were along the lines of the logical and rational—as if they were coming more from her head than from her innards. Karen must have recognized this, too, for she drew in a deep breath, then let it out with a sigh. "I will give you my very abbreviated take on this," she said. "I think we started with two people who were confused about what a real relationship was. I was frightened. Jon was asking himself, Who am I? Is this all there is to my life? Now we've been divorced and had other experiences. I found myself as a sexual, desirable person, which I wasn't in my marriage—there was too much suppressed anger on my part, because Jon was too intimidating, too demanding, too quick to anger. . . . I think I simply went into a shutdown."

She paused momentarily, then went on to say that these days she viewed her first marriage to Jon as a disaster and this second marriage to the same man to be pretty wonderful in many unexpected ways. A faint blush appeared on her face, turning her complexion pink, as she explained earnestly that of course they'd both done a lot of changing and were now very different people. I couldn't help but smile, for her skin had turned rosy and she looked like a bride at that moment.

It seemed to me that she'd put the whole traumatic episode behind her and that her outlook for the future was optimistic—especially since this time around it had been her husband, not his father, who'd done the proposing himself. However, as a trigger of memory was to reveal much later on in time, she was still *holding the experience in her body* without any conscious realization that this was the case.

Chapter Sixteen

—

A TRUSTING MIND, A WARY BODY: KAREN

THAT POWERFUL FIRST EXPERIENCE WITH EMDR HAD LEFT me feeling strangely light-headed, as though I'd been free-associating on fast forward. Not only had I accessed a "forgotten" event that was subtly omnipresent in my ways of being, thinking, and behaving, I'd also managed to evoke the thoughts, emotions, and physical sensations associated with that event in the immediacy of the present tense. Then somehow, in the course of that single ninety-minute session, a marked inner shift—one that left me feeling much more positive and entitled—had taken place. Still, I was far from clear about what had happened. The process had moved along with baffling swiftness, almost *too* swiftly, as if some sleight of hand were involved.

Did this tally with ordinary common sense? We know that the reverse often happens: Traumatic experiences can produce profound effects upon the brain's synaptic pathways in the space of an eyeblink—effects that may persist for years as isolated stress symptoms or emerge as full-blown post-traumatic stress disorder. But could the neural consequences that so often emerge in the wake of malignant events be ameliorated or undone by so simple, if not to say simplistic, a process? How did reprocessing work? What was its underlying mechanism of action?

Despite a large and steadily growing research literature on EMDR—which has been studied more extensively than any other psychological approach to the treatment of traumatic experience—therapists worldwide make liberal use of the method without knowing how its effects are brought about. EMDR has, for example, been recommended by Israel's National Council for Mental Health as one of the three best methods of treating the aftermath of trauma. EMDR has also been cited by Northern Ireland's Clinical Resource Efficiency Support Team as one of the two most effective trauma treatments—and, lamentably, in both Israel and Northern Ireland, there have been ample opportunities to test the various therapies.

Of course, using a treatment method before understanding it completely is not particularly unheard of: Many kinds of *biological* medications have become widely utilized before their mode of operation was deciphered. For instance, penicillin was made available for four decades before scientists could figure out how it worked; and researchers still can't explain, in a definitive fashion, the healing effects of most antidepressants.

So not surprisingly, many clinicians find it acceptable to live with the lack of certainty about just why reprocessing often yields such rapid and dramatic results . . . and the movement continues to gain adherents. Currently there are some forty thousand therapists, working in seventy countries around the world, who have received training in the use of the EMDR protocol. And while they don't truly comprehend the strange alchemy that can transform a malignant memory into one that is bad but *integrated into the self and part of the past*, it seems clear that the so-called neutralizing of highly disturbing memories lies at the heart of the curative process.

This brings me back to an earlier discussion, one having to do with the subject of memory retention at its most basic, which is to say molecular, level (see chapter 3). Due to the tremendous advances in our understanding of human memory functioning, we now know that each and every memory consists of a circuit of nerve cells that are related in such a way that when one member cell fires, the others will fire in synchrony. All of our thoughts, sensory perceptions, ideas, preoccupations, reveries, and so forth consist of such *specific* patterns of neuronal associations. Thus, one nerve cell network may correspond to the experience of a note of music, while another relates to the taste of chocolate, while still other patterns of neural wiring correspond to feelings of anger or of fear.

By and large, memories form when a certain stimulus pattern is repeated frequently. For we don't have to be gazing at a cup of coffee to summon up a sense of "coffee cup–ness"—an image of a cup's shape, and perhaps the steam rising from it, springs readily to mind, as does perhaps a sense of anticipation and pleasure. We hold the patterned information corresponding to "coffee cup" inside our heads, and any cell within its corresponding network of near and distant neuronal associations can light up the entire circuit—a momentary whiff of the fresh brew or merely driving past a Starbucks café are among the profuse number of possibilities.

"Neurons fire in synchrony by setting each other off like particles in a trail of gunpowder," writes British author Rita Carter. ". . . The faster a neuron fires, the greater the electrical charge it punches out and the more likely it is to set off its neighbor. Once the neighbor has been triggered to fire, a chemical change takes place on its surface which leaves it more sensitive to stimulation from that neighbor. . . . Eventually, repeated synchronous firing binds neurons together so that the slightest activity in one will trigger all those that have become associated with it to fire, too."

Thus, it is by means of rote and repetition that many of the memories we've retained within our highly convoluted brains have been created. Yet, as noted earlier, there do exist certain circumstances—those fraught with fierce emotionality—under which *no* such reruns of an initial stimulus are required. Abiding memories form rapidly and at times indelibly in situations that are charged with significance in terms of a person's present or future well-being or survival. A sexual assault while out jogging; the news of a terrifying diagnosis; the sudden impact of a nearby explosion; a natural catastrophe such as an earthquake or flood: All are events that need not happen twice for someone to be deeply affected for years or in some cases for a lifetime.

An important caveat here is that an event clearly qualifying as traumatic—one that involves looking death in the face—will by no means necessarily produce a post-traumatic stress disorder in everyone. As mentioned previously, there is a widely held belief that severe symptoms such as persistent agitation, intrusive thoughts, nightmares, flashbacks, and/or the compulsion to replay the overwhelming experience in some disguised form will be sure to emerge in the wake of such an experience. But the research on trauma tells us otherwise: Only a subset of those exposed to overwhelming experiences (somewhere between 15 and 20 percent) will go on to develop full-blown PTSD.

This is but one among the many confusing qualifiers that make diagnosing trauma, and recognizing its aftereffects, so slippery a proposition. For as EMDR originator Francine Shapiro has pointed out, many experiences that don't seem to rise to the level of "traumatic" in the formal objective sense can hit a person *hard*, subjectively speaking. For instance, a mate's ability to function in her job and in her life may become profoundly disrupted on learning of the partner's betrayal, even though she doesn't perceive herself to be in physical danger. Moreover, the person may be not only responding to experiences happening in real time, but plugging into more distant associations having to do with old, unresolved losses and fears relating to emotional abandonment.

"The truth is that most things that bring someone into a clinician's office are not at the level of major trauma," psychologist Shapiro told me, echoing the observations of Bessel van der Kolk and other specialists in the field. "What motivates most people to seek treatment is typically rooted in *memories* based on earlier life experiences."

As Shapiro sees it, little-t trauma emanates from some of the less dramatic but nevertheless profoundly disturbing occurrences that daily existence sends our way. Nevertheless, she observes, such upsetting, often thoroughly unintegrated experiences can result in some of the same feelings as big-T trauma and have similarly far-reaching consequences in terms of symptomatic aftereffects—most particularly, harshly negative attitudes about the self.

Those life situations that have left a person feeling powerless, humiliated, mocked, abandoned, unable to cope, and so forth frequently leave a residue of self-denigrating beliefs, such as "I'm not good enough," "I'm not lovable," "I'm unattractive," "I'm stupid," "I'm out of control," "I'm a loser," "I'm incompetent," "I can't handle things," and the like. Shapiro maintains that it is these kinds of self-attacking, sometimes crippling belief systems—and the cruel memories that spawned them—that can be readdressed and "detoxified" effectively with the judicious use of her carefully honed and continually updated reprocessing technique.

Follow-up

When next I saw Karen Barry-Freed, she and her husband were in a state of turmoil. I was taken aback, because when I'd called to set up this interview three weeks earlier, she had sounded upbeat and not at all upset.

As soon as we'd sat down, however, she said without preamble, "I have to tell you, Maggie, that I think what people say—you know, that there are no accidents in life?—is right on the mark. I had been wondering when I would hear from you again. . . . It's been so long, and I'd wondered if you were going on with your project."

I felt chastened, for I'd fallen far behind in my usual follow-up schedule. Before I could offer a word of apology, though, Karen continued. "And then, just shortly after you called to make this appointment, I had a really big jolt in my marriage." Her voice was clipped, stark, as if she were reporting details from the scene of an accident.

I stared at her in surprise. There was a clock-stopping silence, and at last I said, "What's going on?"

Karen didn't respond, merely shrugged and raised both arms, palms outward, as if asking "How and where am I to start?" Then she took in a deep breath, let it out, and said, "I was in Santa Fe visiting my parents, and I knew that Jon was having dinner with a certain woman—she works for one of the company's affiliates—and she's someone he's been mentioning off and on for about a year." Jon had told her that he didn't like going out with this person alone, Karen said. In fact, he'd made a point of assuring her that he was arranging things so that there were always other people with them. "I'd say to him, 'That's okay, honey . . . whatever,'" Karen said straightaway, as if to let me know she'd not been harboring groundless suspicions.

But then she amended this account by explaining that there *had* been one occasion—a time when she'd come in after a book club meeting on a night when she knew Jon was having a business dinner with "this person." "I remember driving home and feeling really upset because he'd admitted to me that this woman kind of has fantasies about him. . . . And when I came home I marched right into the bathroom and said to him, 'I just want you to know right now that if this ever happens again, it's *over*. I cannot go through this again, no way! Just tell me, and I'm out of here!' And he was just stunned.

"He said, 'Karen, if this ever, *ever* happened again, *I'm* the one who would be out of here—*my* life would be over! You *are* my whole life, you know that!'" Karen nodded, flushing slightly, as if embarrassed to be repeating this conversation to an outsider. Still, in the wake of that episode, she *had* remained aware that in the course of his regular business activities, Jon was having dinner with the woman at least once a month when she came into town.

I paused, wondering. Had this mention of his female associate's "fantasies" been her husband's way of getting Karen to worry and therefore to focus intently upon him? Jon Freed was someone whose father had supplied him with a daily "fix" of attention throughout much of his adult lifetime. Maybe he was needing to be the center of someone's fixed and dedicated interest at this moment. Given this couple's history, my own perception was that Jon's behavior did sound a somewhat provocative note. However, never having interviewed him directly on a one-to-one basis, I felt that I could discern his silhouette clearly but was missing some of the finely etched details that would have emerged in a fuller, more elaborated portrait.

"Let's give 'this woman' a name, so we won't have to keep calling her 'this woman,'" I suggested gently.

Karen glanced at me, hesitated briefly, and said, "Her name is Margo," in a weary, downbeat tone of voice. Then she went on: Another questionable incident had occurred this past January, which was that Jon had mentioned, in a casual way, that he'd driven his female colleague back to her hotel on his way home from their most recent dinner meeting.

This seemingly innocuous remark had taken Karen by surprise. It had felt like a blow to the belly, making her feel wobbly, as if she were losing her balance. "I asked him why he hadn't simply put her in a taxi after the dinner." Her voice had grown nervous and higher pitched. "*He* said that since he was driving right past her hotel in order to get on the pike, it had just seemed like the 'kind' thing to do. To me it seemed too, I don't know, *intimate*."

She gazed at me searchingly, then said, "*I* felt that certain boundaries were being crossed, but I said nothing. I wasn't going to start some big inquisition . . . but I did think, Am I turning into someone naggy, being overly suspicious and sort of edgy when absolutely *nothing's* really going on?" She looked at me but said nothing further, and in the ensuing silence the question hung in the air.

When Something Bad Is Something Good

Karen seemed far away. "You know," she said at last, "a close friend of mine said that Jon always measures himself by whatever's coming to him from outside, especially from women. She said she thinks *my* greatest challenge will always be to be myself, while Jon will always be checking himself out with other people . . . and most particularly with women."

"As in 'Am I still attractive?'" I asked her with a smile. "And as in 'Am I still young?'" She nodded yes to both questions, her expression grave.

"And as in 'Am I an old man or am I a young stud?'" I continued, and this time she smiled back.

"Really, I don't get it," she said, "taking someone out to dinner who you know has a big thing for you—"

"And then coming home and discussing it with your spouse," I completed her remark, and we both laughed at the silliness of the notion. Then I paused momentarily before saying, in a more serious tone of voice, that I saw it slightly differently from her friend—I could see the whole sequence of events as a phenomenal bid for her attention. For what could alert her more, what could rivet her attention more, what could come to dominate her world more, than those dings of alarm that were going off periodically?

"Well, I will tell you it *has* gotten my attention," Karen said with the lift of an eyebrow.

I smiled, said that I had a private, wholly unsubstantiated theory of my own, which was that neither sex, aggression, nor the so-called will to power was the truly central motivation of human behavior. My theory, based on personal observation, was that a fundamental, driving human force is the compelling need for just plain attention. I was half joking, but

Karen looked at me thoughtfully. However, she made no response, so I went on, "It's clearly true that your husband needs *a lot* of attention, and so in this sense to do something bad is to do something good."

Karen nodded her agreement. "Whatever else, it's *still* attention."

"Yes, and we're talking about someone who was raised on whipped cream in terms of how much attention he got from his parents, particularly his dad, and—" I looked up, noticed that she'd changed color in a moment, turned a delicate, faintly flustered shade of rose. I halted in midsentence and looked at her questioningly.

"I hate to say it, but since all this happened we've come together as a couple—sexually, I mean—more intensely and frequently than we had been. . . . And we're just being *nicer* to each other, too. You know?"

I nodded. I did understand, but what she was telling me did make me wonder. Had Jon perhaps been sensing or feeling that some "creeping distance" was reentering the relationship, and had this been his way, his hugely clumsy, ill-considered, and downright dangerous way, of trying to bridge the distance between them?

This Sick, Sick Feeling

The couple's crisis, which was ongoing, had been triggered by an occurrence as ambiguous as the others—but this time, it had been something that Karen found impossible to shake.

She and her youngest daughter, Laurie, had been out in Santa Fe, visiting with Karen's elderly, retired parents. "I knew that while we were away, Jon would be taking this woman out to dinner. . . . Of course he'd *told* me; this was no secret, unknown thing," she said. I noticed that she was still avoiding the use of Margo's name.

Then she explained that on their return, she and her daughter had had a very long, frustrating day. Their connecting flight had gotten canceled, and eventually they'd had to fly into the Providence airport instead. Jon had met them there, even though he'd had an unusually grueling day himself. There had been a death in his family—his grandmother, who'd been in her late nineties—and he'd been in charge of ferrying members of the family from Boston's Logan Airport to the funeral, to the cemetery, to a luncheon gathering of friends and relatives, and eventually back to

Logan again. After that, he'd had to turn around and come to Providence to pick up his wife and daughter. So on the drive back to Boston, said Karen, everyone in the car had been feeling fairly wrung out.

It was at some point during this journey homeward, though, that Jon had suggested they call the house to let their oldest daughter, Pam, know that they were running very late. Then he'd handed the phone to Laurie, who was in the backseat, saying, "I've got all my numbers stored."

"So she goes flipping through them," said Karen, veering into the present tense, "and she looks at one of the numbers and says, 'Margo? Who's Margo?' And I have to say I—it's hard to find the words—it was like an *explosion* went off—I thought I was going to *burst.*" Karen, her face wearing a look of horror, was pressing both hands hard against her chest as if manually holding her body together.

She had not said another word after the cell phone incident, but due to the general sense of fatigue, no one in the car had taken notice of her silence. It wasn't until they'd gotten home, and she and Jon were at last alone and in their bedroom, that she'd brought the matter up and found herself becoming frantic, completely distraught. "I said to him, 'I cannot *believe*, given what the two of us have been through, that here we are in *this* place again!' I was just hysterical, no two ways about it! And I told him, 'You cannot imagine what this is bringing up for me—how *painful*—how hurt I feel!'"

An emergency alarm within her body had been triggered, but Jon was shocked and said, "My God, Karen, I *need* to call her from work!" Her reaction made no sense to him: How could having Margo's number punched into his cell phone be the betrayal his wife perceived it to be? "I said I felt *in my gut* that it was! Then he got mad and asked me if I trusted my feelings more than I trusted *him.*"

That remark made me laugh. "He really asked you that?" I said.

She nodded and laughed, too. "Yes, he seriously asked me that." Then her expression grew clouded, and she said that many ugly memories had come surging to the surface—*awful* times in their couples' therapy sessions when Jon would say that it wasn't the sex with his lover that mattered to him. The real connection between them was in the *talking,* in feeling close and understood.

"I told him, 'You cannot imagine what this is bringing up for me,'"

Karen repeated bleakly. Then they'd talked and talked, eventually cried together and hugged. "Jon told me that I was the one, the *only* one; he said he'd just have to call off those dinners somehow." She looked at me searchingly, hesitated, and then said, "The real point here is that as secure as I felt in this marriage—and given everything that we'd worked through in the therapy and that I thought was resolved—the mere fact that I saw this woman's number on his cell phone, and that I knew he'd had dinner with her the night before, had undone me in a way that I found astounding. . . . That it was so *painful*—as if none of it had ever been put down, not really."

I nodded in agreement, for a traumatic experience can be like a forest fire that gives every indication of being completely extinguished but has often left behind a residue of kindling that any spark of alarm can set ablaze. Thus, while Karen could reassure herself that there was nothing rational about her response, a presentiment of terrible danger had invaded her.

"I felt *betrayed*—I can't even say at what level. Did I really think that he'd had sex with this woman?" She shook her head in the negative, said the idea was inconceivable. "But I have, since the breakup of our first marriage, learned to be more trusting of my gut responses—and there was something here that didn't feel *right* to me."

"So basically you felt you trusted him in your head, but not in your body?" I asked, as I'd asked her once before.

She nodded. "Yes, that's where these messages, these *powerful* messages, were coming from."

Although she and Jon were about to leave for Europe at that time with three other couples on a long-planned business/pleasure trip, Karen canceled out. She told her husband that she needed that time by herself, and he'd been devastated, beside himself. "But I simply said, 'I'm sorry, I can't do it.' And I couldn't, I *couldn't* go—I felt physically ill. I was going to the bathroom three, four times a day, as I did the first time this happened. . . . I just had this sick, sick feeling."

In truth, said Karen, the intensity and tenacity of her reaction had shocked her just as much as it had shocked Jon. It was as though in the space of that single brief episode—her daughter, sitting in the back of the car and asking, "Margo? Who's Margo?"—she'd been thrust into living contact with a horde of demon memories, terrifying specters of the past that she'd believed had been laid to rest in the rubble of that "first marriage." Yet here she was, feeling *assaulted* by those images of a time when everything about her life had suddenly become unreal, invalid.

The thought that bad things could be happening in *this* marriage did not seem quite believable. Nevertheless, the notion *did* exist side by side with the alarming knowledge that an event that's happened earlier can certainly happen again. "I felt as if this huge rug had been yanked out from under me—no, the very *ground* that I was standing on was giving way. My *trust* had been threatened, and I couldn't get it back . . . so where was I to go with that? How could I ever feel secure? Were we heading for more of the same—the same lying, the same distancing—after all the misery, the breakup, the slow, slow reconciliation, after everything else we'd been through?"

Although Jon had done everything he could to reassure her, and had begged her to reconsider going with him to Europe, Karen remained adamant. "It would have been plain *agony*, putting on a face for those other people," she said without a tinge of regret in her voice. Instead, during the twelve days Jon was away, she'd gone on a personal retreat—used the time to relax, read, do some exercising, and begin regaining some semblance of her former composure and balance.

That had been helpful, at least to some extent, but still, said Karen, about a week after Jon's return from his trip abroad, "an overwhelming sense of sadness" had set in. "Jon picked up on this, and he asked me what was wrong. And I said that I was just feeling very sad—feeling sad for *us*. I told him that it was *inconceivable* that he would lie to me; it was *inconceivable* that he would betray me; but that I felt that his walk was not matching his talk. . . . That something wasn't squaring for me, and that's what I was feeling *in my body*."

"And is that where you are now?" I asked her quietly.

She nodded. "That's where things stand now, though it's healing and sealing over a bit. But basically, we can't just let this drift, ignore it . . . because it's inside me, someplace." Karen's eyes looked watery, and she then said, with a helpless little shrug of her shoulders, that she and Jon were going to see a couples' therapist the following evening—"much as we both dread trotting out all of these old issues, these *hurtful* issues, that we've been through so many times before.

"So this is how things stand at the moment," Karen concluded, "pretty much up in the air."

A Thread on the Rug?

That afternoon, when we parted, Karen promised to get in touch with me in several weeks and let me know how the couples' therapy was progressing. For my own part, driving homeward, I found myself puzzling over the question of what was actually going on (if anything was going on at all). It was impossible to know how much reality did or did not underlie Karen's fears.

But what did come into my thoughts at that moment was a discussion I'd once had with infidelity expert Shirley Glass. In the course of that conversation, Glass had mentioned her irrational but deep-seated fear of snakes, even harmless snakes, and the fact that she lived in a state (Maryland) where these reptiles are not at all uncommon. Once she *had* actually come face-to-face with a large, live, and very long snake, which was slithering across her living room rug and heading straight toward her. She'd gone into an atavistic panic, and even though the situation was handled quickly by a member of her family, the memory of that incident had never lost its power to terrify her. From that day onward, the brisk, very professional Dr. Glass had told me, the sight of a thread on the rug had held the power to send her into a state of immobilizing fear.

It was clearly by no means accidental that this particular story had popped into my mind. For now, thinking about Karen Barry-Freed, I couldn't help but wonder: Was Karen's "gut" reacting to an actual danger or to a mere thread on the living room rug? It was anybody's guess whether her disorienting dread and sense of overwhelming sadness were linked to something real and in the present or something stored in her body but belonging to the past, phantasmagoric.

Chapter Seventeen

REPROCESSING AND INFIDELITY: KAREN

When Karen Barry-Freed called to tell me that she and Jon were dropping out of couples' treatment—although their relationship was still nowhere, in limbo—I decided to talk to her about reprocessing and suggest that she might be interested in giving it a try. Without going into elaborate explanations, I'd mentioned that my own experience with EMDR had proven surprisingly successful.

Actually, in the few months following that initial meeting, I'd decided to target and "detoxify" several other oppressive memories in EMDR sessions with Patti Levin (for instance, the death of the family cat on the day my parents separated). I'd done so periodically, and in the course of this venture, something strange had occurred. I've never been sure *when*, but at some point along the way I realized that the stiff tensing up of my jaw—a lifelong signal of emotional bad weather—had mysteriously ceased to occur. It wasn't that my own allotment of daily pressures had vanished; it was just that this bodily reaction to stress, an old familiar companion, had "gotten off the train" in the course of the reprocessing sessions.

On first hearing about EMDR, Karen was doubtful. She said that she hadn't ever heard anything about this new therapy. Still, she did go on to say that she was currently feeling as "demolished" as she had at the time of Jon's initial treachery so many years earlier. The treatment sounded odd to her, but on the other hand, they'd already *had* so much regular talking therapy—they'd said everything there was to say, and she was still feeling terrible. So the idea of exploring some new approach held some appeal for her.

What follows, then, is part of the story of what happened—or, more precisely, the story of what happened in the course of one particular reprocessing session.

The Ten Worst Memories You Can Think Of

Karen Barry-Freed's assessment interview had taken place two weeks before the meeting to be described. At the close of that first, very lengthy meeting, Patti Levin had asked her to jot down what she thought of as her ten worst memories and then bring this list to the subsequent appointment. These sessions were taking place in Patti's second office in Cambridge, Massachusetts, which has three high, large windows and feels airier and more capacious than her office in New Haven.

Today, Karen had come in with that list of "ten worst memories" in hand. She took a chair directly opposite Patti's, and I placed myself slightly off to one side; I had been invited to attend as a participant-observer. This was to be Karen's first EMDR experience, and I thought she looked nervous, for as she briskly removed a single sheet of printer paper from her handbag, it fluttered in her shaky hand.

Was she apprehensive about how this curious process would affect her? I wondered. I couldn't have known, then, that in the short interval between the previous session and this one she'd encountered another so-called thread in the rug. Something else had happened that had set her highly sensitized alarm bells ringing.

She was gazing fixedly at the sheet of paper on her lap, and as she did so, I felt pretty certain *which* memories would be at the top of her list. An obvious one would be Jon's sudden, crushing announcement that there was another woman in his life and he was leaving the marriage; that would have been an 8 or a 9 on the Richter scale of any unsuspecting spouse's life. Another, more recent "bad memory" would be the unnerving incident with the cell phone, which had exposed her just-below-the-surface sense of mistrust, danger, and vulnerability. Somewhere else on that list, without doubt, would be the memory of hearing about her older brother Scott's sudden death.

Patti had questioned her at length about her reactions at the moment of receiving the news, and she'd described the way her parents called her at her work and reported what had happened in a shockingly abrupt three-word announcement: "Scott's been murdered." These tidings, coming from her former life in the Midwest, had been experienced as unreal, fantastic, almost dreamlike. "I do remember being on the flight back home—things around me seemed to be wavering, somehow. I remember seeing colors, and seeing people, but it was all *different*—nothing looked like it did in real time," Karen said, her voice taut with apprehension.

It was clear that she had displayed traumatic stress responses in the aftermath of every one of these staggering events—symptoms such as emotional numbness, a sense that the world around her was tenuous and unstable, unremitting anxiety, and a range of physical disturbances, including headaches, nausea, and diarrhea. All were episodes that had left her feeling debilitated in their wake, literally *ill* in body and in spirit.

Getting Prepped

"So. Any questions or concerns before we begin?" Patti smiled, flipped back a long strand of dark hair that had fallen forward over her shoulder, and leaned her body in her client's direction.

"No, I think we covered it last time," Karen replied. But she looked uncertainly at the Neuro*Tek* light bar, which had been placed in such a way that both Patti and I would be out of her focal view when the actual eye tracking began.

"Okay, then, let me just show you how this works." Patti pressed a handheld switch, and set the back-and-forth movement of the lights in motion. "It can go faster"—she speeded it up—"or it can go slower. Or if you like, we can move it closer to you. You can put the earphones on; they're just an additional form of bilateral stimulation. Now, just watch the lights. Get comfortable. Basically, the point is to keep your eyes moving at whatever speed is most comfortable. . . . In terms of speed, do you have a preference yet?"

Karen shook her head, seemed wary, said she didn't.

Patti adjusted the speed to a moderate level, then asked, "Can we go like this?"

Karen stared at the moving lights for a few moments, then laughed nervously. "I'm *trying* to follow, but I start seeing all the flashing dots as a line." Patti assured her that the dots would blur out and she wouldn't even notice them after a while.

"Okay," said Karen, "because it's almost like I'm getting a little cross-eyed." She giggled, sounding nervous. Uh-oh, I thought, looking at her flushed cheek in profile, for I'd had an intimation that this might not work for her. I knew that some people had huge reactions to EMDR and some reacted little or not at all.

Patti smiled calmly, then asked Karen if she had a "safe place," real or imaginary, that she could go to and feel comforted and serene. Karen nodded, said she had a real one and an imaginary one.

The therapist looked pleased. She shifted and leaned farther in her client's direction. "Great, then I would like you to just bring it up and let yourself really *feel* it, feel it all through your body. All right? And give it a name or a cue word."

"I guess it would be 'the pond,'" said Karen, her voice subdued. Patti switched the light bar into motion, telling Karen that she wanted her to bring up the image of "the pond" and follow the lights. "I want you to *feel* what it's like to be there, to feel it in your skin, to smell the smells and hear the sounds and *experience* that sense of serenity," she instructed her patient in a low, warm voice.

As Karen's eyes tracked the swiftly moving flashes of light, Patti explained that she was using the bilateral stimulation to "install" this safe place as an internal haven—a place to retreat to in the event that the EMDR became too disturbing. "Does it feel like you've got it securely inside you?" she asked after an interval.

Karen said she thought so, but her voice was uncertain, so Patti offered her a few more back-and-forth passes on the light bar.

"Okay," said Karen after a few moments of eye tracking, sounding more relaxed. She leaned back in her chair.

Patti then instructed her about the two principal metaphors that

EMDR clinicians tend to use, as she had done for me. One, you will recall, was that of getting on a train and traveling from point A to point B, while looking out the window at "the scenery"—which is basically the fragmented, painful material being processed. The second is the image of holding the remote control to a video in one's hand, so that the information being processed is being watched as if on a screen. Also, since the client is holding the imaginary remote, she or he can slow the action down or speed it up, pause it or flick it off.

"If what you're seeing through the train window makes you too uncomfortable, you can avert your gaze and bring it back onto the train," Patti explained. "If you're watching it like a movie, you can blank it out, turn the video off. Right? So *you* have control. Does one or the other of those metaphors appeal to you?"

Karen hesitated for several moments, and as she considered the choices I reflected upon the fact that both these metaphors created a sense of *observing* rather than *experiencing from inside* the memory that still lingered, unresolved. "I think . . . the train," she said at last.

Then, after one final small instruction (to signal a "stop" by raising her hand upright in the "Halt!" position rather than by saying the word aloud), Karen had been fully readied for the journey. What needed to be determined now was the destination toward which she would be heading.

What Would You Rather *Believe?*

"Okay, then, I think this is where we should start." Patti's voice held a bright, faintly official note, like that of a teacher who's announcing to the class that she's now changing subjects and moving on from English to geography. The therapist shifted in her seat and straightened her long slim skirt beneath her.

"So, the next thing we need to do is decide on what we're going to target. My own gut feeling is that we ought to start with—" She caught herself in midsentence. "What is *your* gut feeling?" she asked Karen.

There was a brief silence. Patti prompted gently, "Well, if you think about the original betrayal, and then about the way your body reacted to this most recent experience, which memory feels the most upsetting or disturbing to you?" In other words, did Karen want to look backward to lingering injuries rooted in the past, or did she want to focus upon things that were happening in the here and now?

Karen said in a small voice, "I think the most recent one."

"Good," said Patti, nodding and giving the impression that this was her opinion, too. "So that's where we will start. *Now,* you may find yourself going back to the old experience anyway; you may find yourself going places you can't even imagine. That doesn't matter. Basically, your brain and your body know the way they need to heal. All right?" She gazed directly at Karen, who returned her gaze dubiously.

"Okay, then, when you think of that most recent experience, is there one particular moment—a kind of snapshot, perhaps—that symbolizes that whole experience for you? Perhaps a single sentence that captures the *worst* moment?"

Karen nodded and said, "I think the worst snapshot in my mind is just seeing this woman's name on his cell phone. *Two* of her names! Her regular number and her cell phone number. It was just that, and a bunch of other things, too, that were the culmination of everything else that was happening. Because in that first betrayal, he'd said that it was as much of an emotional need to *talk* with the woman as it was anything else! So that just brought up the whole thing. There was a lot of other stuff that was happening, *little* things, as I've told Maggie—" She glanced over at me as if for corroboration. "But that was the most significant, definitely."

"So then seeing this woman's name on the cell phone," summarized Patti, and Karen nodded her assent. "Okay, when you think of that moment of seeing this woman's name on his cell phone, what is your current negative or irrational belief about yourself?"

"Hmmm," said Karen. "I guess it would be either 'I am being fooled' or 'I am being duped' or 'Am I being taken advantage of in my life?' In other words, 'Am I being totally naive about this?' " Her statements had evolved into questions.

Patti nodded but didn't respond to them directly. She was looking for an "I" statement, a belief about the self that the incident had elicited and fostered. "So when you talk about being totally naive or being duped, what I want to know is what it says about *you*. Does the statement 'I am being totally naive' cover it?"

"Yes, I think so," said Karen.

Patti double-checked by asking, "So 'I am being totally naive' feels like your belief?"

"Yes," repeated Karen in a stronger voice, this time with no hesitation.

The therapist then asked her to cast her thoughts backward to the exact moment of seeing the woman's name on the cell phone. "Picturing that in your mind's eye, rather than believe 'I am totally naive,' what would you rather believe about yourself *now*?"

"Hmmm," said Karen, and a long silence followed. I gazed over at her, waited. She'd come in looking tanned, trim, even taller somehow—she said she was working out with weights and doing a lot of daily walking. Now, however, she seemed to hunch in upon herself, grow more diminutive in size. Her voice sounded tremulous as she replied that she would *rather* believe that it was just a colleague's name, any colleague's name—no different from the fifty or sixty other names, both male and female, listed on her husband's cell phone. She would like to believe that it had no more meaning or consequence than the name of anyone else he needed to talk to for business.

"And what would that say about you?" Patti asked. "I am . . . ?"

"I guess . . . 'I feel secure in myself,'" Karen answered after the briefest pause.

Then the clinician asked her to think back once again to seeing the woman's name on the cell phone and put *that* mental picture together with the words "I feel secure in myself." "How true does that belief feel to you at a gut level? Say, if you put it on a scale where seven equals 'completely true' and one is equal to 'completely false'? And you think of it as it relates to that moment of seeing the name on the cell phone, *not* in your intellect but in your gut?" Here, Patti was making use of the validity of cognition scale (VOSC), a research instrument used to measure the patient's *felt confidence* in his or her positive belief or cognition.

"Thinking back to that moment? I would say, 'Not at all secure in myself,'" said Karen. "I would give it a one or a two," she added with the smallest, infinitely hopeless-looking shrug of her shoulders.

In this exchange, it should be duly noted, Patti had been focusing on her patient's *beliefs* about her own self as they related to that upsetting incident. Next, the therapist would turn the beam of her attention upon the *feelings* that the experience had aroused, feelings that Karen had found intolerable but was unable to shake or put behind her.

Where Do You Feel It in Your Body?

Patti paused to type a few notes into the computer sitting on her lap, then looked up at Karen in a friendly, thoughtful manner. "So. When you think back to seeing this woman's name in his cell phone, and you think of the words 'I am totally naive,' what feelings come up for you now?"

"A whole lot of confusion." Karen's voice was low, strained, hard to hear. "Anger, and just total disbelief. I guess the feeling that the bottom was dropping out from under me. . . . I was flailing, I was in free fall."

"And is that how you're feeling now?" Patti asked.

Karen didn't answer directly. Instead she said while she certainly hadn't made her peace with that scene in the car, she'd been able to make a certain amount of distance between herself and that event by the time of her assessment interview a couple of weeks earlier. "It still hurt, but not with that agonizing kind of sharpness that it had in March, April, and May. Although it's true that the most insignificant thing could set me off."

However, in the interim between the last meeting and this one, she'd gone into a state of true panic, without even understanding what had triggered it. Not until recently, when she'd gotten into a long, confiding conversation with her closest friend, had she become aware of what, precisely, had set it off. "Jon was leaving for work early. We have different wings in the house where we sleep and the girls sleep, and he usually goes in to kiss them good-bye in the morning. So, he went into our oldest daughter Pam's room, which has a full-length mirror; and she, when she came down later on, said, 'Oh, you should've seen Dad, checking himself out in the full-length mirror, turning every which way.' She thought it was so funny, but I felt *blindsided*. Like—'Why is he doing this?' "

Subsequently Karen had mentioned this comment to her husband "jokingly," saying that Pam was amused by the way he'd been checking himself out in her bedroom mirror. And Jon had answered, "I swear to God that was the most expensive suit, and I still don't think the tailor got the pants right. They always look saggy to me."

"Of course, my thought was, Silly me," said Karen, sounding abashed, "but my mind had just skittered off instantly on this. *Why* does he care so much what he's looking like today? Who is he going to see?"

"So there's still a scab there, that gets torn off?" Patti asked sympathetically. Karen nodded, her eyes filling up. I said nothing but was astonished to realize that she hadn't noticed that her danger sirens had been activated by a particularly galling historical precedent—her husband's soliciting her advice about which tie to select to go with which jacket on certain days when he was planning to meet up with his mistress. She felt "silly" because she hadn't remembered or made the connection.

Patti called a short break in the discussion in order to get up and make some small shifts and adjustments in the Neuro*Tek* light bar's position, maneuvering it this way and that until it felt maximally comfortable to her client. "Is that just about right?" she asked at last. Karen, who'd put on the earphones, answered with a nod.

"All right. So, when you think back to seeing this woman's name on the cell phone and thinking the words 'I am totally naive,' and feelings of confusion, anger, and disbelief rise up in you, how disturbing does that feel to you? Let's say if you were to put it on a scale where ten equals 'the most disturbing and upsetting anything could feel' and zero is just 'neutral, no disturbance at all'?"

Karen said that when it happened it had felt like a ten.

"And how does it feel now?" asked Patti. It felt more like a seven, Karen replied. Then the therapist asked her where, in her body, she noticed the disturbance.

"In my stomach and in my chest," said Karen, pointing to those places briefly and then placing both hands upon her abdomen as if to offer herself some support, soothing, and comfort. Here, it should be said, Patti was making use of another well-validated psychological scale—the SUDS, or subjective units of distress scale—which was pioneered by the famed behavioral therapist Joseph Wolpe and has now become a standard component of the reprocessing procedure.

Roadblocks

"*Now,* I am going to lead you along by asking you to hold this information together and follow the lights," said Patti. "I will do that for a little while, and then check in with you and see what you are noticing. If I keep the eye tracking going too long, and you have something you want to say, just say it. Or if I stop too soon and you're in the middle of processing something and you want to keep it in your head, just say, 'Keep going.' . . . Okay? The reins are in your hands."

Karen nodded, and Patti continued: "So, then, I want you to bring up the memory of seeing this woman's name on the cell phone. Hold it together with the words 'I am totally naive.' Notice the feelings of confusion, anger, and disbelief and where they are in your body. And follow the light, letting whatever happens happen." She flicked on the light bar, and the flashes of illumination began moving back and forth.

I shifted my chair slightly, being careful to make no noise, because I wanted to focus on the moving lights even as Karen did. This first pass lasted for about two minutes, after which the therapist halted the movement of the lights. "Take a deep breath," she said to her patient. Then, after Karen had inhaled and exhaled deeply, Patti asked her what she was noticing.

Karen, sounding confused, asked, "I'm just supposed to be holding on to that image—?" She laughed briefly, a high-pitched, nervous sound.

"Yes, but don't worry if it drifts. Whatever happens is what should be happening," said Patti, and switched on the light bar once again. This time she let the reprocessing continue for an even longer time, and when she switched it off, she told Karen to take a deep breath once again. "What are you noticing?" she asked.

"You know, I was thinking mostly about the light," Karen admitted, laughing again and sounding embarrassed. "I mean, I was holding the image of being in the car coming home from the airport when Laurie was scrolling through the cell phone, but then . . . I just started focusing on the lights."

"Okay, go back to that image," Patti said softly. She set the lights into motion, and silence fell as her client began tracking their steady back-and-forth movement. I, too, was doing some eye tracking in the background, but my own sense that the reprocessing wasn't going to be particularly helpful to Karen was growing ever stronger. Sure enough, after the next pause and deep breath, she giggled apologetically and said, "Wow, I'm beginning to realize that it's hard for me to focus on two things at once. I find that when I look at the moving light it's hard for me to keep the image of being in the car with the cell phone. My mind *did* wander to other things, but when I came back to the light, it was all I could focus on. So not a whole lot is really coming up."

Patti suggested that she keep her eyes closed and go back to the image they'd started out with—the scene in the car with the cell phone. Karen would then not be distracted by the lights and could focus on the bilateral stimulation offered by the oscillating ear tones. But this alternative proved equally unsuccessful.

For this time when Patti asked, "What are you getting?" Karen answered in the frustrated voice of a schoolgirl who simply can't make any sense of the problem she's supposed to be solving: "I *did* start off by putting myself in the situation, but then I started listening to the beeps. You know, this beep is louder than this one. . . . Is this one a little higher than the last one? And that's all I was able to focus on." There was that slightly discordant, embarrassed laugh once again.

Patti smiled. "So, what do you think is happening?"

Karen stopped laughing and said that she thought she was blocking somehow. "It's just *hard* to keep that image. It's as if I can't focus on two things at one time."

Patti explained that holding on tightly to that initial image wasn't necessary. It was perfectly fine to let go, to let it drift, to let it change. . . . "No matter what happens, let it happen. Whatever happens is fine," she assured her patient. Then she suggested that Karen go back to whatever the last image had been, to use that image as a starting point and then go anywhere.

"It's kind of funny," Karen said, "but I can't *remember* the last image I was seeing."

Patti suggested that in that case they should go back to the original image and start from there. "Notice where it is in your body and just *go* with it. Don't judge what comes out; don't judge where it goes or what you think or feel . . . just let it go wherever it wants to go, okay?" Karen nodded, and the therapist turned on the earphones once again. By now, however, my own hopes for a "minor miracle" or even a favorable outcome of this session were fading.

Sure enough, when this next interval of sound tracking had ended,

Karen reported that while she *had* found herself able to visualize sitting in the car, she'd gotten no further than that. "We are sitting in the car," said Karen, "but I can't maintain a dialogue and listen to the beeps."

"Does your mind go anywhere else?" asked Patti.

"No, I find I'm really following the beeps," the client replied. She shrugged. "Maybe it's because I meditate, and I focus on the breath. So I'm used to shutting down and staying focused on one thing. And in *this* instance, it's the beeps." There was that off-putting laugh once again. As far as I was concerned, the fact that this was going nowhere seemed glaringly apparent.

Perhaps Karen was erecting internal roadblocks—automatically walling herself off from the painful reexperiencing of a shock that had left her feeling physically and emotionally sick. Surely her reactions to former traumatic events had always been similar—freezing and emotional numbing, resulting in avoidance and a state of nonfeeling. On the other hand, reprocessing simply might not work for her, for any of a variety of other reasons.

Now the therapist said, with no hint of impatience and a friendly smile, "You *don't* need to focus on the beeps. Or the light. I want you to let them just be there, in the background. The only reason for their being there is to keep the bilateral stimulation going, and they will do that whether you listen to them, or watch the light, or you don't. What I want is for you to let go, so that your mind and body can make whatever associations they need to make, so they can find whatever route they need to take." She looked at Karen intently and said with a small shrug, "And who knows what path that might be—your brain and body will find the way they need to go."

Karen met her gaze but made no reply. "So we'll just keep trying," said the clinician, "and you can listen to the beeps, watch the lights, it doesn't matter." She switched on the light bar as she spoke. "So let's begin again with that image we started with, and once again, notice how it feels in your body."

"Okay," said Karen, and a long interlude of EMDR followed.

"What's going on now?" Patti asked when it had ended.

Karen shook her head, said that she still saw them all sitting in the car, and nothing felt very different. "But it's true, I don't feel quite as tense, and maybe I'm feeling slightly warmer . . . ? My hands felt cold when I came in." She sounded as if this puzzled her.

"Okay, go with that," said the therapist, "you're doing fine."

She switched the slowly alternating light into motion once again. But at the close of this pass, once again, Karen shook her head. "I was just sitting in the car. Not talking. I'm finding that I have this whole dialogue in my head—that I'm telling myself not to keep analyzing so much. Because I do that too much—analyze and pass judgments. And I'm conscious of making an effort *not* to do that, but . . ."

She shook her head again, as if to say that the effort to be nonjudgmental was proving unsuccessful. This particular approach wasn't working for her, and she was sounding as if she blamed herself. At this point I was feeling pretty blameworthy, too, for I had been the enthusiastic sponsor of what was turning out to be an obvious and decisive failure. But now Patti said to Karen, "Okay, go ahead with that. Try not to judge whatever happens." Then she turned on the light bar (and also, I assumed, the earphones) yet again.

This time Karen's report was different. "I was thinking"—she began laughing—"that this is sort of funny. I'm sitting in the car, and Laurie is going, 'Margo? Margo? Who's Margo?' And for some reason I'm thinking it's *funny*!" She stopped laughing and said seriously, "I don't know if I'm thinking it's funny because that situation was funny, or because I'm judging that I'm not doing so well with this? . . ." She looked at Patti questioningly, but her voice was trusting.

Instead of responding directly, the therapist instructed her to go back to the target memory—the scene that had unfolded on the way home from the airport—and describe what she noticed about it now. Karen paused, then said, "Well, we are driving in the car and I'm looking at that number on the cell phone, and I just think it's *funny* that Laurie's going, 'Margo? Margo? Who's Margo?'" I stared at her, astonished. Whatever did she mean by the word *funny*? I wondered. Funny as in "strange" or funny as in "ridiculous"?

Patti, looking pleased, said, "So on that scale of zero to ten, where ten is 'the most disturbing something can be' and zero is 'neutral or no disturbance,' how does it feel to you now?"

"It doesn't feel that disturbing." Karen sounded baffled. "I don't know if that's because . . . I just *don't know*. It just doesn't; it feels *funny*. Which is—" She stopped, shrugged as if to say that she wasn't sure exactly where this last remark had been heading. Then, after a brief pause, Patti asked once again if she could rate how she felt on that imaginary scale where zero was no disturbance and ten was the worst disturbance possible.

"I don't know, maybe a three or a four," Karen answered uncertainly.

"What do you think keeps it from going lower?" asked the therapist. "What's still disturbing about it that keeps it at a three or a four?"

"I think I'm telling myself it *should* be disturbing," Karen admitted with a smile.

Patti returned the smile, said, "Okay, go with that," and set the light bar back into motion. After a briefer period of reprocessing, she stopped it, waited while her client took a deep breath, then asked, "Where are you now?"

"Well, I once more have to say it's really not disturbing. I just think it *should* be!" Karen reiterated, sounded pleased, if somewhat taken aback. "But it seems like . . . it doesn't *feel* disturbing. It feels fine. That's how it feels." She turned and looked at me as if hoping I had the explanation of what had just happened. I just smiled and raised both hands outward in a gesture that said, "I don't have any idea."

Patti then asked her to bring up the original image and whatever was left of the memory, then follow the moving flashes of light one more time. "What are you getting?" she asked when this last pass had been completed.

Karen said, "Well, I still think the whole thing is funny." She laughed, and this time it was a lighthearted sound.

For my own part, I was having trouble making rational sense of what had just happened. What nodal moment had I missed seeing that might explain the sudden turnaround that had just occurred? But Patti didn't leave me much time for reflection.

"Now remember," she was saying to her client, "what you said you would *rather* believe when you think back to that memory, which was, 'I feel secure in myself.' Do those words still fit the situation? Is that what you would prefer to believe when you think back to what is left of that old memory? Or is there a better way to put it, perhaps some other words that would describe the way you would *rather* think about yourself?"

"I guess those words are about the right ones," said Karen, sounding much less strung out and more self-possessed. "Somehow, I just don't feel as threatened as I did."

Point A to Point B

If I myself felt nonplussed by this abrupt shift in the dynamics of the session, Patti Levin didn't appear fazed in the slightest. She tossed back the long strands of hair that had now fallen forward on both sides, typed a few notes into her laptop, then looked up at her client brightly. "So. On a scale of one to seven, where seven is 'completely true' and one is 'completely false,' how true do the words 'I feel secure in myself' feel when you bring up that old memory? How true do those words feel *in your gut*?"

Karen answered without hesitation, "I'd say I feel secure in myself as it relates to that old memory," then added that she would rate this feeling at about a five or a six on the scale.

Patti asked her, in a curious but friendly tone of voice, What stopped it from going higher? What prevented it from being completely true? Her patient thought about that for a moment, then said that it just seemed *too easy*. "Maybe it's my cynical self, but I just think, How easy can this be? That I'd just look at this light and picture the scene in the car and start thinking the whole situation is *funny*!" She smiled and said, "I guess I'm making judgments again." She was blushing.

Without responding to these remarks directly, Patti smiled and said softly, "What I want you to do now is bring up whatever is left of that old memory and your feelings about it. Hold it together with the words 'I feel secure in myself,' and just follow the light." A long interval of eye tracking followed, after which the therapist asked, "How true do those words feel?"

"Well, it's true, when I thought about it, I *do* feel secure in myself," said Karen, sounding pleased and even lighthearted, if perplexed. "It's just that I think I *should* still have some residual . . . I don't know . . ." It made no sense to her that this sense of foreboding and all of the suffering of the past few months should simply dissipate in this way. "It's just too easy. I mean, looking at these lights and then feeling like this whole thing is *funny*!"

"It took on a different meaning for you," Patti said.

"I guess so, because the only feeling I got was that it was funny. *Silly* funny!" She laughed.

The therapist smiled and said, "As opposed to serious, meaningful, tragic?" Then, after leading Karen through a last interim of reprocessing —this one a body scan, a surveillance of her internal world to check for any lingering areas of discomfort—the session seemed to be drawing to a close. "Do you have any questions?" she asked her patient.

"*Yes!* How does it work?" It was less a question than a bewildered demand.

Patti only shrugged and held her arms outward in a "Who knows?" kind of gesture. "Nobody's really explained it, though there's been a huge amount of research," she said. Nevertheless, she herself had the delighted but surprised look of a magician who's just pulled a rabbit out of a hat without any clear idea of how it got there. She turned to me and asked, "Anything you want to say here, Maggie?"

I simply held up a hand, signaling her to wait a moment, for the reversal that had just taken place was so startling that I was having trouble absorbing and comprehending it. Then I said, in a low voice, that because I knew what Karen had been through, the sudden denouement of this session had left me feeling ready to cry.

"Using that metaphor of leaving the train journey, I never *did* experience the train as leaving the station," I told her, then turned to Karen directly. "At each standstill I kept thinking, It's not happening, so I believed it wasn't going to work for you. I thought it was a shame. I thought, I guess there are some people it doesn't work for. . . . And suddenly there you were, you'd arrived! It was as if you'd taken the express train from point A to point B with no station breaks in between!" I laughed, feeling elated, turned back to Patti. "The way it happened was a big shock for me," I admitted. "But I found it very moving, and I'm so *glad* it worked for her."

"Me *too*," piped up Karen, exhaling deeply and sounding profoundly relieved, as if a malevolent spirit were leaving her body.

Chapter Eighteen

THE AFFAIR AS GUERRILLA WARFARE: JOANNA GRAVES

DURING THIS SAME PERIOD I WAS ALSO TALKING WITH A number of women who were, or had been recently, involved in extramarital affairs—no surprise, given that any series of interviews on the subject of secrets, betrayals, and their often traumatic aftereffects is sure to touch frequently upon the subject of infidelity. I soon noticed that a particular motif seemed to pop up time and again in the course of these conversations. This motif or theme had to do with the *justification* for the affair, which the person often portrayed as having to do with her survival—as one participant put it, "the survival of my self as a valid human being."

Confirmation of One's Worth and Dignity

There are, of course, countless motivations and rationales that an individual will cite for having gotten into an extramarital involvement, ranging from plain and simple sexual curiosity to a need for affirmation of one's physical attractiveness to being swept away by a sudden, overwhelming passion. But what I seemed to hear with surprising frequency were accounts in which the underlying but decisive reasons for the affair had to do with someone's desperate search for confirmation of her worth and dignity as a person. Many of the women I talked with were people who'd been dominated and bullied over time—made to feel inadequate, unbecoming, dim-witted, clumsy, or basically *all wrong* by their contemptuous, critical partners.

This kind of situation was typified by the plight of thirty-nine-year-old Joanna Graves, who at the time of our series of interviews was mourning the breakup of a passionate, yearlong affair. When she spoke with me about her lover (who I thought sounded like a bit of a scoundrel), Joanna's face came alive. She described this man as warm, affectionate, deeply interested in her as a person, and truly caring about everything happening in her life. He could enjoy a joke, and he was *fun* to be around.

Admittedly, the affair had had its destructive side, for she'd begun drinking heavily while it was in progress. In defense of her ex-lover, however, Joanna acknowledged that she'd never expected the involvement to be a lasting one. He had been honest with her from the outset, told her that his executive career involved extensive travel, and warned her straight out that he was "something of a philanderer." But at the same time he'd been so attentive, understanding, and *there for her* that any thoughts of "endings" had seemed remote and been banished from her mind.

Joanna's husband, Roger, whom she described as withdrawn and overcontrolling, was now fully aware of that yearlong relationship. In fact, it was Roger who, when he'd learned of it, had confronted the lover and threatened to cause serious damage in both the man's own marriage and his professional life. This male-to-male encounter had brought the affair to its precipitous close, and in its stormy aftermath, the couple had ultimately reconciled. Roger had graciously "forgiven" his wife. But life within Joanna's marriage, and life within her family, too, was "bleak" these days, for she'd returned to a situation that felt as empty and unrewarding as it had been when she'd first made her attempted escape.

She explained that her husband, a person who hadn't ever liked to touch or be touched in the best of times, had been sexually passionate for a short period of time after the affair ("He was marking his territory," she said wryly) but had then become angry and withdrawn. Moreover, a cloud of family blame had descended upon her, so that whatever school or behavior problems arose in regard to any of their three children were always ascribed to "*bad*, no-good Joanna's behavior"—her period of drinking and going AWOL emotionally.

"I do accept the guilt and the blame for that," she told me, her expression taut, "but I can see that Roger's never going to let go, never put it down." There was never a question of getting him to look at the difficulties within the marriage that had led to her going outside it. As her husband saw it, the glaring defects in her own sorry character were all the explanation needed. This marriage, as had already become clear in the course of the interviews, was one of those top dog/bottom dog pairings in which the wife had been the thoroughly subjugated partner almost from the outset.

Historically speaking, so had Joanna's own mother, and Roger's mother, too. This was the fundamental system for being in a male-female relationship that both members of the couple had witnessed in their own families of origin. Thus, both had come by their internal model for how a man and a woman will predictably interact in the most clear-cut manner possible—by growing up in an emotional world in which no other option or way of being had ever been presented to them.

The truth, however, is that *no one* is ever really victorious in the marriage of the tyrannizing partner and the disadvantaged spouse. For the intractable problem in these kinds of oppressive relationships is that while maintaining dominion and control over someone else's thoughts, feelings, wishes, and behavior may appear to be effective in the short run, it is always doomed in the longer one. As I have written elsewhere (see *Intimate Worlds: Life Inside the Family*), ". . . like murder, human complexity will out—and inevitably, as in other totalitarian systems, a rebellious fifth column develops." And for obvious reasons, in this era of enhanced sexual possibilities and relaxed social mores, this rebellion often takes the form of an affair.

In Joanna's case, the extramarital love affair had been brought to a precipitous ending; but the couple's sex life was now distant and perfunctory, almost nonexistent. When she told me this, Joanna hastened to add that it wasn't just *sex* that was missing from her marriage, "though I think I would like to have sex," she said, sounding doubtful. "No, it's really more that—oh, I would just like to hold hands, or have Roger put his arm around me sometime. . . . But if I bring it up, he'll say it's just that he's tired, or feeling a cold coming on, or things are so stressful at the office."

She shrugged, gave me a long, assessing look, then said forthrightly that she was "coming to the realization that at least she'd had something *good*" with her lover. "Something *very* good," she underscored, a defiant note sounding in her voice. True, she was currently in despair over the loss of that relationship, but she would never, ever regret it. "It taught me that I could laugh and enjoy myself, that I could be spontaneous . . . that I was intelligent and worth listening to . . . I could be sensual and give affection and receive it, too." She sighed deeply, then said she'd learned a lot about who she really was as a person.

"And if, for example, you take your husband's hand or put your arm around *him*, what happens then?" I asked, meeting her gaze directly.

Joanna shrugged and said dryly, "Roger was going away on a business trip this very morning, and he came down the stairs first, and I *did* put my arms around him. But he backed off and he said, 'No, no, no.' Then he wrote out a list of things I was supposed to do that day—he's great on lists, there's always a list of things for me to do! I didn't raise any objections, but he said, 'Well, walk out to the car with me.'

"I did walk out, and he sort of apologized, said he was sorry, but he had to make the list. And I said he could have made the list another time." She shrugged hopelessly, like a prisoner who's been thrown back into a small dark cell after the briefest taste of joy, light, and freedom. I felt sorry for her, in terms not only of her present pain, but of her past experiences and the future that loomed ahead. She murmured something about Roger needing her as a "presence," not a person—someone in the background of his life who was a helpmate and a mom but not a real woman with whom he could ever become close and intimate.

I already knew, from earlier interviews with Joanna, that there had been a lot of barely suppressed rage in her family of origin. One of the constant refrains of her childhood had been her distant, easily irritated dad telling her more outgoing, high-spirited mother to "hush *up*, Priscilla, for heaven's sake!" As a young girl, Joanna had also witnessed intermittent physical violence visited against an adopted younger brother by her dogmatic, short-tempered father (in this regard, her early history was reminiscent of that of Claudia Martinelli).

Joanna's mother had died when Joanna herself was in her late teens, "just as I was getting to really know her," she'd told me wistfully. Now she seemed stuck in a time warp, one in which a tense, oppressive early history had reemerged in her tense and troubled present-day life. I knew that traditional therapy, which she'd tried, hadn't changed the situation; and that

Roger wouldn't go for joint counseling. So on a compassionate impulse, I suggested throwing a wild card into this seemingly unresolvable marital stalemate—a few sessions of EMDR with Patti Levin or some other reprocessing facilitator.

One of Life's Small Miracles

Once under way, Joanna Graves's course of EMDR proceeded at a surprising pace. I'd been invited to sit in while she targeted certain memories for neutralizing and detoxifying and had placed myself off to one side while she faced Patti Levin directly. The subject of the first and most dramatic of these reprocessing sessions involved a memory she hadn't really given much thought to in a long, long time: witnessing her dad's savage beatings of her kid brother.

Subsequently, over the course of some five or six therapeutic meetings—alternating sessions of EMDR and straight talk therapy—the treatment began to have a clear-cut, in fact transforming, effect upon Joanna's sense of herself as a valid human being. For the first time in her married life, she was finding herself able to marshal the inner resources to confront her husband's abusive put-downs, disapproval, and blaming and to do so from a position of dignity and self-respect.

Moreover, when she held her ground in this way, calmly yet firmly, there were many instances in which she could get him to back off—often in ways that surprised her. She had never thought this to be possible before. And certainly I, in my role as participant-observer, felt that I was watching one of life's small miracles occurring.

Part Four

DEIRDRE

THE POWER THERAPIES

CREATING "NEW" MEMORIES

Chapter Nineteen

POWER THERAPIES: ACCESSING WHAT THE BODY KNOWS

Reprocessing is but one among a small group of what are called "power therapies," so named because they often prove effective with astonishing rapidity—especially when compared to the far slower-paced, traditional "talking" methods of treatment. These comparatively new techniques and procedures rely heavily upon what the body knows, or "somatic memory." Other than the meticulously researched EMDR, the most well known power therapies are thought field therapy and Hakomi.

These body-centered approaches vary widely and can *look* very different. Still, they do have a crucial feature in common: All are focused upon retrieving and integrating scattered bits of data stored within the patient's *physical* as well as mental being. All of them seek to promote a state of heightened bodily awareness by *actively summoning up a person's feelings, emotions, and sensations*—for instance, what was felt, seen, touched, smelled, and heard during certain critical events or time periods of the individual's life.

The body's "memory" is thus put into play as a way of gaining access to regions deep within the "old," emotional brain where hugely oversensitized networks of reacting have been established.

The Psychomotor Approach

According to trauma expert Bessel van der Kolk, one of the less widely known but remarkably compelling of the alternative therapies is Pesso Boyden System Psychomotor. This innovative form of treatment (often referred to as "psychomotor" or by the acronym PBSP) unites a conventional "talking therapy" approach with a variety of bodily experiences—touching, holding, and the like. Psychomotor techniques have a special way of gently coaxing extremely accessible and vulnerable feeling-states into being. These feeling-states, in turn, become the impressionable medium in which freshly manufactured "memories" can be created. These new "memories" are, basically, imaginary scenes that are dramatized and enacted. The ultimate goal is to introduce into the patient's internal being *a taste of what it would be like* to have had a different, more benign past and thus to engender more hope-filled expectations about the future—expectations that are rooted in the body and yet not grounded in the negativity and pain of the past.

Frozen Emotions

PBSP's originators, Al Pesso and Diane Boyden-Pesso, entered the world of therapy by an improbable route. When they first met, these long-married partners were highly trained creative dancers; later on, when they were no longer primarily performers, they opened a studio in the Boston area and became teachers of dance.

It was in their role as teachers that the Pessos became increasingly aware that certain technically experienced students could at times become virtually immobilized when it came to performing particular movements. It was as though some wordless but profoundly felt emotion had frozen a certain body part in place; and the couple soon recognized that such happenings were often deeply connected to the dancers' earlier life experiences.

Intrigued, the Pessos began to develop a series of exercises and procedures designed to foster exploration of the relationship among inner mental states and the ways in which inner states became manifest in outward, bodily expressions. It was in the course of this process that the couple began to realize that their "emotional movement" sessions were actually bringing about enduring changes in their students' personal lives.

Soon the couple began focusing less upon the teaching of dance *per se* and more upon physical expression as an alternative route into the world of the unconscious.

It was indeed from this curious, almost accidental beginning that the Pesso/Boyden system began its slow development into the highly elaborated method of treatment that exists today. What had started out as a series of therapeutic body movement exercises (and, along the way, become well recognized for its effectiveness by an ever growing number of colleagues) had kept on broadening and taken on a pronounced psychodynamic flavor.

Currently, the psychomotor movement claims groups of adherents in a loose connection of cities throughout the nation. Bands of followers have also sprung up all over the globe; there are Pesso/Boyden outposts in Belgium, Holland, Denmark, Switzerland, Germany, and Brazil. However, the central hub of the worldwide association is a sprawling establishment in northern New England. The place is called Strolling Woods and is located on Webster Lake, near the small town of Franklin, New Hampshire.

At Strolling Woods, the Pessos preside over a spread of some 215 acres, which encompasses hills, densely wooded areas, a large main house, and various outbuildings. Owing to a fire that swept through the property several years after I attended a first, weeklong training workshop there, some of the original structures have been rebuilt. But at the time of that initial visit, which was in the late 1990s, a charmingly rickety white Victorian-style farmhouse stood atop a high promontory, and we participants in the workshop bunked in this rambling central building. For our working sessions, however, we gathered in a smaller place called "the shed," which was at the base of a long, grassy slope and had once served as a guesthouse.

Structures

We met for three sessions daily: morning, afternoon, and evening. Our agenda consisted of 1) lectures on psychomotor theory; 2) demonstrations of the emotional information embedded in various bodily postures and movements; and 3) participation in the intense fifty-minute therapy sessions called "structures."

A structure is best characterized as a carefully constructed mini–theatrical event, presided over by a therapist who functions as a kind of "coach" or stage manager. That is, the therapist guides the choice of certain of the speaking parts, props, and placements-in-space of the various participants in the story, while overseeing the unfolding *and revision* of critical elements of the principal actor's life drama.

These "healing" dramatizations were all presided over by Al Pesso, and I soon noticed their tendency to take on a certain recognizable pattern or rhythm. The therapeutic structure would begin slowly, haltingly, as full of conversational stops and starts as a jet plane inching slowly toward its designated runway before accelerating its engines for takeoff. Then, often with a suddenness that could be breathtaking, the session would lift off and zoom upward into heights of emotionality, sometimes so intense that they teetered on the edge of the unbearable.

At first I found this disorienting, even frightening; but soon I realized that as each individual's structure began drawing to a close, so too would the tension level begin its descent. And eventually, the "protagonist" of the drama would gently bump down to earth once again—having come to rest in a drastically different place than she or he had been in at the session's beginning.

Antidotes

Before describing a prototypical PBSP structure, let me say a bit about the psychomotor method in more general terms. A basic tenet of this theory is that internalized, often very early memories of experiences that *felt* catastrophic foster ways of looking at the world that are filled with negative expectations. Rather than active maltreatment, such memories may involve woeful parental neglect.

In any case, such deeply pessimistic belief systems—often buttressed by feelings of profound hopelessness—may be grounded in the individual's long-ago history, but they bias his or her ways of seeing and comprehending the ongoing events of everyday life in the present. Like chaotic, scrambled bits of raw data that haven't ever been processed and organized into a meaningful whole, these scattered images and memories—of feeling alone, unprotected, overwhelmed in an uncaring universe—create an underlying but all-pervasive outlook on life. It is with the goal of creating alternative, symbolic experiences that can act as mental "antidotes" to this negative worldview that the Pessos' therapy has been created.

But can there be antidotes in the present for injuries that occurred long ago? Common sense would suggest that what once happened *did* happen and that the past cannot be altered retrospectively. For instance, if someone has grown up as the daughter in an alcoholic, occasionally violent household, there is no way to alter her recall of the awful events to which she has been the involuntary, frightened witness. Given that certain menacing, disturbing events *did* take place, they've inevitably become part of the developing person's inner reality, then part of the basic structure of her later, adult existence.

Here, it's important to emphasize that the psychomotor clinician's efforts are *not* directed at making bad memories disappear. Rather than trying to erase the recollection of parental indifference or emotionally or physically abusive events that *did* occur, this therapy is geared toward creating "symbolic, supplemental" memories—an internalization of the simulated experience of growing up in a loving, caring environment where such wounding things could never have happened. Creating a structure, in the psychomotor sense of that word, involves developing a completely novel option for being in the world—one that's hitherto been beyond the individual's imagining, given the psychologically injurious experiences that the client actually did suffer.

Basically, a therapeutic structure involves the creation of an alternative or countermemory, a memory replete with "virtual" images of basic human needs that *were* met and profound hopes that *were* satisfied—*at the right time* (early in life, when the developing person's map of the world was slowly forming) and *by the right people* (the beloved parental caretakers). This "synthetic, supplemental memory" comes into being slowly, and with surprising naturalness, in the course of an intensely moving dramatization. In what follows, I shall try to explain how this comes about and is made to feel surprisingly believable and authentic during the slow construction and acting out of a therapeutic scenario.

Finding a Place

On the first day of the workshop, each member of the group seemed to gravitate toward a preferred place to sit, and most of us returned to that place throughout the course of the weeklong conference. It was a kind of territoriality that I didn't take much note of until one afternoon when I found someone else sitting in my designated spot on one of the couches.

That incident rattled me, partly because the passionate self-reflection generated by the workshop had created an all-around heightened level of intensity. More to the point, however, Al Pesso had been lecturing about the metaphoric aspects of "place"—in this instance, meaning "place in the world." The questions we were being prompted to ponder had to do with the very beginnings of our lives: Had we been born into an environment where a "nest" had already been prepared for us in our parents' dreams, fantasies, hearts, and thoughts? Had we been welcomed joyously into the family's preexisting world, so that we'd felt protected and nurtured—or, alternatively, had we experienced ourselves as unbidden, accidental visitors whose presence had strained our caretakers' thinly stretched emotional, financial, or other resources?

This discourse on "place" had in fact triggered a disturbing recollection, one having to do with a Thanksgiving visit from my oldest sister. On that occasion, my young family and I had just returned to the East Coast after a long sojourn in California. That holiday was the first time in a long time that we adult siblings had been able to bring our growing families together, and naturally, reminiscences were in order. After a big turkey dinner, when we were all sitting in the living room having coffee, my sister said that she recalled very vividly my arrival from the hospital as a newborn.

She herself had been close to six years old at the time, she said. But then she added, with a surprising bite in her voice, that my entrance into the family had created a certain space problem in the household. It had in fact caused my father to tell his grown daughter by a former marriage—her name was Mary, and she was the child of his deceased third wife—that she would have to move out and find a place of her own. This piece of information shocked me. I stared at my older sister, for I hadn't heard anything about this until that very moment.

In truth, there had been so much family silence about the very existence of these half-siblings that I couldn't recall ever having heard the name "Mary" before. Nevertheless, elaborating upon this event, my sister told the gathering at large how close she herself had felt to this kind, mothering older girl and how upsetting it had been to see her tossed out of the household. The message wasn't hard to miss: My coming into the world had been the cause of this deprivation. In any case, my sister concluded this story by saying dryly with a short bark of a laugh, "As far as *I* was concerned, it was a bad bargain."

Could she possibly have thought this to be a lighthearted tale about the good old days when we were children? I've no idea, but given the circumstances of that moment, I chose not to respond. What I remember most about what followed is that one of my little daughters slid down along the sofa, flung an arm around my neck, and nestled her head sweetly against my shoulder.

Speed-Dialing to the Unconscious

The obvious link between discussions of "place," that recollection, and the discovery that my usual place on the couch had been usurped wasn't particularly obscure; what surprised me was the robustness of the memory of that incident, once that network of associations had been set off. It was such a vivid illustration of the ways in which we view the small events of our present-day lives—such as hearing a lecture and finding your usual seat occupied—through the lens of everything that happened earlier and how those experiences were interpreted at that time.

Generally speaking, we workshop participants sat in rows on one side or the other of the two long, wide sofas that lined both sides of the rectangular room. These sofas were strewn with an exorbitant number of throw pillows of differing sizes and colors; there was also a lavish assortment of floor cushions scattered throughout the room. This abundance of pillows and cushions was not, as I soon came to realize, merely decorative in nature. For as soon as the intense work on structures got under way, these objects began being pressed into service as props. For example, a large green pillow could serve to symbolize aspects of a certain figure—say, the remembered good side of a bullying older brother. A well-worn coral cushion might stand in for a certain locale or setting—perhaps the neighbor's house, where you felt safer and more welcome than in your own home.

More important, we members of the group were expected to role-play important figures in one another's lives, and we did so on a regular basis. On one occasion, you might be enrolled as someone's angry mother; on another, a rejecting father or the ideal parent that the enactor of the structure had longed for but never had. The request to play such a role always came from the client, who chose someone in the group who seemed to fit the part well enough. If the person asked to role-play felt uncomfortable about enacting a certain figure, he or she had the right to refuse—and on rare occasions, someone did.

Al Pesso, in his dual role as lecturer and supervising coach of the therapeutic structures, always sat in his own particular spot. It was a low, cushion-covered bench that stood just to the right of the large fieldstone fireplace that occupied most of the wall at the far end of the conference room. At the opposite end, close to the narrow entry door, was an eclectic assortment of freestanding chairs. These were always occupied by those members of the group who preferred to sit at some distance from Pesso and closer to the exit.

As for the attendees, there were some sixteen of us, and we were as polyglot a gathering as could be imagined. Some of those present were psychotherapists who'd come either for basic grounding in psychomotor techniques or for further technical know-how in terms of creating therapeutic structures. Then there was a small European contingent, all executives with a state-owned Belgian utility. These were people who'd attended psychomotor meetings abroad and had flown in expressly to attend this weeklong workshop.

There was also a woman who was working on her Ph.D. at Harvard and a young, haunted-looking housewife with long, shiny dark hair who was a trauma patient of Bessel van der Kolk's. She had come here at Dr. van der Kolk's suggestion. Other people at the conference were therapy clients, too—people who had heard of Pesso's work through the grapevine, had seen him at one of his frequent lectures or symposia, or were among a group of longtime devotees. One of the latter was a tall, mild-mannered pastor of a church in the Greater Hartford area.

Another was a slim, elegant, fiftyish Chilean-born lawyer. This man told me that he'd suffered from an ongoing, debilitating asthma condition before getting into psychomotor treatment. He said that as long as he could remember, he'd been dogged by nameless anxieties and feelings of imminent danger—an irrational, ever-present sense of threat that had no basis in his real-life circumstances. These symptoms had dissipated slowly in the course of a series of psychomotor therapeutic structures.

Still another frequent returnee, a middle-aged manager in an international banking concern, told me that he appreciated this form of therapy because it had "a focused way of getting to the heart of the matter, and doing so rapidly." Clearly, this was a person who placed a high value on his time. He told me that in his opinion, the Pesso/Boyden approach was "less burdened with abstractions and closer to reality" than other forms of therapy he'd tried, including a long Freudian psychoanalysis that he'd undergone in his early thirties. He said he didn't know whether Al Pesso was an unusually gifted therapist, or some kind of magician, or whether he'd developed a method of speed-dialing to the unconscious.

A Witness for Deirdre

It was Wednesday in a week of training that had begun the previous Sunday afternoon, and the weather was brutally hot. The psychomotor workshop was taking place during that most unusual of northern New England happenings, a heat wave during the first days of July. The conference room in which we were meeting, which was lined with wooden paneling, would have been comfortable and cool in more typical New Hampshire weather. But in these searing temperatures we were roasting, despite the best efforts of an old standing fan and a rumbling, cranky air conditioner.

It was early evening, and the first person scheduled to do a structure was Deirdre Carmody, a woman in her early thirties who was a doctoral candidate in the School of Public Health at Harvard. At the moment Deirdre sat stone-faced and silent, cross-legged on the floor in the center of the room, her gaze fixed upon Al Pesso.

A few members of the group were still chatting with one another quietly, and their low voices were punctuated by the drone of the air conditioner and the labored turning of the fan in the background. The blinds had been pulled down over every single window, but the pitiless rays of a slowly setting sun were poking through the bamboo slats.

I knew very little about Deirdre Carmody, who was one of the more diffident members of the group. She was an attractive person, with hazel eyes, dark wavy hair, and a slim, softly rounded figure; but when she spoke it was in a muted voice, almost a whisper, as if the conversation were taking place in a library. Given her air of extreme reserve, I thought that Deirdre's structure would get off to a very slow start, if it ever got moving at all.

Al Pesso, sitting on his customary bench, was looking from person to person as if waiting for the group to grow still. Pesso is a short, stocky man who exudes an air of zest and high energy, as well as a fund of benevolence and respect. He has strong features and a bald crown, rimmed with a halo of curly gray hair. During the development of a structure, when every word that's spoken *matters*, he always dons a set of earphones to enhance his partially compromised hearing. This gives him the air of an exuberant aviator, about to take the protagonist aloft on the trip of a lifetime.

Slowly, the room was becoming silent. Pesso fixed his gaze upon Deirdre and lifted his shaggy eyebrows as if to say "The next move is yours to make." It was up to her to raise a personal issue, a concern that was troubling her, to talk about anything that came into her mind at that moment. But she said nothing, and my thought was that it must be hard for someone like Deirdre to find herself at the center of so much focused attention. She did look dumbstruck, as if she were sorting desperately through her mental files for some topic, any topic, that she felt able to talk about in so public a setting as this one.

I wasn't optimistic about her finding anything and so almost jumped in my seat when she blurted out in a loud, hoarse voice, "My emotions are running really *high* this evening! I think it's because I've been watching people changing here—taking risks—" She stopped as if unable to continue speaking, as if she'd choked up on her words. Looking around, I could see that I wasn't alone in my surprise. Deirdre's structure seemed to be taking on altitude without even pausing at the runway.

Pesso nodded at her, then observed kindly, "*Moved* by that."

She nodded back, assenting. "Yes, very. But maybe I'm being emotional about something that isn't actually the thing I'm struggling to get to. Because I'm only halfway there, if you know what I mean?" She paused and looked at Pesso, whose expression was puzzled. He shook his head as if to say he didn't understand.

"Well, there's something that's been blocking me for about two years now," she said. "It happens when I start writing—not just the routine stuff that I turn out for my part-time job—but when it's for *me*. When it's *my own stuff,* work on my papers or my thesis, that's when I get into the problem." She paused, as if she were having trouble continuing. "I just feel . . ." She was choking up again, and her eyes were glistening. "I feel this kind of . . . echoing loneliness," she said, then wiped her eyes on her sleeve.

Al Pesso met her gaze fully, his large brown eyes full of compassion. He said nothing for a few moments, then gestured upward toward the ceiling. "Let's put a witness figure in the air. A witness would see how devastated you feel when you think of that echoing loneliness. Is that right?"

"Yes!" She sounded relieved. Pesso had begun the process of "microtracking"—that is, carefully noting each momentary expression of emotion as it appeared on Deirdre's features, then stating aloud what he was seeing. "Devastated and frightened," continued the therapist.

Deirdre, with an eager nod, assented. "And I'm *not* one of those people who always has to be with somebody to feel complete! I mean, I mostly do enjoy my own company. But when I'm working on my own project, something that I need to do for school—" She halted, fighting back tears again. Emile, a member of the Belgian contingent, got up and brought her a box of tissues. Deirdre wiped her eyes and said, "It just feels like . . . like there aren't enough people around."

"Saddened and full of grief that there aren't enough people around," Pesso said softly. He himself was taking on the role of the "witness," a role that on many occasions he would assign to someone else in the group. The "witness figure" makes an appearance very early in the development of a therapeutic structure and serves as an accepting, tolerant observer of the states of feeling that the client's facial expressions are communicating.

The witness not only *names* the protagonist's visible emotion (thereby validating its existence and reality), but *locates* it in the context in which it arose. Here, repeating Deirdre's own spoken words, Pesso had said that "there weren't enough people around" when she tried to work on her own projects. Clearly, this lack of people around her was having a devastating impact upon her ability to function and produce, for she nodded, looking stunned by grief. "Yes, it's like there's someone missing . . . ," she whispered, then began sobbing with abandonment as she pulled a fresh tissue from the box. She patted her eyes, blew her nose, then looked up at Pesso again.

"*Longing* for someone." His voice was gentle, probing.

Deirdre nodded and said almost inaudibly, "Yes."

"Who is it that you'd long for at those moments?" asked the therapist; and for some reason, Deirdre's expression brightened.

"When I was growing up, I did all my studying and writing right in the middle of the house," she said. The memory seemed to cheer her; it even brought a hint of gaiety in her voice. "I'd sit on the sofa and do my work, and there'd be all this *life* going on around me!" She threw her arms wide in a gesture meant to imply the buzz of family activity with which she'd been surrounded. A moment later, though, she grew teary again and used her fingers to wipe below her eyes as if she thought that some eye makeup might be dripping down. Then, surprisingly, she giggled.

Pesso tilted his head to one side, looked interested. "You laugh at that. Why?" he asked.

Deirdre said that most people would have found it impossible to concentrate under such circumstances, but for her it had felt exactly right.

"So that was a lovely remembrance?" Pesso asked, and when she nodded, he said, "A witness would see how *fond* you feel when you remember all that life around you in the house."

"Yes," Deirdre breathed, fresh tears springing to her eyes. "I'm just—missing them. . . . And part of it is that . . . my mother being dead . . . that piece of my life will never come back."

Pesso met her gaze, said quietly, "A witness would say, 'I see how much grief you feel that that piece of your life, when your mother was alive, will never come back.' So your mother is in your mind now?"

Deirdre, weeping, nodded. But then she said that this was part, but by no means *all*, of what weighed on her mind at this moment. Another piece had to do with her father and the fact that his professional life—he'd been a water resource specialist—had always involved frequent travel to developing countries everywhere across the globe. During those periods when her dad had been at home, the climate of the family had become thick with tension, fear, and pressure.

"So now, thinking about your father, you *feel* that anger and that stress coming from him?" inquired Pesso.

A frightened look crossed Deirdre's features, and she nodded; but then she added quickly that there had been long periods of time when he'd been away from home on his trips. "I guess it's good times like that I'm remembering, really. When he was gone, the household was . . . well, it was *happy*." The rough sketch of a scenario, the domestic tableau in Deirdre's mind, was slowly emerging.

This basic tableau involved a lively, friendly family atmosphere that had encompassed and supported her in her strivings and had felt joyful during her father's frequent absences. Deirdre Carmody seemed to be not only mourning the passage of an era when her mother was alive and her siblings had surrounded her, but also grieving about the angry, disgruntled parent who'd never been a caring, loving presence in the first place.

A Voice of Warning

For reasons that she'd never really understood, Deirdre's father had responded to her with less rage and irritability than he had to her four siblings. "I remember him hitting me just once—maybe it happened more times, but I can only remember that once—but I have vivid memories of the many, many times he hit the others. Watching that was very painful."

"You remember how painful it was to watch him hitting the others." Pesso was, once again, adhering closely to her own language as he confirmed and validated Deirdre's experience.

She nodded, her gaze fixed upon his. Then she said that in a way it had been like a wartime setting, one in which the victors make an example of some of the villagers. "You know, they pick some out and shoot them just to let the others know they'd better behave."

"So, he was like a tyrant or a Nazi," said Pesso.

"*Yes!*" The word seemed to burst out of her, as if she were excited by hearing that ugly truth said aloud. Yet at the same time she was clearly taken aback by hearing it stated in such stark, unvarnished terms, for she quickly backtracked and leapt to her father's defense. "He didn't *mean* to be, but that's the way it happened," she countered.

"A witness would see how protective you feel toward him. Because you said, 'He didn't mean to be,'" the therapist clarified her statement sympathetically.

She nodded. "I see now that my father got thrown into parenting and family life when he was way too young a man." She shrugged. "Still, I was left with the memories. . . . And now that I'm married myself, I thought it would be a different kind of life. But in many ways, it isn't. Because I've come to realize that even though my father didn't actively go *after* me as much, there was an awful lot of neglect!" Her expression was stricken.

"*Struck* by how much neglect there was," Pesso, in his role as witness, responded.

Deirdre nodded. "And at the same time, having to pretend that everything is fine!"

"That's a voice," said Pesso, raising his arm, the palm of his hand flattened upward, toward a different area of the ceiling. "And the voice is saying, '*Pretend that everything is fine!*'" He was placing that disembodied voice in the air, as he'd placed the witnessing figure earlier in the sequence.

"Yes, because if I didn't pretend that everything was fine, then *I* would get hurt, too," Deirdre elaborated.

Pesso gestured upward toward the ceiling once again, saying, "So, that's another voice—a voice of warning." Then he said, in a low, foreboding tone, "'*If you don't pretend that everything is fine, you'll get hurt, too!*'" Deirdre stared at him, seeming almost mesmerized by what he'd said. Then she blushed deeply and nodded, as if to say she fully accepted the validity of that statement.

Fragment Figures

In psychomotor theory, the witness figure and the various voices (of which there are many, including the voice of truth, the voice of warning, the voice of caution, the voice of doom, and the voice of negative prediction) are known as "fragment figures." That is to say, they are not full role players in the dramatic scenario that slowly emerges as the therapeutic structure develops.

The function of the witnessing figure is simply that of *seeing and naming* ongoing states of feeling, as expressed in micromovements of the facial muscles of the protagonist. This provides constant feedback about whatever emotion the person appears to be experiencing in the here and now of the current moment. (Let me interject here that when I myself did a structure, I found that this steady feedback process made me feel ever safer, more clearly heard and understood.)

The work of the voices is to state openly the thoughts that gave rise to whatever emotion is being observed. In other words, the voices serve as explicit, outward expressions of internalized beliefs, values, and rules for living that have been established early on and considered to be beyond question. In Deirdre Carmody's case, the directive "Pretend everything is fine!" was a clear example of a voice of caution or a voice of warning. In that instance, it was even more—a rule of behavior, a belief, and a pattern of being all rolled up in one internalized injunction.

I should add that there are many instances in which an enactor's statement calls forth *both* a witnessing figure and a voice. For example, in one of the structures that took place during the workshop, the pastor had said in a forgiving tone of voice, "I can't blame my father for being unable to protect me from my mother's crazy rages." At the same time, the expression on his features was one of stark fear. Immediately Pesso had gestured upward, placing a voice of caution in the air: "*'Don't blame your father for being unable to protect you from your mother's crazy rages!'*" But this was followed by a soft word from the witnessing figure, who'd said empathically, "I see how *terrified* you feel as you remember that situation."

Dependably, as a therapeutic structure develops and is elaborated upon, the enactor's internal map, or "blueprint for being," becomes externalized, visible, and surprisingly tangible. This blueprint consists of a relatively coherent set of perceptions, thoughts, and feelings, patterns of behaving, and ways of looking at the world. It can be thought of as the precipitate of an individual's accumulated experiences of living in his or her body and interacting with the human environment by which he or she has been surrounded.

Deirdre Carmody had commenced her structure by talking about a here-and-now concern: She was finding herself paralyzed by a sense of desolation and echoing loneliness whenever she tried to move forward on her own personal work—primarily, work on a research paper or on her doctoral thesis.

But this manifestly current-day issue, cruelly self-punitive in its effects, was obviously connected to memories that went far back into her personal history. For one thing, she was clearly in a state of desperate mourning for the loss of the family camaraderie that had existed when her mother was alive and her father was away on one of his journeys. For another, she was preoccupied by ambivalent feelings about a household tyrant who'd behaved abusively and uncaringly toward the family and had ignored and neglected her in ways she was just beginning to recognize. Her father had made her feel that "pretending that everything was fine" was a condition of her psychological survival. Moreover, at the present time—so Deirdre had hinted—this rejecting male figure from her past had reemerged in the present, in the figure of a neglectful, invalidating spouse.

A Theater of the Imagination: Role-Playing Figures from the Past

Slowly a symbolic arena was coming into existence—an imaginary theater stage upon which we fellow members of the group would enact the major figures of Deirdre's past and present life in a dramatic presentation fashioned and produced (under Pesso's supervision) by the protagonist herself. In the course of this work, we would be following Deirdre's cues and suggestions meticulously, as we role-played figures and scenes from her remembrances of the world-that-was. Then, importantly, we would begin to enact hypothetical figures in a far more affirmative kind of family world and create a "virtual reality"—one that placed her securely in the world-that-could-have-been, a world that was completely different from the one remembered with such pain.

Chapter Twenty

CHOREOGRAPHING THE SCENE

"PRETEND EVERYTHING IS FINE!" THIS WAS THE INNER DIrective to which Deirdre Carmody had always conformed, as if fending off some nameless but formidable danger. Now, however, hearing this internalized decree stated explicitly and in the form of a command—a voice of warning—she'd hesitated, her forehead narrowed in a thoughtful frown.

This particular internal rule, never before questioned, had guided Deirdre in steering her way through life, and it had governed many of her patterns of relating. But as she sat there, staring straight ahead, she looked disconcerted and—was I mistaken?—somewhat defiant.

This kind of reaction to the statement of a "voice" isn't unusual. The paradoxical effect of hearing an inner rule stated aloud—sounding as if it emanates from a control center outside the self—is that there's an automatic tendency to muster some resistance to it. Simply hearing the order "Pretend everything is fine!" has a way of making a person stop and say to him- or herself, "Wait a minute, everything is *not* fine. Why should I act as if it is?"

Thus, it wasn't surprising that the link between the voice's injunction —"Pretend everything is fine!"—and things that were happening in Deirdre's marriage sprang to the front and center of her thoughts. She and her husband were about to celebrate their third anniversary, she said, adding that she had waited a long time before marrying because she wanted to choose very carefully. "Also, I wanted to have a strong enough core so I wouldn't get—you know, *lost*."

"A witness would see how *resolved*, how resolute, you feel when you remember that you waited, and you wanted to have a strong enough core," Pesso said.

She sat up straighter, then nodded. (This confirming nod is a response that the psychomotor therapist always waits for before continuing; it is the signal that the witness's observation was an accurate one.)

"And I really feel like I *do* have a good, solid core," Deirdre said. "And yet I'm noticing"—she inhaled deeply—"neglect happening." It sounded odd, the way she had stated it: not "I am being neglected," but vaguer, as though neglect were occurring somewhere out there in the world.

"A witness would see how pained, and regretful, you feel . . . that neglect is happening," the therapist said.

"Yes!" Her face seemed to brighten in the way that it does when someone feels accurately heard. She waited, gazing at him expectantly.

"So, then, the neglect of your father is being repeated in some way by the neglect of your husband?" Pesso asked.

"Yes." Deirdre sounded energized, as if they were two hunters who were finding their way along the right trail. "And it's the same thing. My husband means well—but *not* well enough!"

There was a brief silence, during which that flurry of excitement dissipated; Deirdre's spirits seemed to droop, and she looked disconcerted. The therapist, sitting there and meeting her gaze while this transformation occurred, said, "A witness would see how discontented you are, that it's *not* well enough."

She nodded, and then Pesso asked her if she would like to choose two members of the group, or even two objects—perhaps a couple of pillows?—one to represent the neglectful part of her real father and the other the neglectful part of her husband. Deirdre nodded, then looked around, scanning those present one by one.

She chose Ernesto, the elegant, lanky Chilean lawyer, to be the neglectful part of her real father. Then she chose Jean-Michel, one of the Belgians, to play the role of the neglectful part of her husband. Each of them enrolled in his part formally, and then Pesso asked Deirdre to place them in the room as she saw them in relation to herself.

She directed Ernesto, as the neglectful part of her real father, to sit up tall and straight, at the maximum possible distance—the far end of a long sofa on the opposite side of the room.

Jean-Michel, as the neglectful part of her husband, was situated on the nearer sofa, somewhere in the middle, and just a few feet away from her.

Pesso, glancing at her choice and placement of the parent figure, said, "So your father is tall?"

Deirdre nodded. "Also, he lives a long way away." She looked comfortable, as if it felt right to have him at that distance.

"And what is your husband's name?" asked Pesso.

His name was Nikos, and he was Greek. He had been born in Alexandria, she replied, then sat there looking from one male role player to the other. After a few moments, Pesso inquired thoughtfully, "What happens as you feel the presence of these two figures?"

Deirdre's Adam's apple bobbed up and down before she said in the muted tone of voice in which she usually spoke, "They're fun, they're good people."

"A witness would see how content a part of you feels—" began the therapist, but then he stopped in midsentence. "But you don't *look* content," he stated.

Deirdre nodded, shrugged, said the fact that they were good company was merely something superficial. Pesso gestured airily toward the ceiling. "That sounds to me like a voice, the voice of reasonableness. It's saying, 'They're good company.'" He then observed that her two role players had been placed in the structure as neglecting figures, and it was interesting that she'd begun by describing them as good company.

"Well, neglect is not very easy to lay your hands on," explained Deirdre. "It's done in ways"—she'd begun to choke up again—"that not many people can see."

Pesso nodded understandingly and suggested that just for now, it should be made clear that Ernesto's role was that of the *neglecting* part of her father, and Jean-Michel's was that of the *neglecting* part of her husband. "We want them out here, in this space, as aspects of your father and your husband that can be *seen* by everyone present. There may be other, 'good company' parts of Nikos and your real father, but right now these two are the neglecting parts only. Is that okay?"

"Yes." Deirdre was looking intently from one man to the other, then back and forth again, as if these two role players were truly those neglectful persons incarnate. And when she spoke again, it was in that same hushed voice. "It was very hard on me to have to—well, to *lie* all the time, growing up," she said.

"A witness would see how pained you are, knowing you had to lie all the time, growing up. And that would be a voice, too." Pesso paused.

Deirdre nodded, offered the voice's statement spontaneously: "'*Say things were one way when they were really another way!*'"

He smiled and said, "Yes, that's a voice of warning: '*Say things were one way when they were really another way!*'"

"'Because if you don't, things will be worse,'" she added immediately. The therapist nodded and repeated her statement. Then he suggested that somewhere along the way they might invent a different family setting where she would be able to tell the truth and wouldn't have to lie. He looked at her questioningly, as if asking if he were still on track, but she shook her head in the negative, saying something here didn't feel completely right.

"Actually, I *could* tell the truth, but the thing was that I couldn't act on it. . . . I was trapped," Deirdre said. It wasn't clear what she meant.

The therapist didn't probe further. "A witness would see how helpless you feel, knowing you were trapped," he said.

"Yes, I was trapped," she agreed, looking miserable.

"Maybe, when we create the antidote, we'll invent the ideal family where you could both tell the truth *and* act on the truth. So then you wouldn't be trapped," suggested Pesso.

At this, Deirdre's expression brightened, as if an inner dimmer switch had suddenly been turned up to full capacity. "Yes, oh! I'd *like* that," she said.

The Voice of "Lower Your Expectations"

Speaking in terms of real time, or "here and now" time, Deirdre Carmody was in this room, in the presence of the workshop leader and the other members of this group. But as she sat there, gazing in turn at each of the two role players representing the neglectful aspects of the most significant males in her life, she was clearly somewhere else as well. In her mind's eye, she was also in historical time, the "then and there" time of experiences that were in the past.

And when she spoke again, she seemed to be musing aloud. "People say that if a husband is a good husband, you can tell it's so, because he doesn't get addicted to things, and he doesn't run around with other women, and he doesn't hit you."

Pesso repeated these words back to her in the oracular tones of a voice: "People say he's a good husband if he doesn't get addicted to things, he doesn't run around with other women, he doesn't hit you."

Deirdre nodded. "And to me that implies another, different voice—a powerful one—a voice that's saying, 'You'd better lower your expectations.'"

"You'd better lower your expectations, that's the best you can get," the therapist intoned, and Deirdre's eyes began filling.

"Yes," she half whispered, head hanging down.

"A witness can see how heartbroken that makes you feel, is that right?" Pesso asked, and she nodded, repeating that she'd waited a long time because she'd wanted more than that.

"So there's a longing for more than that." He was sticking to her own language as closely as possible. "And we can invent that. . . . Why don't we pick someone else to be the kind of husband you longed for?"

"Hmm." Deirdre raised her teary face and looked around the group thoughtfully. Then she asked Jim, the Hartford pastor, if he would take that role.

"I'm Jim, and I will enroll as your longed-for husband," he agreed, using the formulaic words of assent. Deirdre smiled at him, and Pesso intervened to ask her if this choice worked for her, if it felt like a good fit.

Eyes fixed steadily and even yearningly upon Jim, she nodded, and the therapist said quizzically, "You're looking at him with a kind of hope . . . and an expectation . . . ?"

"Yes," she said as the tears began rolling down her cheeks.

"And I can see how much pain you feel as you remember not having that—that hope, that expectation," Pesso said, stepping into his function as witness.

She nodded, unable to speak momentarily, her shoulders shaking with gusts of grief. Then she took out a fresh tissue, wiped her eyes, blew her nose gustily, and grew more composed. "To give an example, I live in this big old house, and the windows fall down really fast, because they don't have ropes or chains. And in many cases, the sashes are broken. So they're heavy, and they come down *hard*. And it's hard to get the storm windows in and out, because they're old and warped. It's hard, grueling work, and it's *hard* to do it alone!"

"A witness would see how pained and lonely you are, knowing that you have to do that alone," said Pesso. He was validating her experience.

Deirdre nodded, looking relieved to have voiced this complaint aloud and been heard. Still, when she spoke, she sounded angry and upset. "As it is, I end up covered with bruises. So okay, I don't have a husband that beats me, but still I'm covered with bruises! You might ask, 'What's going on here?'" she demanded.

"A witness would see how unjust that feels—" Pesso began, but Deirdre interrupted to say heatedly:

"There's something very wrong here!"

"It feels like there's something wrong," echoed the therapist, who then turned to Jim, in his role of the longed-for husband. "Maybe *this* husband would lift the windows," he said speculatively, raising his bushy eyebrows.

Deirdre turned to Jim, too, smiling through her outrage and her tears. "He might even help me *fix* the windows!" she said.

Then the pastor, in his role as the ideal husband she had longed for, was instructed to say, "If I had been your husband, and we lived in that big old house, I would have helped you fix those windows."

"Yes," said Deirdre, staring at him. She was growing calmer, looking mollified.

Pesso then suggested that the ideal husband go on to say, "And you wouldn't be covered with bruises." Jim did so, but this statement brought forth a fresh outburst of grief. Deirdre reiterated, in a despairing tone of voice, that her marriage felt "like a repeat, somehow."

"A witness would see how helpless you feel that you're in a repeat," said Pesso, and she nodded. "A repeat from your father to Nikos."

She looked appalled and said once again that she'd promised herself this would never happen—she would give herself a better fate than that.

"Shocked," said Pesso, "by your disappointment. Because you'd promised yourself more than that." Then he observed that because an older pattern seemed to have made this present-day pattern possible, it might be useful for them to travel backward in time. "Maybe, instead of an ideal husband, we should go back and get an ideal father. Do you want to see what that would feel like?"

"Well . . . I'm willing to try it" was Deirdre's somewhat dubious reply.

Autobiographical Memory and Evolutionary Memory

A basic tenet of psychomotor theory is that human memory falls into two broad general categories. One is "autobiographical memory," a blank tablet at birth, upon which our unfolding experiences in the environment will be inscribed. The other class of memory is "human evolutionary memory," by which is meant a prepackaged set of innate, genetically based programs that are geared toward survival of the self and of the species.

The latter—human evolutionary memory—is conceived of as part of our hereditary endowment and can best be understood in terms of certain fundamental needs that *must be met* in order to promote the growing child's optimal development. These basic requirements fall into five different headings: 1) the need for nurturance; 2) the need for protection; 3) the need for limits; 4) the need for support and 5) the need for "place"—which is, of course, that wonderful sense of belonging in a world that has been primed for and welcomes our arrival.

An apt example of the first of these genetically based programs—the need for nurturance—would be early attachment behavior. As a huge accretion of infant research has now demonstrated, newborns of our species come into existence ingeniously "prewired" for falling in love with *and inspiring the love of* their all-important caretakers, the parents. And, as a raft of important studies has made evident, these earliest, hugely powerful love bonds will have vast consequences in terms of the developing youngster's mental and physical well-being.

As Albert Pesso has written, "Our genes are the source for the information that guides our cells to construct the very systems and neural processes that give rise to perception and action in the first place. We naturally and without thinking access that gene-inspired information—

perfectly suited to provide avenues, strategies, perceptions and actions that can lead to successful outcomes. . . . It is as if our genes 'anticipate' our individual demise and have built into us a craving for sexual and social interactions that can result in the continuity of our species. From that genetic source we yearn to find our mates, find our calling and make our contributions to the world."

To put it plainly, we come into life just raring to form those kinds of passionate attachments that will result in individual survival and the perpetuation of our species. It follows, therefore, that first and foremost on every human being's inborn agenda is the intensely felt hunger for the stable, tender, responsive kinds of experiences with the first nurturers that will foster healthy maturation. And, according to Pesso, those of us who have been fortunate enough to have had the *right* relationships with the *right* kinship figures (the parental caretakers), at the *right* times, will naturally form the expectation that our lives will contain a fair portion of meaning, pleasure, satisfaction, and emotional connectedness. On the other hand, when fortune has dealt us a less favorable hand of cards, we come to anticipate pain rather than pleasure, incoherence rather than meaning, and isolation and alienation instead of a satisfying sense of connection and involvement.

Of course, this kind of theorizing about the fateful importance of early life experience does not represent a radical departure from traditional clinical thinking. What *is* different about the psychomotor approach is the hands-on way in which early deprivations are handled therapeutically. For a basic premise of this work is that there are reliable continuities between what is happening in the current moment and the things that happened earlier; and that our stored memories, *embedded not only in the mind, but in the "body's mind,"* provide the all-important bridge between a person's current state of being and the way in which those four genetically based human needs (for nurturance, protection, limits, and place) were well met or went miserably unsatisfied.

Thus, human memory is seen not only as crucially important in the organization and composition of an individual's present-day consciousness, but as *the* crucially important determinant when it comes to the patterning of his or her future. Again, the notion that our inner expectations, based upon past experiences, mold and shape the lives that are to follow is by no means a completely novel idea. On the contrary, it's so old that it's reflected in the writings of the Buddhist sages and appears in an ancient text called the Dhammapada. There it is written, "What you are now is the result of what you were. What you will be tomorrow is the result of what you are now."

Constructing an Internal Neural Network

In terms of therapeutic action, however, the question remains: Can what an individual will be tomorrow, based on what he or she is now, actually ever be changed or even modified? Psychomotor clinicians do believe it can be done. Their endeavor is to change the client's future (that is, avoid what Deirdre had called "a repeat") by creating a virtual stage upon which comforting "synthetic, supplemental memories" of a far less painful or depriving past can be devised and constructed. These healing scenarios are meant to provide the client with something often completely unknown—an internal action pattern, or neural network, for something that he or she has typically never even had a taste of earlier. That is the *felt sense* of a world in which the earliest caretakers hailed your arrival, held you devotedly, protected you solicitously, and met your normal developmental needs in the most satisfying, fulfilling ways imaginable.

. . . But the Heart Was Wrong

Deirdre's choice of the person to play her ideal father surprised me. She selected David Lucas, a large-framed, bulky therapist in his early forties. Dave, who'd come here accompanied by his wife—she was also a therapist—wore a perpetually aggrieved expression upon his face, as though his life had proven disappointing.

"I will enroll as your ideal father," he said to Deirdre immediately, looking flattered.

Then Pesso asked her where, in this room, she wanted him to be placed. "Let's see," she said thoughtfully, looking around, "somewhere within reaching distance . . ."

The therapist gazed at her, then said, "So maybe he says, 'If I had been your ideal father, I would have been within reaching distance.' Is that all right?"

Deirdre nodded, indicated a small vacancy on the sofa nearest her, and asked two of the women in the group if they'd mind if Dave sat between them. They shifted over, made a space available. There was a long silence as she stared at Dave in his ideal parent role.

"What happens when you see him beginning to take on that function?" Pesso asked softly. When Deirdre made no reply, he asked her if she wanted this ideal father sitting even closer to her.

She didn't hesitate: "Yes." She looked at the person sitting closest by on the sofa, and he, without a word, rose and moved to a floor cushion on the opposite side of the room. Deirdre, still cross-legged on the floor, shifted on her haunches until she was seated no more than a foot away from Dave. Then she sat there staring at her "ideal father," saying nothing but looking somehow absent, as if her thoughts were wandering elsewhere.

"What happens now?" Pesso asked, his voice low.

"Oh . . . uhm," was Deirdre's vague reply, as if speaking out of a reverie or daydream.

"What's coming into your mind?" inquired the therapist, and Deirdre turned to face him as she answered slowly.

"I was thinking . . . about a time when I was sick. . . . I must have been about nineish or tenish, something like that, and we were living in Egypt. It was some sort of tropical disease, one of these things that goes up and down. . . ."

"An undulate fever?" asked the therapist, and she nodded eagerly.

"Yes, that was it! So anyway, my parents kept sending me to school because my temperature was always down in the morning. But after a while it started going up in the early afternoon, and the teachers noticed, and they sent me home."

Pesso, gesturing with his head in Dave's direction, advised Deirdre to keep checking in with him, then asked what she would have wanted her ideal father to do in this situation and what her real father had actually done.

She had wanted her father to *believe* her when she said she wasn't feeling well, she cried out, sounding very young and scared. Dave needed no prompting: "If I had been your ideal father, I would have *believed* you when you said you weren't feeling well," he assured her. She gazed at him irresolutely, as if she yearned to take this statement in and find it credible.

"Anyway, when the teacher sent me home, there was no way to *get* home. There was only one car, and my father had it, and it was many miles across the desert to where we lived. So even if I'd been well, I couldn't have walked it! And he was out drinking at a club."

"So they called him?" asked Pesso, and she shook her head, said that, no, there was no way to reach him. "So then, how—" the therapist began, but Deirdre interrupted to say that her brother had walked her over to her father's club, which wasn't that far away.

"He was in a certain room where kids weren't permitted to go. So we got . . ." She halted, put her right hand over her chest as if to hold her heart in place, and began weeping again. "We got the waitress to go and tell him I was there, and I was sick. . . ." She drew in a breath that became transformed into the despairing sob of a forsaken child. "But he stopped to have another drink first, and in the meanwhile I threw up on the floor."

Pesso said, "So he stayed away, saying"—here, he switched into the pontificating tone of a voice—"'*I'm having another drink!*'" He was highlighting the facts of her real father's actual behavior.

Deirdre nodded, saying that the waitress had been the one to clean up the mess. "But it should have been my father who was doing that!"

The therapist looked at her thoughtfully, glanced briefly at Dave and then back at Deirdre. "So what would *he* say?" he asked her, sounding tentative. "If I'd been your ideal father, and I was at the club—"

"I would have come out right away!" Deirdre completed the sentence indignantly.

Dave then told her that if he had been her ideal father, and had been at his club, and she was sick, he would have come out right away. "And I wouldn't have stopped to have another drink," Pesso instructed him to add.

"And I wouldn't have stopped to have another drink," Dave repeated, gazing at Deirdre compassionately. But her own expression was unreadable.

"What happens when he says that?" the clinician asked.

Deirdre shrugged, said it was helping, but she felt as if they were still in the outer layers of the onion. "The thing is that this incident is just one of many, but it's a picture that gives the whole—" She halted, made a wide, sweeping gesture with both arms as if to say this episode was merely a small, representative piece of a much larger, more highly stratified and complex reality.

"Like a hologram," Pesso suggested.

"Exactly," she said. "So everything *looked* okay on the outside. After all, he did come out eventually."

"That's a voice of truth: 'After all, I did come out eventually.'"

"Yes, and brought me home," she agreed.

"'And I brought you home,'" echoed Pesso, still speaking in the oracular tone of the voice of truth.

"'And I made sure you had a good doctor,'" she said.

"'And I made sure you had a good doctor,'" intoned the therapist.

"But the heart was wrong!" Deirdre burst out, stretching her arm outward in Dave's direction, palm upward, fingers bent around it as if she were literally holding a heart in her hand.

"A witness would see how pained you are to know that the heart was wrong," said Pesso, and Deirdre nodded as tears began rolling down her cheeks. Then, slipping into his role as choreographer of the scene, he addressed Dave: "Talk about his heart. . . . And could you hold your hand the way she held hers when she said the word *heart*?"

Dave nodded and extended his own arm in Deirdre's direction, holding his own "heart in his hand" in the same way she had done. "What happens when you see him make that gesture?" Pesso asked her in a tone between an embrace and a whisper.

She looked affected, even shaken. "An ideal father would have . . . a connection," she said, placing both hands over her own heart. There was a silence.

Pesso turned to Dave, telling him to place his hands over his own heart, then feeding him his lines. "Say: 'I would have had that connection.'"

Dave, placing both hands over his heart, said feelingly, "If I had been your ideal father, I would have had that connection."

Deirdre nodded, looking spellbound. "And it would have told you how to act."

"And my heart would have told me how to act," Dave agreed. Again, Deirdre stretched her arm toward him, her hand cupped as if holding her heart inside it; and Dave, as ideal parent, mirrored the gesture, as if offering his own heart in return.

"Yes" was all she said. "Exactly."

There was a long, long pause, during which everyone present seemed to be holding his or her breath. "What's happening? What are you feeling?" Pesso asked at last.

Deirdre told him that there had been a lot of knots in her chest at the outset of the structure, but now she could feel them beginning to open up. "This one's opened, this one's going," she said, pointing to various places on the left side of her chest.

"Make a sound from the part that hasn't opened up yet," said Pesso, but Deirdre only exhaled deeply. "As you exhale, make a *sound*," he then prompted her. I expected to hear a loud expulsion of air, a profound sigh or even a groan. But shockingly, what emerged was a loud, wrenching, atavistic kind of sound, the kind of groan you'd expect to hear from someone under torture.

When it was over, though, it seemed to leave her feeling better, not worse. She looked relieved.

"And what about your hand?" the therapist asked her in a kindly, curious tone of voice. It had remained extended toward Dave, her ideal parent, still cupped upward as if she were offering her beating heart to him. Deirdre stared at that hand for a moment, almost as though it belonged to someone else. But her only comment was that it felt very steady.

"And the meaning of it?" Pesso asked.

"The meaning is that when people care about each other in a certain way, there's a connection across distance," she replied.

Pesso turned to Dave and asked him to send this statement back to her; and he, in his role as ideal parent, obliged by saying feelingly: "When people care about each other in a certain way, there's a connection across distance."

Deirdre looked moved, deeply gratified.

"A witness would see how convinced you feel about that," said Pesso.

"That *is* the way I feel," she replied unhesitatingly.

We had reached a moment of calm and serenity, and a feeling of peace descended upon all of us—one that seemed sanctified by a sudden chorus of evening birdsong. Dusk was gathering, and those sitting nearest the table lamps began to turn them on. It seemed to me that Deirdre's structure was winding down to its natural conclusion; but in this I was mistaken. For it soon became evident that there yet remained some deeper, more sensitive and painful "onion peeling" to be accomplished.

Chapter Twenty-One

ANTIDOTE: CREATING "VIRTUAL, SUPPLEMENTAL" MEMORIES

IN HIS ROLE AS CHOREOGRAPHER OF THIS EMERGING SCENARIO, Pesso now turned to Dave Lucas and asked if he could make a suggestion. Could Dave, as Deirdre's ideal parent, move himself a little closer to her, near enough so that their two cupped hands could connect physically?

Dave nodded and shifted his body to the edge of the sofa on which he sat; and Deirdre, cross-legged on the floor, shimmied closer to him on her haunches. They reached a position in which they were leaning toward each other and stretching their arms forward until their concave hands touched lightly at the backs of the knuckles.

After a long pause, Deirdre murmured, "It feels very warm."

Pesso, leaning forward on his low bench, said to her, "He might say: 'You could *feel* my warmth.'" She nodded her acceptance of this statement, then looked up at Dave with a childlike expression on her face; and he, with genuine sympathy in his voice, said that if he'd been her ideal father, she could have felt his warmth. She looked at him gratefully, let out a sigh of contentment.

"Imagine getting father warmth that way," said Pesso. "What does it feel like?"

"It feels like I can breathe more easily," she replied, the ring of relief in her voice.

The therapist then forwarded this new line of ideal father script directly to Dave, who duly repeated it. "If I had been back there then, you would have been able to breathe more easily," he said.

"Yes, and not just me, but my brothers and sisters, too!" said Deirdre, who, while still with us, had in some sense left this setting and everyone present. She had gone into an alternative space, the imaginary world of the-way-it-could-have-been.

Pesso glanced meaningfully at Dave, who repeated her words: "Not just you, but your brothers and sisters, too!"

"Yes," said Deirdre, looking deeply affected.

"A witness could see how convinced you are of that possibility," said Pesso.

Yes, she replied, adding that in reality her brothers and sisters had all suffered from asthma. Then tears began welling up in her eyes once again, and she looked searchingly at Dave, her ideal parent. "We wanted so to miss you when you were away," she said to him mournfully.

Here, the structure leader intervened to tell her that she had left the healing scenario momentarily. "Now you're talking about your *real* father," he said, then turned to Dave and asked him to say that if he had been her ideal father back then, she would have missed him when he was away.

"Yes." Deirdre's voice was girlish but hopeful sounding. "Yes, I would have missed you."

"A witness would see how touched you are by that realization," Pesso observed quietly.

She nodded and said, "Yes, that's what we all wanted." This line became quickly incorporated into the "virtual" memory they were developing; and Dave, as ideal parent, repeated her words as she had said them.

"It would have been the way all of you wanted it," he told her firmly. His cupped hand and Deirdre's cupped hand, both holding their symbolic hearts, were still touching. Her eyes were shining.

"Yes," she said, "yes."

There was a silence. Then Pesso said to Deirdre in a low, inviting voice, "Take that inside yourself, at that age—maybe around nine or ten years old. . . . That kind of heart connection with a father."

She didn't answer, merely emitted a long, peaceful breath. She looked deep into Dave's eyes, then said, "If you were my ideal father, you would *know* what you were doing!" But this seeming criticism was muted by a small, forgiving little giggle.

Dave, smiling, said, "If I were your ideal father, I would *know* what I was doing."

She nodded, still smiling. Here, the therapist intervened to remind her that earlier on she had spoken about her father's having married too young. "Yes," she said, and Pesso turned to Dave with the suggestion that he say, "I would have raised a family *knowing* what I was doing."

This brought a broad grin to Deirdre's face, and she laughed aloud again, saying that this last comment had caused a voice of reason to pop into her head. "And, you know, that voice of reason was saying, 'Hey, he was only twenty years old!'"

In that case, responded Pesso, the ideal father might say, "I would have started a family at—" He halted in midsentence. "At what age, do you think?" he asked Deirdre.

"*Much* later!" she answered merrily.

Then Dave said, "I would have gotten married *much* later."

"Yes," she breathed, gazing at him, looking contented.

"A witness would see how relieved you are by that reassurance," the therapist said. Deirdre nodded, sighed deeply, kept looking fixedly into her ideal parent's eyes. She seemed transported, but she said nothing aloud.

Addressing the "Glut"

As Deirdre and Dave sat facing each other, arms outstretched, cupped hands touching lightly at the knuckles, Pesso urged her once again to *feel* that relief at whatever age she had missed it. "Because you're feeling real relief right now, is that right?" he asked.

Deirdre said that she was indeed feeling relief, but that leaning toward Dave and holding her arm in this outstretched position was beginning to make her shoulder muscles ache. This led Pesso to suggest that the pair move even closer to each other in order to diminish the physical strain upon their arms and still retain their linked "heart in their hands" position. The two then shifted and rearranged their positions until both were comfortable, and Deirdre said, "This feels much better, this feels fine to me."

From this nearer vantage point, she fixed her gaze upon her ideal father, and Dave Lucas met that gaze unflinchingly. "What's happening?" Pesso asked her softly. "What do you see when you look at him now?"

"I see a lot of . . . soul," said Deirdre, her eyes beginning to fill.

"Maybe he says, 'If I had been your ideal father, I would have had a lot of soul.' Does that sound right?"

Pesso was checking in with her about every aspect of this synthetic memory in the making, and now he looked at Deirdre questioningly. Eyes glued upon Dave, she didn't speak; she merely nodded her assent. But when Dave, in his role as ideal parent, said he would have had a lot of soul, she answered energetically, "You wouldn't have been *afraid* of it, either!"

"I wouldn't have been afraid of it, either," Dave agreed.

"*Yes,*" she said with a profound sigh, as if she'd unloaded a painful burden. A moment later, though, she inhaled, and her expression turned to one of grief; she exhaled, a sound that was somewhere between another deep sigh and a groan.

"What's happening?" Pesso asked.

Deirdre turned from Dave to him and said, "I feel as if most of the knots are gone." She gestured toward her upper chest. "There's still one here"—she pointed to a place just below her left clavicle—"but it's like this—this *glut.*" She looked embarrassed and laughed lightly, as if trying to downplay something shameful.

Pesso looked at her thoughtfully. "I can give you a good way to deal with that," he said. "If you take a deep, deep breath, and tighten hard at 'the glut'—then tighten even harder, harder, harder—and make a *sound* with that tightness . . ." Deirdre, who'd been following these instructions even as he spoke, suddenly emitted a loud racking cough so intense and full of spluttering choking sounds that her body doubled over in pain. It seemed to come out of nowhere and was awful to see, frightening to listen to—like watching someone trying to exorcise a demon or cough up the phlegm of a lifetime.

What had Deirdre said earlier? Hadn't she described herself as the one child in her family of origin who'd been asthma free? This terrible, grinding, hacking episode made you wonder. The coughing fit receded slowly, ending with an extended, long, sobbing, indrawn breath.

"That's the remains of the grief. Do you hear the cry, the desolation, in there?" Pesso asked her softly. She nodded but seemed chagrined and did not look up to meet his eyes. Then he told her that he had another suggestion to make, one that would help her to feel safe and supported as the process of addressing "the glut" continued.

Let the Cry Come

According to Albert Pesso, there are many clients who cannot possibly be helped if approached by means of verbal psychotherapy alone. These are people who have dealt with their unbearable thoughts and feelings by walling them off and who experience their suppressed emotionality in the form of bodily symptoms and sensations—for instance, Deirdre Carmody's "glut." As the therapist now explained to Deirdre, she was going to need the reassurance of what, in psychomotor parlance, is known as a "contact figure."

A contact figure is simply someone in the group whose reassuring physical touch serves to communicate the message that he or she will *be there* to help the protagonist handle whatever painful feelings emerge as work on the structure continues. "I say this because when you cry in that way, it sounds to me like you need someone to hold you," Pesso said. "So, do you want to pick a contact figure? . . . Because I think you have a lot of grief in there, and if we touch it once again, I'm certain it's going to come out."

Even as he spoke, Deirdre was looking around the room for a member of the group who felt right to her when it came to taking this particular role, but she couldn't seem to settle on anyone. "This is so hard for me, I can't seem to choose," she said at last, sounding flustered, even scared, as if no one in this room felt strong or safe enough to be given this particular assignment.

Pesso waited quietly as she scanned the group again, but once more she shrugged, shook her head, looking confounded. Then Pesso, glancing at Dave Lucas, said to Deirdre, "Perhaps he could hold you?"

She nodded. "I'll just move over," she said, and then placed herself, like a child seated on the floor at her parent's foot, next to Dave's right shin.

"I will enroll as your contact figure as well as your ideal father," he said formally.

Then she curled up next to his leg, her head facing downward, her arms entwined around her own torso. She was facing outward to the room, and Dave, seated on the low sofa, was instructed to place a caring, protective arm around the backs of her shoulders.

For a brief while they sat there, the picture of parent/child tranquillity. At last the therapist said, "Tighten that spot in your chest again," and Deirdre did so, then released the breath. This was followed immediately by a long bout of that same racking cough, a cough so hard and wrenching that she doubled over again. Given the peaceful interlude that had preceded this eruption, I felt shaken by the raw pain of this scene. So did others in the group, I thought, for when I looked around all heads were lowered, as if in prayer, and nobody met my eyes.

I glanced at Pesso, who seemed unfazed. He now suggested that Dave put one arm all the way around Deirdre's shoulder, and then hold her forehead with his open palm. The coughing fit petered out slowly, and the pair of them remained in this position for a while. Then the clinician said to Deirdre gently, "Let the cry come. . . ." She drew in a long, shuddering breath that sounded like a sob.

"Hear that?" Pesso asked her encouragingly, and those words seemed to penetrate some kind of internal dike or seawall. The resultant flood of grief and sorrow that came pouring forth was alarming, even given the long bouts of hacking and choking that had gone before. Once again, there were those deep, rasping fits of coughing, but this episode sounded far more desperate. Deirdre was struggling to catch her breath, then getting some air in, then sobbing wildly, coughing hard again. It was hard to sit there simply watching because you wanted to jump up and help. She seemed so much like someone drowning—going under, coming up, gasping and flailing, going down again, and then surfacing anew as if in a mad struggle to take in some swallows of scarce, life-giving oxygen.

At last, as abruptly as it had begun, the horrible episode ended. Deirdre's coughing receded, and she sat up, reached for the tissues box, and began to wipe her eyes and blow her nose. "Wait," said Pesso, as if to say that this episode had not yet reached completion. He asked her to take Dave's hand and place it on her chest just where she felt "the glut," then tighten that spot once again.

"Hold on a moment," she said, "I can't breathe."

"Yes, that's the emotion," Pesso responded.

After a brief time-out, during which she inhaled and exhaled deeply several times, Deirdre placed Dave's hand above her left breast in the spot where she'd have put it if she were saluting the flag. "Now, take another deep breath, and tighten hard, and *sound*!" the structure leader coached her.

Deirdre inhaled deeply, and as she exhaled the breath it became that same deep, racking cough, interspersed with sobs and asthmatic-sounding, indrawn gulping for air.

"It is terrible, terrible sorrow," Pesso commented sympathetically.

Deirdre nodded, head down, still struggling for breath, though the rasping, choking sounds, interspersed with cries of sorrow, were slowly diminishing in intensity. Now the therapist asked Dave, in his combined role of contact figure/ideal parent, to wrap both arms around Deirdre's shoulders even more tightly and hold her forehead firmly in his grasp. As he did this, she let out a sudden anguished cry, a deep, howling "Aaaaah!" that sounded as if it had bubbled up from the inmost recesses of her being.

"It's deep grief you're feeling," Pesso said again. "Did you hear it, those sounds? What did they sound like to you?"

Deirdre sat up, pulled away from Dave, and ran a distracted hand through her wavy dark hair. Then she pulled some more tissues from the box, wiped her eyes, blew her nose, and looked at the therapist directly. "Whatever I might have said, or *not* said earlier, I guess I didn't say how much pain I was in," she said in a wondering tone of voice, sounding amazed to realize it herself.

It Really Got into Your Body

Now Pesso suggested that Dave say to Deirdre, "If I had been back there then, you could have said how much pain you felt."

She nodded, eyes wide and trusting. "Yes, I could," she breathed.

The structure leader smiled and observed that she was gazing at Dave with such a young look on her face. "You look about seven or eight years old . . . you must have felt that way at seven," he said. Then he pointed out the way she was now hanging on to Dave's hand by his little finger, the way that a little girl might have hung on to her daddy's hand.

"Maybe he could say, 'You could have held my hand like this when you were seven,'" Pesso suggested.

Deirdre nodded and laughed with pleasure at the notion; but before Dave could say another word, that laugh had become a sob. She was weeping openly as her ideal parent said, "You could have held my hand like this when you were seven."

She looked up at him through her tears and said, "If you were my ideal father, you would not have let life get so on top of you that you couldn't . . ." She left the sentence incomplete.

"Be there for you?" suggested Pesso.

Deirdre shook her head. "Treat us kindly," she said.

"If I were your ideal father, I wouldn't have let life get so on top of me that I couldn't treat you kindly," Dave said, and she nodded.

"Because we would have been more *important* to you than all those other things that were going on!" She said, her voice charged with reproach.

Dave, as ideal father, said understandingly, "Because you would have been more important to me than all those other things going on."

"Yes," she said, "yes." She sighed again, mollified.

"When you let the air out, let a sound come, too. See what comes of it," the therapist advised her. Deirdre inhaled, exhaled peacefully. "Feeling relief now," Pesso commented.

Deirdre nodded, breathing in and out calmly for a few moments. Then, suddenly, she turned to Dave with a fresh accusation. "There's another thing—if you had been my ideal father, it would have been safe to make noise around you!"

"If I had been your ideal father, it would have been safe to make noise around me," he assured her.

Deirdre breathed in and out deeply, crisscrossed her hands across her chest. "I'm feeling my back letting go as well, this is good," she announced to no one in particular.

"A witness can see how relieved you are—how *pleased* you are—to feel your back letting go," Pesso said. Then, in his capacity as impresario, he turned to Dave and suggested that he repeat that remark in his ideal parent role.

"If I were your ideal father, you could have let your back go like that, when you were young," Dave told her, and Deirdre nodded, began to cry.

"A witness can see how touched you are, to experience that possibility," Pesso said gently.

She nodded, said through tears, "I wouldn't need the armor."

"If I had been your ideal father, you wouldn't have needed the armor," Dave said.

Deirdre nodded, met his gaze, and said in a childish, somewhat truculent voice, "I *like* making noise!"

Pesso quickly interposed himself and instructed Dave to say, "I like *hearing* your noise," and this elicited an excited laugh from Deirdre—a laugh that turned into a sob, then into racking cries of grief. She began rocking back and forth, like a soul in deep mourning, mourning for the way things had really been, so far from the deeply satisfying tableau being created.

Then, as unexpectedly as it had begun, the episode passed. She straightened up, blew her nose, and said with a self-mocking laugh, "This is beginning to look like a video ad for Kleenex tissues!" Her social self was reasserting itself, but her complexion was plaster white and her eyes so rounded and bulging that she looked like a frightened ghost. She jumped when the *beep-beep* of Pesso's timer sounded.

This meant that forty minutes had passed, and the structure had a mere ten minutes left to run. "Okay, I think I'm almost done," Deirdre said quickly, half rising from her seat on the floor. But Pesso, waving her back into place, told her that the beeping signal didn't mean she had to rush, only that the time left to them was limited now.

Sinking back against the side of her ideal father's legs, she sighed peaceably, as if it felt good being back there again. "Let a sound come every time you exhale," the structure leader suggested. Deirdre sighed again, more loudly this time, and Pesso said, "That sounds like relief."

"Yes," Deirdre said quietly, then inhaled and exhaled deeply several more times. "Yes, that feels really *good*," she said, snuggling even closer and resting her head against Dave's thigh trustingly.

"At what age would you have wanted this kind of contact?" the therapist asked her, and Deirdre paused thoughtfully. Then she said that her father had in fact given all his children some measure of contact, but it hadn't been consistent with his other behavior.

"So maybe he'll say, 'If I had been your ideal father, my behavior would have been consistent,'" said Pesso. Deirdre nodded and twisted her position slightly so that she could look directly up at Dave's face as he echoed this statement.

"Yes." She sighed deeply, sounding consoled. "The picture would have matched the inside."

"The picture would have matched the inside," Dave said, needing no prompting.

"Yes," she said, and Dave said, "Yes," right back to her.

Deirdre seemed to sink into a reverie and said nothing for a period of time. "What are you thinking?" Pesso broke the silence to ask her.

"I was thinking that I would have felt safe at night," she said.

"You would have felt safe at night," Dave, as her ideal parent, assured her. A beatific expression settled over her features.

"Go back, now, to some of those nights when you didn't feel safe," Pesso suggested, "and bring this experience back there. See what happens when you do that."

Deirdre closed her eyes, was silent for several moments, then began to cry brokenheartedly. "A witness could see how much you suffered when you were younger," the therapist told her. She nodded, reached for more tissues, and dabbed at the tears rolling down her cheeks.

Pesso, glancing at Dave, said to her, "So maybe he says, 'I would have brought you this safety back then'?"

She nodded and turned to Dave, who repeated this statement with genuine compassion in his voice. Clearly, he had become swept up in the role he was playing. "I would have brought you this safety back then," he said, and she nodded, sighed with relief, then began to cry again.

"I didn't think that it got to me as much as it did," she said, tears streaming down her face.

"A witness would say, 'I can see how surprised you are to realize it got to you as much as it did,'" said Pesso. Then, stepping out of the witness role, he added, "It really got into your body, though you kept it from reaching your mind."

Deirdre nodded and said that all the other kids had gotten asthma, but somehow she hadn't.

"You just got those knots in your chest," the therapist observed, and this remark elicited a huge sigh.

"Yes, I think we would have all been more well—"

Interrupting, Pesso turned to Dave and said, "Say that: 'If I had been—'"

Dave stepped in smoothly and said, "If I had been your ideal father, you would all have been more well."

Deirdre, gazing up into his eyes, said, "Yes," and once again, Dave said, "Yes," back to her immediately. She sighed contentedly, took out a fresh tissue, and blew her nose again. "It's important to me to be able to breathe," she said.

"It would have been important to me that you would have been able to breathe," Dave, as her ideal parent, repeated her words.

"Yes, it would have mattered a lot to me," Deirdre said wistfully.

"It would have mattered a lot to me that you would have been able to breathe," Dave echoed with real caring in his voice.

"So . . . he would have been interested in your breathing. He would have been *present*," Pesso prompted softly.

"I would have been interested in your breathing; I would have been present," her ideal father assured her.

Deirdre sighed deeply, said in a little girl's voice, "And you wouldn't have given up on me."

"I wouldn't have given up on you," Dave said firmly.

She nodded, sighed again, looked at the therapist, and said she was ready to derole and "chew on what had happened." But he merely smiled, pointed out the childlike way in which she'd taken hold of Dave's little finger once again. "So then, *remember* the grip, and remember the touch, and remember the relief in your breathing." Pesso's voice was low, hypnotic. "And put all of that back in time, into a context that has to do with your ideal father being *there for you* at that age. So that all of these sensations, with their life-altering possibilities, get linked in your mind. And they're there *inside you*, at that age level."

Deirdre, listening with her eyes closed, looked as if she were feeling serene, at ease. "I am trying to bring all of this back into that house, into those rooms," she said, as if reporting from a location that she saw in her mind's eye.

"Good," Pesso said encouragingly, for the ultimate goal was to insert something new into Deirdre's internal narrative—not a replacement of her real personal history, but something in the nature of a "supplemental" memory. This satisfying, reassuring "virtual" memory had been developed and designed in such a way as to instill in her a reassuring, vivid sense of having been loved unconditionally by the first important male she had ever known, for it was the memory of having been loved by the *right* person in the *right* kinship relationship at the *right* time of her life.

"Those rooms, where we felt so unsafe. Yes . . . it was very dramatic, but it could have been so different if we'd known we were safe. We could have laughed so much off." Deirdre's reflections were drifting ones; she was musing aloud.

"You would have had another perspective," the therapist agreed.

She nodded, sighed deeply, peacefully. The session ended there, with the process of "deroling." The voices in the air—the voice of truth, the voice of warning, the voice of "lower your expectations," the voice of reasonableness—were all dissolved by successive waves of Pesso's hand. The neglecting parts of Deirdre's father and her husband, Nikos, stepped out of their roles formally and told her that they were resuming their true identities now; they were Ernesto and Jean-Michel once again.

Jim, the pastor, resigned from his part as ideal husband, and then Pesso waved his hand, erased the witness figure from the airy space above him. Last of all, Dave Lucas said, "I derole and am no longer your ideal father. I am Dave." But Deirdre, with a child's stars in her eyes, looked at him and said worshipfully, "I'm grateful . . . thank you." She seemed a bit dazed, as if a part of her yet remained in the world of "then and there" and hadn't yet returned to this time, these people, this wood-paneled shed in the hills of northern New Hampshire.

A Life Worth Living

At the outset of the workshop, Al Pesso had told me that in my role as invited observer I should by no means feel pressured to do a structure of my own unless I so desired. But in the meantime I'd observed the other conference participants "taking a risk" (as Deirdre had phrased it) and profiting mightily from having done so.

I knew that if I did volunteer to do a structure, I would want to work on the subject of "place," for the jarring vision that had surfaced—of having come home from the hospital, as a newborn, to a household that was overfilled and unready to receive me—had raised certain basic, fairly daunting questions in my mind. These questions had to do with things that had been said during Pesso's lectures. People whose "place" in the world has not been prepared for them, the therapist had observed, often struggle with a sense of "Where do I belong?" and sometimes even question their fundamental right to existence.

At week's end, as the psychomotor workshop was drawing to a close, I took a brief hike around a nearby lake along with Deirdre and Bea Ellis, another member of the group. Bea, a tall, elegant African American academic in her mid-fifties, had come to this conference with a specific, well-defined goal in mind. She had been widowed a year earlier, and though she was mourning her husband's loss and missing him desperately, she'd found herself unable to weep. She said she felt "waterlogged with grief," but her tears seemed locked inside her, and crying had proven impossible.

Bea Ellis had done two extraordinary structures during this week, and neither of them had left her (or most of the rest of us) dry-eyed. Both structures had involved large casts of characters and long interchanges with role-playing figures; and I myself had taken part in one of them, enrolling as her "ideal maternal aunt" at her request. Actually, Bea's two healing scenarios could not have been more different from Deirdre Carmody's structure, which had involved far fewer speaking roles and just a handful of people—Dave Lucas more than anyone. In Deirdre's case, the work had focused pretty exclusively on one particular life course–setting relationship—her relationship with her dictatorial, neglectful father, which had erupted into the present and was being reenacted with Nikos, her spouse.

"The past falls open anywhere," the Irish writer Michael Donaghy has written. But as I strolled along with these two women, I wondered if the creation of virtual, supplemental early memories could really intervene and prevent that from happening. Certainly Bea Ellis had become able to cry openly about her husband's death and to connect her long emotional shutdown with certain earlier experiences that had taught her *not to feel* things that seemed too painful to handle. But did her newly minted, happier early "memories" have the real stamp of authenticity?

I had so many questions that I wanted to put to Bea, and to Deirdre, too, about how they'd been affected during and after their structures. I couldn't do this, though, because we participants had been enjoined to respect one another's internal processes and basic privacy by not getting into discussions about the highly personal sessions we'd witnessed. So as we walked along, the three of us chatted lightly, enjoying the beauty of the scene and the fact that the weather was finally cooling down. I was preoccupied by, but didn't even mention, my own most pressing concern—the decision I was struggling with about whether or not to do a structure before the workshop ended. But along the way, I was checking out my companions carefully—Deirdre especially, since we'd both had explosive, neglectful fathers—and trying to take my cues from their behavior, how well they appeared to be doing.

Deirdre *did* seem different in the wake of the session that I've described, most especially in terms of her voice: It was firmer and had lost the hushed quality that so often made it difficult to hear her. Now, as we women strolled down a wide woodland road alive with the humming sounds of summer, she paused and raised her hands in front of her in prayer position, then spread them wide in a huge circle as she inhaled deeply. Bea and I stopped, waited. Deirdre held her breath a moment, then exhaled with a deep "Ahhhh," the sound of satisfaction. Without preamble, then, and apropos of nothing we'd been talking about before, she said, "When I go home I'm letting my husband know something: Either the marriage will change or the marriage will end. . . . And if it *does* end, that's okay, because what's become clear to me now is that I need to get a life worth living."

Once again she spread her arms wide, as if to encompass the whole world, then inhaled and exhaled deeply. And at that moment I decided I would volunteer to do a structure of my own.

EPILOGUE

When Claudia Martinelli called to tell me that she and Paul had reconciled, I can't say that I was completely surprised. It seemed to me that she'd answered her own anguished question—What lesson am I not learning?—by surrendering to the belief that, at least in her own case, any new relationship would prove to be as damaging as all the past ones. The lesson was one that would never be learned, so she had "settled," as her mother had done.

She was quick to tell me that the marital climate had improved—a change in the weather that she ascribed to the fact that she was now taking Prozac. I received this news somewhat dubiously. I knew that Prozac could be helpful, in terms of blunting the uncomfortable messages her body was sending her, but Claudia still seemed to be making use of massive repression and denial. It was as if she were discounting the effects of her husband's emotionally abusive behavior and suggesting that all their problems had been resolved by a magic bullet into her own brain, Prozac; Paul's periodic aggressions seemed to have vanished from her thoughts. Claudia seemed *not* to want to "know" about (much less confront) his episodic attacks any more than she'd wanted to "know" about her father's physically abusive behavior in the first place.

Of course, Claudia had grown up in a family where violence was occurring (her father was beating her brother "to the point of blood"), one in which everyone knew that there are things *you're not supposed to talk about.* And so not telling other people—or your prospective mate—the truth about yourself was a familiar re-creation of the world she had lived in as a child.

The last time that we met for a face-to-face interview was late in her pregnancy with her daughter Jessica. In the intervening time, Claudia and Paul had bought a new house in a pleasant Connecticut town. They were moving soon and would be living close to one of her sisters, she told me enthusiastically. But then, without warning—and apropos of nothing to do with the conversation we were having—Claudia burst into tears and buried her face in her hands. I was startled, shaken.

I leaned forward, put a light hand on one of her trembling shoulders. "What's happening, Claudia?" I asked her.

She looked up at me and said, "I'm so *ashamed* . . . so *ashamed* . . ." At the same time, she was shaking her head from side to side in the negative, as if to ward off any further questions I might ask her. So I sat there silently, and eventually she murmured something to the effect that Paul was throwing ugly tantrums now and then, episodes that ended with his stomping off and sleeping in another room.

I didn't press the matter further—she was too upset—but I did wonder whether her husband was slapping her around as well; men who are abusive often become even more so during a partner's pregnancy. After a while, Claudia's sobs lessened. She wiped her cheeks with her hands and shuddered briefly, a signal that the crying spell was over. But she said nothing further about what was troubling her so deeply.

It wasn't until months later, during one of our occasional telephone conversations, that I returned to the subject of Paul's stalking out of the bedroom and asked her if this had continued to happen. Claudia said that this *did* go on from time to time, but she didn't feel as startled or shaken up about it anymore. "We'll go through periods where we're very sexual, and we're very close, and then he turns it off; he'll just be really *nasty*. And nowadays, I don't say anything when he sleeps in the other bedroom." She laughed dryly. "I'm almost seeing the positive side, because I can get a good night's sleep and I don't have to listen to anyone's snoring. . . ."

At a surface level, Claudia's life seemed much less stormy. For now that the pregnancy was over, she was back on Prozac, and this served as a palliative to her body's uncomfortable inner state; this medication decreases bodily hyperarousal. She was also attending Al-Anon meetings as the spouse of a "dry drunk" and getting a lot of support from those she'd come to know in that setting. She was back in therapy, too, with someone who was a specialist in alcohol and drug addiction. All of the above, plus the fact that her energies were now focused upon her baby daughter, was serving to take the pressure off the marriage.

On the other hand, these same things were helping Claudia to remain in denial about her inability to build a healthy relationship—and, by doing so, break the intergenerational cycle and build a healthy role model for her daughter. For basically what I was hearing was that nothing in the marriage had changed. In the midst of a subsequent telephone conversation, during which she was describing the way in which Paul could be harsh with their daughter on some occasions but "melt" at other times, Claudia stopped suddenly, in midsentence, and said, "Let's face it, I married my father."

To which I responded, "So the great question on my mind is this: Will Jessica grow up with 'the Bickersons' as the model in her mind?" This question was met with a stunned silence. I asked her then whether Paul ever carried on the way her father had done. "I mean, does he ever lose it and hit people?"

"My father never hit anybody," she replied immediately.

"I mean . . . he hit your brother," I said, confused.

She paused a long moment, then said haltingly, "Ummm . . . they *are* similar in that they both suffer, I believe, from depression. They're both introverts. They're both uncomfortable in social situations." Claudia was still adept at finding rationales and excuses for her father's and her husband's behavior. It was as if she were always erecting walls inside her head so that she wouldn't have to face the full extent of what was really happening; and it occurred to me that the safest way of not telling a secret—in this case, one that had to do with the existence of intermittent emotional abuse—is not even "knowing" what the secret is in the first place. She seemed to be pedaling away furiously without realizing that she was on a stationary bicycle.

Did It Last?

My conversations with Claudia raised an inevitable question in my own mind: Would one of the body-oriented therapies have proven more effective—made a real difference—if she had ever moved in that direction? It was highly likely that some reprocessing would have helped her to contain her emotions, as the Prozac was now doing, and have done so without any of that medication's potential side effects—for example, loss of libido. Also, and very significant, a course of reprocessing might have enabled Claudia to *reassociate what had happened to her as a child with what was happening to her in her current life*. This would have freed her to live more fully in the present and to stop reenacting the events she had witnessed in the past.

Of course, where Karen Barry-Freed was concerned, the foremost question was: Had the effects of reprocessing lasted? For this reason, I called her periodically to ask if the EMDR treatment's effects had held up over the long term. Karen's response, on all these occasions, was similar: "It held, it definitely held. . . . I don't understand why it worked, but it did. And really—I'm a bit of a skeptic; I thought the whole idea seemed kind of"—she paused—"out there." Initially, she told me, she'd been unsure about whether or not she'd had a simple placebo reaction. "When I left that day, I thought that maybe it had worked because I'd *wanted* so much for it to work. . . . I did feel much better, but I had my doubts. And so my thought was, Well, we'll see what happens. . . ."

It will be recalled that when she'd first come in for therapy, Karen Barry-Freed was experiencing body symptoms (severe headaches, nausea) that had been activated by symbolic reminders of the original traumatic shock—one such trigger was the realization that "this woman's" numbers were inscribed on her husband's cell phone, and the other trigger was hearing that Jon had been primping in front of the mirror before going to the office on a particular morning.

Karen was also being plagued by what are called "intrusive thoughts" —ugly thoughts and images of Jon and "this woman" sharing an intimate, romantic dinner—and the notion that she herself was being gulled and betrayed once again. "In the time leading up to my work with Patti Levin, I'd had a lot of sleeplessness, too," Karen said. "As soon as I'd shut my eyes, it would all start flashing up at me; and I'd have to get out of bed and wander. I was so confused, so dazed. It was as if I'd been punched in the stomach and had the wind knocked out of me."

This state of affairs had persisted for months, while the Barry-Freeds' "second marriage" hung in the balance. "Jon was frightened, really *scared*, he was sure he was losing me. And I myself don't know where we would have been without the EMDR. . . . The funny thing is that I couldn't understand why staring at this moving light would have any effect at all. I *still* don't understand how it works, but for me it was like a 'snap!' moment. It was right away, in that first session that something happened—it was like I'd been zapped back into my normal life. You know, I was in one place, and all of a sudden, wow! It wasn't a subtle thing. It was just—boom!"

It was so immediate, so sudden, that in the aftermath of that first EMDR session (she'd had four sessions in toto), Karen had deliberately tested out the treatment's effectiveness by intentionally bringing those tormenting mental scenes to the center of her awareness. "I would think of these horrible, painful images *on purpose*. I'd picture the incident with the cell phone—I'd picture Jon with that woman—images that had been tearing at my gut for months and filling me up with all those sick, angry, hurt feelings." But these internal tableaux had lost their cruel power. "The whole thing just stopped being an issue. And there hasn't really been an issue like it since that time. Basically, I'm feeling grounded these days—I feel as if I know who I am as a person, and who I am in relationship to Jon."

I wondered—and couldn't resist asking Karen—where she thought she would have been right now if she had never had that reprocessing experience. "I don't know what I'd have done or where I would have been without the EMDR," she replied slowly, thoughtfully. "I think that even *if* I had stayed in the marriage, I would have become a chronic worrier. You know, one of those people who worry and worry and worry, and who imagine that if they just *worry* enough, it's going to have some impact on their world and on whatever happens. And of course, it doesn't." Karen laughed ruefully.

Then she added quietly, "I honestly think I was heading that way, continually revisiting that scene in the car with the cell phone, continually filling myself up with all of these horrible, sick feelings. I was just playing that scene over and over in my mind—as if by playing it over, I'd arrive at a different outcome. . . ." After that initial EMDR session, though, the scene's virulent impact was gone; its noxious force had dissipated entirely, and the awful feelings associated with it had not ever returned.

I Can Breathe

Deirdre Carmody told me that she and her husband were now separated. It was only after their separation that she had truly realized the degree of stress and tension she'd been living with; her hair, which had been graying rapidly, had actually stopped losing color in the aftermath.

"It's sad. There are so many things I liked about Nikos, and still *do*—his intelligence, his wit," said Deirdre. "But he's always had this underhanded way of scuttling things that promised to be fun. Say, if I was looking forward to a family event, he would often pick a huge fight just before starting out. It so happens that there are some really terrific people in my extended family, but I'd arrive feeling all shaken up because of his having picked a fight, and the evening was ruined already." Her husband was, she added, a person who was just *filled* with boiling resentment and hatred, especially toward his mother; but as his wife, it had been Deirdre herself who was bearing the brunt of it. Finally, she'd reached a point at which she felt she couldn't handle all that anger and vitriol anymore.

"By the way, this may be off the subject, but something really *strange* happened to me after doing that structure," said Deirdre, shifting the thrust of our conversation on the spot. Her voice took on a buoyant tone as she explained that throughout her life she'd loved to sing. Even now, though she was a full-time graduate student, singing was a serious avocation; currently, she was part of a group of professional performers.

"We've cut CDs, and things like that," explained Deirdre, "but my problem has always been with my breathing—I wasn't always able to sing to the end of a line. I'd have to take a quick breath halfway through, and it didn't sound as professional as I would have liked." She had, she reminded me, been the only one of her siblings who hadn't developed asthma; and she had always thought she'd gotten off lightly. Nevertheless, she said, "in the house in which I grew up you had to be really careful about what you said, and you couldn't make noise. And I suppose I'd always assumed that this was what was keeping me from breathing freely in my singing."

In the course of creating the structure, however, the central focus had been upon "father issues"; and Al Pesso had suggested that there was often a connection between a lack of father-energy and problems in breathing. "That idea came to me as a revelation," Deirdre told me. "I mean, that the problem was *really* about father absence—about a father who was emotionally absent, even when he was at home. And actually, while I was doing the structure—most specifically, during the times when I was connecting to the fellow who played my ideal father—there were moments when I felt very, very safe, as if I could truly 'breathe easy.' . . . As if I could breathe easier, and breathe more deeply, than I ever had before."

Over time, said Deirdre, the effects of this experience had proven to be surprisingly wide-reaching. "One of the first things I noticed after doing that structure—and this is something that's only gotten better over time—is that the breathing aspect of my singing wasn't troubling me, and I was singing much better. Not only was my breathing improved, but all of a sudden, band members were asking *me* for tips on how to improve their singing!" Deirdre laughed. "Also, people who came in as guest singers began inquiring, 'Do you give singing lessons?' "

She laughed again. Gone, I realized, was the whispery voice that was the first thing I'd remarked upon in regard to Deirdre Carmody. "So it wasn't just *me*, noticing a difference; it's clear that other people were noticing, too, that I was changed. . . . Which proved to me that these kinds of traumatic experiences really do lodge in your body in some way." Deirdre paused, then went on to say that during this selfsame time period, she'd had ample opportunities to be exposed to her father's "toxic interaction style."

Then she giggled and said, "Excuse the jargon, but 'toxic' is what my father *is*." To take an example, there had been a recent family reunion during which her father had invited—"by name"—an aunt, an uncle, one of her siblings, and her sibling's husband, to join him at a vacation villa that he'd rented in Italy for the following July. "He'd invited everyone *by name*, except for me. At first I thought that maybe I was being oversensitive. . . . So, after everyone left that evening, I asked him about the dates he was going to be there, so that I could see if I was free. And he frowned, his face darkened—he was really, really *angry*. . . . It was very *obvious* that he hadn't meant to invite me."

And equally obvious, she pointed out, was the fact that her father had wanted her to know she wasn't being invited; otherwise, he could have called the others on the telephone and not invited them right in front of her. So, as a way of defending herself, Deirdre had done her best to summon up the "happier" father memories that had been created during her structure.

"When my real father was targeting me in that way, I tried to imagine the things my 'ideal father' would have been saying. . . . I tried to place that figure in the room and have him say, 'Well, of course I meant to include you! Why else would I have talked about it with you there?' And that helped some. . . . But what helped much *more* was trying to send my body memory back to the structure—to the way my body had felt during the session." In other words, explained Deirdre, "when I felt my body going into the embattled, unloved state—which was what my father wanted—I would send my thoughts back to the structure. . . . I would go back to that moment when Al Pesso was saying to me, 'Now let this feeling of safety, of being loved, of being accepted, extend back into your past and forward into your future. Imagine that *this* is the way that you grew up.' And I would try to recapture that good feeling, hook it into my body again."

And had she been successful? I asked her.

Deirdre paused, then said that to some degree she really had been. "For example, about a week after that incident happened with my father, I was driving along and thinking, Oh, what a mean thing he did. But I didn't take my whole body into it. I could see the clear reality of the situation—he was behaving like a fool—and yet I could remember it without my body getting sucked up in the experience." Then, almost as an afterthought, she added that—at least in her view—that was the basic thing about traumatic memories. These were the memories your body got sucked into, the ones that could take you over completely.

Am I Different?

Although Deirdre's father and my own father bore a distinct resemblance to each other—both had been negative, emotionally absent figures in our early lives—the notion that this lack of "father-energy" might be connected to breathing or vocal problems resonated with nothing in my own experience. My reaction to this situation had been to develop a smoothly competent, self-sufficient exterior, through which no glimmers of neediness might ever become visible.

This required a good deal of vigilance on my part, for even though I thought of my life as divided into two separate segments—one that had to do with an uncared-for little ragamuffin, the other involving a successful wife, mother, and career woman—there was always the danger of leakage from the first narrative to the second one.

Without quite realizing it, I was living on high alert, always scanning for danger, and at the same time always finding some other person—a friend in trouble—to shower with compassion. This was, of course, a reenactment, in my current life, of a familiar scenario: one involving the wary, fearful child of an affectively absent, unpredictable father and a lonely, powerless mother who was in need of comforting.

In brief, while on the outside I looked as if I were unflaggingly secure and in charge, on the inside I was working *hard*, in a state of constant, watchful tension. And this state of hypervigilance, which was reflected in a taut body musculature, often left me feeling one cup short of physical energy; I tended to run out of juice far too easily. These themes and issues tumbled out very rapidly in the course of my first psychomotor structure: It was as if the therapeutic process simply lifted me up, transported me backward in time, and then put me down in the heart of the seemingly discarded part one of my life's story. That portion of my life had to do with a child who'd had hurts and needs of her own, which she'd learned how to ignore and which had gone unattended.

What I remember most clearly from that first structure—I have done others since that time—was the sense of terrible homesickness that assailed me. As Milan Kundera has written, the "Greek word for 'return' is *nostos*. *Algos* means 'suffering.' So nostalgia is the suffering caused by an unappeased yearning to return." In my case, it was a piercing, unappeased yearning to return to a home that had never even existed—the home in which my ideal father had loved my ideal mother and held her firmly in his embrace while she nurtured and cared for her children. What a chasm had existed between my "real" parents and the ideal ones that Pesso helped me to create during that structure! At some point during the session, I felt an almost physical sensation of something moving inside my body. It was like a boulder rolling away from the mouth of a cave, where so much hurt and grief had been hidden—from my own view as well as the view of those around me.

That particular structure, like all others, had ended with a long, peaceful coda. In this instance, the man who played my ideal father and the woman who played my ideal mother sat just in back of me, their arms entwined around each other affectionately. I, their little child, was snuggled down against and between them, and their free arms were holding me closely and enfolding me securely. It was, for me, an experience of complete relaxation, of being well and unstintingly nurtured by parents who—because of their love for each other—were freely able to love, support, and care for me, their adoring, dependent child. It was a deeply satisfying tableau—a tableau of the family life that I had never known—and I was instructed to linger there awhile, to take it inside me as a "supplemental memory," to *feel* as if I now lived inside a body whose earliest experiences of the world had been different.

Had this experience actually changed me? The best answer I can give is that in the course of researching the various body-oriented methods of therapy—and focusing most intently upon reprocessing and psychomotor structures—I have found that it isn't only the muscles in my jaw that are more relaxed; I feel far more relaxed all over, simply easier in my skin. I have more energy as well.

While I continue to hold the view that there is much that is very valid about the conventional talking therapies, I now believe it to be true that unprocessed, painful memories are often lodged within the nervous circuitry in *physical* locations and are not addressable by means of traditional forms of treatment. These body-based memories, which are very primitive, are not connected to speech or understanding; and they have a way of reasserting their enormous power over a person when they're triggered by a stimulus—being in a similar context, or getting into the same internal state, or experiencing a similar sensation, such as a smell or a taste—that is reminiscent of the original insult. When this happens, the emotions connected to them can surge through the body like a tidal wave and overwhelm the executive functions—the thinking, reasoning powers of the brain.

For my own part, having held so many interviews with secret holders of all kinds and consulted with a variety of researchers in associated fields (as well as having experienced two kinds of body/mind therapy myself), I come away impressed by the ways in which these body-oriented treatments can access not only a person's frontal lobes, but his or her limbic system—the seat of our emotions.

"Have you found me different, in any way, since I've been working on this project?" I asked my husband recently.

"Enormously so, and in important ways," he answered without hesitation.

The research work I'd been doing had, he said, not eliminated any painful childhood memories—it couldn't, obviously—but it had made the hidden places of the past more available to me. "You're just more able to see those things in perspective, as what they are, more finite in size." And as a result, he said, I no longer seemed to hold on to injuries.

Thus, when something from my earlier, familial life was triggered by an event happening in the present—when somebody had hurt my feelings, or I was feeling excluded, or one of our kids was behaving in an uncaring way, or a friend was neglecting me—I was able to separate the current incident from the past. Life's everyday needles and insults didn't linger with me: They were comprehensible, assimilable, not overwhelming. "And that's a matter of *extreme* importance," he repeated, "because the hurt is so diminished, so seen in perspective." That, he said once again, was the most important change he'd seen.

But then he added, "I *love* the person you've become. . . . I've always loved you, loved lots of things about you, but I've felt the shadow of your father. But now I love your ability to love *me*—to look at me through your *own* eyes, not through the eyes of *his* daughter. And that's a matter of extraordinary importance in our relationship, because it means you can trust me and see me as who I am, the *real* me, with all the bad and the good."

Appendix 1

—

SEEKING TREATMENT

1. Reprocessing, or EMDR

For those readers who want to know where to go for further information about the evolving research on EMDR (reprocessing) therapy, or who are interested in a treatment referral, the following suggestions are provided:

Choosing a Clinician

EMDR (or reprocessing) should be administered only by a licensed clinician specifically trained in EMDR. Take time to interview your prospective clinician. Make sure that he or she has the appropriate training in EMDR (basic training is a two-part course) and has kept up with the latest developments. While training is mandatory, it is not sufficient. Choose a clinician who is experienced with EMDR and has a good success rate. Make sure that the clinician is comfortable in treating your particular problem. In addition, it is important that you feel a sense of trust and rapport with the clinician. Every treatment success is an interaction among clinician, client, and method.

Ask:

1. Have they received both levels of training?
2. Was the training approved by the EMDR Institute?

3. Have they kept informed of the latest protocols and developments?
4. How many people with your particular problems or disorder have they treated?
5. What is their success rate?

Background Information: The EMDR Institute

The EMDR Institute has trained over 50,000 clinicians in the EMDR methodology since it was founded in 1990. It maintains an international directory of Institute-trained clinicians for client referrals and trains only qualified mental health professionals according to the strictest professional standards. Trainings authorized by the Institute display the EMDR Institute logo.

For further information on training or referral, the Institute can be reached at:

PO Box 750
Watsonville, CA 95077
(831) 372-3900
fax (831) 647-9881
e-mail: inst@emdr.com
website at http://www.EMDR.com

2. Psychomotor Therapy (PBSP)

For those readers who want to know where to go for further information about the evolving research on PBSP (psychomotor) therapy, or who are interested in a treatment referral, the way to make contact is as follows:

To reach the Pesso Boyden System Psychomotor international office, or to reach Albert Pesso directly, or to inquire about a workshop with Albert Pesso, or for the name of a psychomotor therapist in your area, please get in touch with the Psychomotor Institute, Inc., PBSP International Office in New Hampshire. The address is:

Pesso Boyden System Psychomotor
Lake Shore Drive
Franklin, NH 03235
(603) 934-5548
fax: (603) 934-0077
e-mail: pbsp1@aol.com
website: www.pbsp.com

Appendix 2

THE PEACE AT HOME WARNING LIST

Emotional and Economic Attacks

- Destructive Criticism/Verbal Attacks: Name-calling; mocking; accusing; blaming; yelling; swearing; making humiliating remarks or gestures.
- Pressure Tactics: Rushing you to make decisions through "guilt-tripping" and other forms of intimidation; sulking; threatening to withhold money; manipulating the children; telling you what to do.
- Abusing Authority: Always claiming to be right (insisting statements are "the truth"); telling you what to do; making big decisions; using "logic."
- Disrespect: Interrupting; changing topics; not listening or responding; twisting your words; putting you down in front of other people; saying bad things about your friends and family.
- Abusing Trust: Lying; withholding information; cheating on you; being overly jealous.
- Breaking Promises: Not following through on agreements; not taking a fair share of responsibility; refusing to help with child care or housework.
- Emotional Withholding: Not expressing feelings; not giving

support, attention, or compliments; not respecting feelings, rights, or opinions.

- Minimizing, Denying, and Blaming: Making light of behavior and not taking your concerns about it seriously; saying the abuse didn't happen; shifting responsibility for abusive behavior; saying you caused it.
- Economic Control: Interfering with your work or not letting you work; refusing to give you or taking your money; taking your car keys or otherwise preventing you from using the car; threatening to report you to welfare or other social service agencies.
- Self-Destructive Behavior: Abusing drugs or alcohol; threatening suicide or other forms of self-harm; deliberately saying or doing things that will have negative consequences (e.g., telling off the boss).
- Isolation: Preventing or making it difficult for you to see friends or relatives; monitoring phone calls; telling you where you can and cannot go.
- Harassment: Making uninvited visits or exits; following you; checking up on you; embarrassing you in public; refusing to leave when asked.

Acts of Violence

- Intimidation: Making angry or threatening gestures; use of physical size to intimidate; standing in doorway during arguments; out-shouting you; driving recklessly.
- Destruction: Destroying your possessions (e.g., furniture); punching walls; throwing and/or breaking things.
- Threats: Making and/or carrying out threats to hurt you or others.
- Sexual Violence: Degrading treatment or discrimination based on your sex or sexual orientation; using force; threats or coercion to obtain sex or perform sexual acts.
- Physical Violence: Being violent to you, your children, household pets or others; slapping; punching; grabbing; kicking; choking; pushing; biting; burning; stabbing; shooting; etc.

- Weapons: Use of weapons, keeping weapons around which frighten you; threatening or attempting to kill you or those you love.

For further information, please contact:

Peace at Home
PO Box 440044
Somerville, MA 02144
e-mail: peaceathome@aol.com
website: www.peaceathome.org
1-877-546-3737

Appendix 3

—

COMMON RESPONSES TO TRAUMA

After a trauma—either of the *little-t* (discovering a partner's infidelity) or *big-T* (witnessing a homicide) variety—individuals may display some or many of a variety of typical reactions and responses. Such reactions may be evidenced not only in people who experienced the trauma firsthand, but in those who witnessed or heard about the trauma, or who have been involved with those immediately affected. Many traumatic stress responses can be triggered by persons, places, or things associated with the trauma. Some reactions may appear totally unrelated to the original event or events.

Here is a list of common physical and emotional reactions to trauma. In some real sense, these symptoms and problems can be thought of as normal reactions to sudden, unexpected, frightening experiences that *feel* overwhelming and compromise our capacity to cope.

Emotional Reactions

1. shock and disbelief
2. fear and/or anxiety
3. grief, disorientation, denial
4. hyperalertness or hypervigilance
5. irritability, restlessness, resentment

6. overreactions, including outbursts of anger or rage
7. emotional swings—such as crying and then laughing
8. worrying or ruminating—intrusive thoughts of the trauma
9. nightmares
10. flashbacks—feeling like the trauma is happening now
11. feeling of helplessness, panic
12. increased need to control everyday experiences
13. minimizing the experience
14. attempts to avoid anything associated with trauma
15. tendency to isolate oneself
16. feelings of detachment
17. concern over burdening others with problems
18. emotional numbing or restricted range of feelings
19. an altered sense of time
20. difficulty trusting and/or feelings of betrayal
21. memory lapses or difficulty concentrating
22. feelings of self-blame and/or survivor guilt
23. shame
24. diminished interest in everyday activities or depression
25. unpleasant past memories resurfacing
26. loss of a sense of order or fairness in the world; expectation of doom and fear of the future

Physical Reactions

27. low energy
28. sudden sweating and/or heart palpitations (fluttering)
29. changes in sleep patterns, appetite, interests in sex (more or less than usual)
30. constipation or diarrhea
31. easily startled by noises or unexpected touch
32. more susceptible to colds and illnesses
33. increased use of alcohol or drugs and/or overeating

Developing problems and symptoms in the wake of severely stressful experiences is *not* a sign of personal failure, weakness, or deficiency. Many mentally well-adjusted and physically healthy people will react to awful, uncontrollable life events—either immediately or at a later point in time—with a random assortment of the responses and reactions named above. Moreover, the difficulties inherent in such situations are compounded when the trauma goes underground—when it is felt to be too shameful to discuss with anyone else, or, in some instances, too painful to remain in conscious awareness. Therefore, a vital first step on the pathway to managing the symptoms of trauma is understanding *exactly what they are*, and the range of options now available for treating them.

For further information, see:

The Trauma Center of Boston: www.traumacenter.org
International Association for Traumatic Stress Studies: www.iatss.org

SELECTED BIBLIOGRAPHY

Abramson, M. "Keeping Secrets: Social Workers and AIDS." *Social Work*, 35(2):169–173, 1990.

Allen, Jon G. *Coping with Trauma: A Guide to Self-Understanding*. Washington, D.C.: American Psychiatric Press, 1995.

American Psychiatric Association. *Diagnostic and Statistical Manual of Mental Disorders*. 4th ed. (DMS-IV). Washington, D.C.: American Psychiatric Association, 1994.

Amichai, Yehuda. *A Life of Poetry 1948–1994*. Selected and translated by Benjamin and Barbara Harshav. New York: HarperPerennial, 1994.

Amini, F., et al. "Affect, Attachment, Memory: Contributions Towards Psychobiologic Integration." *Psychiatry*, 59:213–239, 1996.

Arnsten, A. F. T. "The Biology of Being Frazzled." *Science*, 280:1711–1712, 1998.

Bach, George R., and Wyden, Peter. *The Intimate Enemy: How to Fight Fair in Love and Marriage*. New York: Avon, 1968.

Bok, Sissela. *Lying: Moral Choice in Public and Private Life*. New York: Random House, 1989.

———. *On the Ethics of Concealment and Revelation*. New York: Pantheon, 1982.

Botwin, Carol. *Men Who Can't Be Faithful*. New York: Warner, 1988.

Bradshaw, John. *Family Secrets: The Path to Self-Acceptance and Reunion*. New York: Bantam, 1995.

Bremmer, J. Douglas. "Does Stress Damage the Brain?" *Biological Psychiatry*, 45:797–805, 1999.

Brown, Emily M. *Patterns of Infidelity and Their Treatment*. 2nd ed. Philadelphia: Brunner-Routledge, 2001.

Cahill, L., et al. "Beta-adrenergic Activation and Memory for Emotional Events." *Nature*, 371:702–704, 1994.

Carter, Rita. *Mapping the Mind*. Berkeley, Calif.: University of California Press, 1998.

Curran, D. *Tyranny of the Spirit: Domination and Submission in Adolescent Relationships*. Northvale, N.J.: Jason Aronson, 1996.

Damasio, Antonio R. *Descartes' Error: Emotion, Reason, and the Human Brain*. New York: Avon, 1994.

———. *The Feeling of What Happens: Body and Emotion in the Making of Consciousness*. New York: Harcourt Brace & Co., 1999.

DiBlasio, Frederick A. "Decision-based Forgiveness Treatment in Cases of Marital Infidelity." *Psychotherapy*, 37(2):149–158, 2000.

Dutton, D. *The Domestic Assault of Women*. Vancouver: UCB Press, 1995.

Dutton, D., and Painter, S. L. "Traumatic Bonding: The Development of Emotional Attachments in Battered Women and Other Relationships of Intermittent Abuse." *Victimology: An International Journal*, 6:139–155, 1981.

Eaker-Weil, Bonnie. *Adultery, the Forgivable Sin: Healing the Inherited Patterns of Betrayal in Your Family*. Seacaucus, N.J.: Carol Pub., 1993.

Edelman, Gerald M., and Changeux, Jean-Pierre, eds. *The Brain*. New Brunswick, N.J.: Transaction Pub., 2001.

Efran, J. S. "Mystery, Abstraction, and Narrative Psychotherapy." *Journal of Constructivist Psychology*, 7:219–227, 1994.

Evans, Patricia. *Verbal Abuse Survivors Speak Out: On Relationship and Recovery*. Holbrook, Mass.: Adams Media Corp., 1993.

———. *The Verbally Abusive Relationship: How to Recognize it and How to Respond*. Holbrook, Mass.: Adams Media Corp., 1996.

Everstine, Diana S., and Everstine, Louis. *The Trauma Response: Treatment for Emotional Injury*. New York: W. W. Norton, 1993.

Figley, Charles R. *Treating Stress in Families*. New York: Brunner/Mazel, 1989.

Figley, Charles R., and Kleber, Rolf J. "Beyond the 'Victim': Secondary Traumatic Stress," in R. J. Kleber, C. R. Figley, and B. P. R. Gersons, eds., *Beyond Trauma: Cultural and Societal Dynamics*. New York: Plenum Press, 1995.

Follingstad, D. R., et al. "The Role of Emotional Abuse in Physically Abusive Relationships." *Journal of Family Violence*, 5:107–120, 1990.

Ford, Charles V. *Lies! Lies!! Lies!!! The Psychology of Deceit*. Washington, D.C.: American Psychiatric Press, 1996.

Forster, E. M. *A Room with a View*. New York: Dover Pub., 1995.

Freyd, Jennifer J. *Betrayal Trauma: The Logic of Forgetting Childhood Abuse*. Cambridge, Mass.: Harvard University Press, 1996.

Friedman, Sonya. *Secret Loves: Women with Two Lives*. New York: Crown, 1994.

Geller, Janet A. *Breaking Destructive Patterns: Multiple Strategies for Treating Partner Abuse*. New York: Free Press, 1992.

Gerhardt, Pam. "The Emotional Cost of Infidelity." *Washington Post*, Health, March 30, 1999.

Glass, S. P. "Beyond Betrayal: Post-Traumatic Reactions to the Disclosure of Infidelity." *Professional Counselor*, 13(1), Feb. 1998.

Glass, S. P., and Wright, T. L. "Clinical Implications of Research on Extramarital Involvement," in Robert A. Brown and Joan R. Field, eds., *Treatment of Sexual Problems in Individual and Couples Therapy*. New York: PMA Pub., 1988.

———. "Justifications for Extramarital Relationships: The Association Between Attitudes, Behaviors, and Gender." *Journal of Sex Research*, 29(3):351–357, 1992.

———. "Reconstructing Marriages After the Trauma of Infidelity," in W. K. Halford and H. J. Markman, eds., *Clinical Handbook of Marriage and Couples Interventions*. New York: Wiley, 1997.

———. "Sex Differences in Type of Extramarital Involvement and Marital Dissatisfaction." *Sex Roles*, 12:1101–1120, 1985.

Goldner, Virginia, et al. "Love and Violence: Gender Paradoxes in Volatile Attachments." *Family Process*, 29(4):343–364, 1990.

Goleman, Daniel. *Vital Lies, Simple Truths: The Psychology of Self-Deception*. New York: Simon & Schuster, 1985.

Greenacre, Phyllis. "The Impostor." *Psychoanalytic Quarterly*, 27:359–382, 1958.

———. *Trauma, Growth, and Personality*. New York: W. W. Norton, 1952.

Greenough, W. T., Black, J. E., and Wallace, C. S. "Experience and Brain Development." *Child Development*, 58:539–559, 1987.

Grolnick, Lawrence. "Ibsen's Truth, Family Secrets, and Family Therapy." *Family Process*, 22(3):275–288, 1983.

Grotstein, J. "Nothingness, Meaninglessness, Chaos and 'the Black Hole,' II: The Black Hole." *Contemporary Psychoanalysis*, 26(3):377–407, 1990.

Herman, Judith L. *Trauma and Recovery*. New York: Basic Books, 1992.

Imber Coppersmith, Evan. "We've Got a Secret! A Non-marital Marital Therapy," in A. S. Gurman, ed., *Casebook of Marital Therapy*. New York: Guilford Press, 1985.

Imber-Black, Evan. *The Secret Life of Families: Truth-Telling, Privacy, and Reconciliation in a Tell-All Society*. New York: Bantam, 1998.

Janoff-Bulman, Ronnie. *Shattered Assumptions: Towards a New Psychology of Trauma*. New York: Free Press, 1992.

Kandel, E. R. "A New Intellectual Framework for Psychiatry." *American Journal of Psychiatry*, 155(4):457–469, 1998.

Karpel, Mark A. "Family Secrets." *Family Process*, 19(3):295–306, 1980.

Kaslow, F. "Attractions and Affairs: Fabulous and Fatal." *Journal of Family Psychotherapy*, 4:1–34, 1993.

Kendler, K. S., et al. "Stressful Life Events and Previous Episodes in the Etiology of Major Depression in Women." *American Journal of Psychiatry*, 157:1243–1251, 2000.

Kernberg, O. F. "Aggression and Love in the Relationship of the Couple." *Journal of the American Psychoanalytic Association*, 39:45–70, 1991.

Kessler, R. C., Sonnega, A., and Bromet, E. "Posttraumatic Stress Disorder in the National Comorbidity Survey." *Archives of General Psychiatry*, 52(12):1048–1060, 1995.

Kirkwood, Catherine. *Leaving Abusive Partners*. London: SAGE Pub., 1993.

Kreisman, J. J., and Straus, H. *I Hate You, Don't Leave Me: Understanding the Borderline Personality*. New York: Avon, 1989.

Krystal, H. "Trauma and Affects." *Psychoanalytic Study of the Child*, 33:81–116, 1978.

Lachkar, Joan. *The Many Faces of Abuse: Treating the Emotional Abuse of High-Functioning Women*. Northvale, N.J.: Jason Aronson, 1998.

Lawson, Annette. *Adultery: An Analysis of Love and Betrayal*. New York: Basic Books, 1988. Lecovin, K. E., and Penfold, P. S. "The Emotionally Abused Woman: An Existential-Phenomenological Exploration." *Canadian Journal of Community Health*, 15(1):30–47, 1996.

LeDoux, J. E. *The Emotional Brain: The Mysterious Underpinnings of Emotional Life*. New York: Simon & Schuster, 1996.

LeDoux, J. E., Xagoraris, A., and Romanski, L. "Indelibility of Subcortical Emotional Memories." *Journal of Cognitive Neuroscience*, 1:238–243, 1989.

Lerner, Harriet G. *The Dance of Deception: Pretending and Truth-Telling in Women's Lives*. New York: HarperCollins, 1993.

Levine, Peter A., and Frederick, Ann. *Waking the Tiger: Healing Trauma*. Berkeley, Calif.: North Atlantic Books, 1997.

Lewis, Michael, and Saarni, Carolyn, eds. *Lying and Deception in Everyday Life*. New York: Guilford Press, 1993.

Loring, Marti Tamm. *Emotional Abuse: The Trauma and the Treatment*. San Francisco, Calif.: Jossey-Bass, 1994.

Lusterman, Don-David. *Infidelity: A Survival Guide*. Oakland, Calif.: New Harbringer Pub., 1998.

Marans, Steven, and Adelman, Anne. "Experiencing Violence in a Developmental Context," in J. Osofsky, ed., *Children in a Violent Society*. New York: Guilford Press, 1997.

McDougall, Joyce. *Theaters of the Body: A Psychoanalytic Approach to Psychosomatic Illness*. New York: W. W. Norton, 1989.

———. *Theaters of the Mind: Illusion and Truth on the Psychoanalytic Stage*. New York: Brunner/Mazel, 1985.

McGaugh, J. L. "Involvement of Hormonal and Neuromodulatory Systems in the Regulation of Memory Storage." *Annual Review of Neuroscience*, 12:255–287, 1989.

———. "Significance and Remembrance: The Role of Neuromodulatory Systems." *Psychological Science*, 1:15–25, 1990.

McGoldrick, M., and Gerson, R. *Genograms in Family Assessment*. New York: W. W. Norton, 1985.

Mishkin, M., and Appenzeller, T. "The Anatomy of Memory." *Scientific American*, 256(6):80–89, 1987.

Nagy, L. M., et al. "Open Prospective Trial of Fluoxetine for Posttraumatic Stress Disorder." *Journal of Clinical Psychopharmacology*, 13:107–113, 1993.

Najavits, Lisa M. *Seeking Safety: A Treatment Manual for PTSD and Substance Abuse*. New York: Guilford Press, 2002.

Napier, Augustus Y. *The Fragile Bond: In Search of an Equal, Intimate and Enduring Marriage*. New York: Harper & Row, 1988.

Napier, Nancy J. *Getting Through the Day: Strategies for Adults Hurt as Children*. New York: W. W. Norton, 1993.

Neubeck, Gerhard. *Extramarital Relations*. Englewood Cliffs, N.J.: Prentice-Hall, 1969.

NiCarthy, Ginny. *Getting Free: A Handbook for Women in Abusive Relationships*. Seattle, Wash.: Seal Press, 1986.

Nisenbaum, L. K., et al. "Prior Exposure to Chronic Stress Results in Enhanced Synthesis and Release of Hippocampal Norepinephrine in Response to a Novel Stressor." *Journal of Neuroscience*, 11:1478–1484, 1991.

Notarius, Clifford, and Markman, Howard. *We Can Work It Out: Making Sense of Marital Conflict*. New York: Putnam, 1993.

Othmer, E., and Othmer, S. C. *Life on a Roller Coaster: Coping with the Ups and Downs of Mood Disorders*. New York: Berkley, 1989.

Ornitz, E. M. "Developmental Aspects of Neurophysiology," in M. Lewis, ed., *Child and Adolescent Psychiatry: A Comprehensive Textbook*. Baltimore, Md.: Williams & Wilkins, 1991.

Osofsky, J. D. "The Effects of Exposure to Violence on Young Children." *American Psychologist*, 50(9):782–788, 1995.

Panksepp, Jaak. *Affective Neuroscience: The Foundations of Human and Animal Emotions*. New York: Oxford University Press, 1998.

Pesso, Albert, and Crandell, John, eds. *Moving Psychotherapy: Theory and Application of Pesso System/Psychomotor Therapy*. Cambridge, Mass.: Brookline Books, 1991.

Pitman, R. K. "Post-Traumatic Stress Disorder, Hormones, and Memory." *Biological Psychiatry*, 26:221–223, 1989.

Porterfield, Kay Marie. *Violent Voices: Twelve Steps to Freedom from Verbal and Emotional Abuse*. Deerfield Beach, Fla.: Health Communications, 1989.

Reiser, Morton F. *Mind, Brain, Body: Toward a Convergence of Psychoanalysis and Neurobiology*. New York: Basic Books, 1984.

Rich, Adrienne. *On Lies, Secrets, and Silence*. New York: W. W. Norton, 1979.

Rosenbaum, A., and O'Leary, K. D. "Marital Violence: Characteristics of Abusive Couples." *Journal of Consulting and Clinical Psychology*, 49:63–71, 1981.

Rosenblum L. A., and Andrews, M. W. "Influences of Environmental Demand on Maternal Behavior and Infant Development." *Acta Paediatrica*, Supplement 397(83):57–63, 1994.

Rothschild, Babette. *The Body Remembers: The Psychophysiology of Trauma and Trauma Treatment*. New York: W. W. Norton, 2000.

———. "Defining Shock and Trauma in Body Psychotherapy." *Energy and Character*, 26(2):61–65, 1995.

Sampson, Ronald V. *The Psychology of Power*. New York: Pantheon, 1965.

Sartre, Jean Paul. *Being and Nothingness: An Essay on Phenomenological Ontology*. New York: Philosophical Library, 1956.

Schneider, J. P., Corley, M. D., and Irons, R. R. "Surviving Disclosure of Infidelity: Results of an International Survey of 164 Recovering Sex Addicts and Partners." *Sexual Addiction and Compulsivity*, 5:189–217, 1998.

Schuham, A., and Bird, H. W. "The Marriage and the Affairs of the 'Anxious' Man of Prominence." *American Journal of Family Therapy*, 18(2):141–152, 1990.

Seagull, E. A., and Seagull, A. A. "Healing the Wound That Must Not Heal: Psychotherapy with Survivors of Domestic Violence." *Psychotherapy*, 28:16–20, 1991.

Shapiro, Francine. *Eye Movement Desensitization and Reprocessing (EMDR)*. 2nd ed. New York: Guilford Press, 2001.

Shapiro, Francine, and Forrest, Margot S. *Eye Movement Desensitization and Reprocessing (EMDR)*. New York: Basic Books, 1997.

Shay, Jonathan. *Achilles in Vietnam: Combat Trauma and the Undoing of Character*. New York: Maxwell Macmillan International, 1994.

Shengold, Leonard. *Soul Murder: The Effects of Childhood Abuse and Deprivation*. New Haven, Conn.: Yale University Press, 1989.

Singer, Jefferson A., and Salovey, Peter. *The Remembered Self: Emotion and Memory in Personality*. New York: Free Press, 1993.

Southwick, S. M., et al. "Role of Norepinephrine in the Pathophysiology and Treatment of Posttraumatic Stress Disorder." *Biological Psychiatry*, 46:1192–1204, 1999.

Spanier, G. B., and Margolis, R. L. "Marital Separation and Extramarital Sexual Behavior." *Journal of Sex Research*, 19(1):23–48, 1983.

Spence, Donald P. *Narrative Truth and Historical Truth: Meaning and Interpretation in Psychoanalysis*. New York: W. W. Norton, 1982.

Sperry, L., and Maniaci, H. "The Histrionic-obsessive Couple," in L. Sperry and J. Carlson, eds., *The Disordered Couple*. Bristol, Penn.: Brunner/Mazel, 1998.

Spiegel, D., and Cardeña, E. "Disintegrated Experience: The Dissociative Disorders Revisited." *Journal of Abnormal Psychology*, 100:366–378, 1991.

Spring, Janis A., and Spring, Michael. *After the Affair: Healing the Pain and Rebuilding Trust*. New York: HarperCollins, 1996.

Squire, Larry R., "Mechanisms of Memory." *Science*, 232:1612–1619, 1986.

———. "Memory and the Hippocampus: A Synthesis from Findings with Rats, Monkeys, and Humans." *Psychological Review*, 99:195–231, 1992.

Squire, Larry R. and Kandel, Eric R. *Memory: From Mind to Molecules*. New York: Scientific American Library, 2000.

Steiner, Claude M. *Scripts People Live: Transactional Analysis of Life Scripts*. New York: Grove Press, 1974.

Stosny, Steven. *Treating Attachment Abuse: A Compassionate Approach*. New York: Springer Pub., 1995.

Straus, M. A. "Victims and Aggressors in Marital Violence." *American Behavioral Scientist*, 23(5):681–704, 1980.

Strean, Herbert S. *The Extramarital Affair*. New York: Free Press, 1980.

Subotnik, Rona, and Harris, Gloria G. *Surviving Infidelity: Making Decisions, Recovering from the Pain*. 2nd ed. Holbrook, Mass.: Adams Media Corp., 1999.

Suomi, S. J. "Early Stress and Adult Reactivity in Rhesus Monkeys," in G. Bock and J. Whelan, eds., *The Childhood Environment and Adult Disease*. New York: Wiley, 1991.

Taylor, Richard. *Having Love Affairs*. Buffalo, N.Y.: Prometheus Books, 1982.

Tolman, R. M. "Psychological Abuse of Women," in Robert T. Ammerman and Michel Hersen, eds., *Assessment of Family Violence: A Clinical and Legal Sourcebook*. New York: Wiley, 1992.

Tosone, Carol, and Aiello, Theresa, eds. *Love and Attachment: Contemporary Issues and Treatment Considerations*. Northvale, N.J.: Jason Aronson, 1999.

Uno, H., et al. "Hippocampal Damage Associated with Prolonged and Fatal Stress in Primates." *Journal of Neuroscience*, 9:1705–1711, 1989.

Van der Kolk, Bessel A. *Psychological Trauma*. Washington, D.C.: American Psychiatric Press, 1987.

Van der Kolk, Bessel A., McFarlane, Alexander C., and Weisaeth, Lars, eds. *Traumatic Stress: The Effects of Overwhelming Experience on Mind, Body, and Society*. New York: Guilford Press, 1996.

Walker, Lenore E. *The Battered Woman*. New York: Harper & Row, 1979.

Webster, Harriet. *Family Secrets: How Telling and Not Telling Affect Our Children, Our Relationships, and Our Lives*. Reading, Mass.: Addison-Wesley, 1991.

Weiner, Marcella B., and DiMele, Armand. *Repairing Your Marriage After His Affair: A Woman's Guide to Hope and Healing*. Rocklin, Calif.: Prima Pub., 1998.

Weitzman, Susan. *Not to People Like Us: Domestic Abuse in Upscale Families*. New York: Basic Books, 2000.

Wiederman, M. W. "Extramarital Sex: Prevalence and Correlates in a National Survey." *Journal of Sex Research*, 34:167–174, 1997.

Wilson, S. K., Cameron, S., Jaffe, P., and Wolfe, D. "Children Exposed to Wife Abuse: An Intervention Model." *Social Casework*, 70(3):180–184, 1989.

Winter, David G. *The Power Motive*. New York: Free Press, 1973.

Wolf, Marion E., and Mosnaim, Aron D., eds. *Posttraumatic Stress Disorder: Etiology, Phenomenology, and Treatment*. Washington, D.C.: American Psychiatric Press, 1990.

Yehuda, Rachel, ed. *Psychological Trauma*. Washington, D.C.: American Psychiatric Press, 1998.

Young, G. H., and Gerson, S. "Masochism and Spouse Abuse." *Psychotherapy*, 28(1): 30–38, 1991.

Index

A

B

G

Q

R

S

T

About the Author

MAGGIE SCARF, the author of *Unfinished Business, Intimate Partners,* and *Intimate Worlds,* is a senior fellow at the Bush Center in Child Development and Social Policy at Yale University and a member of the Advisory Board of the Poynter Fellowship in Journalism at Yale. She is currently a contributing editor to *The New Republic* and has served on the Oxygen/Markle Pulse Advisory Board; she also served as a member of the advisory board of the American Psychiatric Press for a decade (1990–2000). She has been a Ford Foundation fellow and a Nieman fellow in journalism at Harvard University, an Alicia Patterson Foundation fellow, has twice been a fellow of the Center for Advanced Study in the Behavioral Sciences at Stanford University, and is a grantee of the Smith Richardson Foundation, Inc. She has received several National Media Awards from the American Psychological Foundation. She lives in Connecticut with her husband and is the mother of three married daughters.

About the Type

This book was set in Electra, a typeface designed for Linotype by W. A. Dwiggins, the renowned type designer (1880–1956). Electra is a fluid typeface, avoiding the contrasts of thick and thin strokes that are prevalent in most modern typefaces.